Derrida's Secret

Incitements

Available

Return Statements: The Return of Religion in Contemporary Philosophy
Gregg Lambert

The Refusal of Politics
Laurent Dubreuil, translated by Cory Browning

Plastic Sovereignties: Agamben and the Politics of Aesthetics
Arne De Boever

From Violence to Speaking Out:
Apocalypse and Expression in Foucault, Derrida and Deleuze
Leonard Lawlor

Agonistic Mourning: Political Dissidence and the Women in Black
Athena Athanasiou

Interpassivity: The Aesthetics of Delegated Enjoyment
Robert Pfaller

Derrida's Secret: Perjury, Testimony, Oath
Charles Barbour

Resistance and Psychoanalysis
Simon Morgan Wortham

Visit the series web page at: edinburghuniversitypress.com/series/incite

Derrida's Secret

Perjury, Testimony, Oath

Charles Barbour

EDINBURGH
University Press

Edinburgh University Press is one of the leading university presses in the UK. We publish academic books and journals in our selected subject areas across the humanities and social sciences, combining cutting-edge scholarship with high editorial and production values to produce academic works of lasting importance. For more information visit our website: edinburghuniversitypress.com

Edinburgh University Press Ltd
The Tun - Holyrood Road, 12(2f) Jackson's Entry, Edinburgh EH8 8PJ

Typeset in Bembo
by R. J. Footring Ltd, Derby, UK, and

Printed and bound by CPI Group (UK) Ltd, Croydon, CR0 4YY

A CIP record for this book is available from the British Library

ISBN 978 1 4744 2499 8 (hardback)
ISBN 978 1 4744 2501 8 (webready PDF)
ISBN 978 1 4744 2500 1 (paperback)
ISBN 978 1 4744 2502 5 (epub)

Contents

Acknowledgements

My sincere thanks go, first, to the editors of the *Incitements* series, Peg Birmingham and Dimitris Vardoulakis, for their encouragement and support throughout the duration of this project. Dimitris in particular has been a great friend and consistent supporter of my work ever since my arrival in Australia in 2009, and much of what I have accomplished here and elsewhere would not have been possible without his wisdom and generosity.

The School of Humanities and Communication Arts and the Philosophy Research Initiative at Western Sydney University (and all of its members) have also contributed considerably to whatever I have accomplished here. The latter is an extremely exciting place to be working right now – long may it reign! My editor at Edinburgh University Press, Carol Macdonald, and her assistant Ersev Ersoy, are superlative, and I greatly appreciate all of their efforts.

I would also like to mention two mentors – Professors Thomas Kemple and George Pavlich – both of whom edited special issues of journals in which elements of the present book were first published, and both of whom were integral in helping me navigate academic life over the early years. The reviewers of the manuscript have also contributed immeasurably to its realisation.

Parts of this research have been published in other places, although everything has been altered significantly for the current monograph. Still, I must credit the support of a number of academic journals: *Theory, Culture and Society*; *Societies*; *Parallax*; *Philosophy and Social Criticism*; and *Law, Culture and the Humanities*.

Finally, I would like to express my deep gratitude to my family, Erin Kruger, and Jacob and Sofia Barbour. We are an unconventional little family, no doubt – but a family nonetheless.

List of Abbreviations

Quotations from Derrida's work are followed by abbreviations for the text in question and a page number. With one or two exceptions, in the cases where the reference is to, not a monograph written by Derrida, but a collection of essays all of which are written by him, I make clear which essay I am dealing with in the text, and then refer to the book. In the cases where the reference is to an essay written by Derrida and published in a collection with more than one author, I refer to the specific essay rather than the collection as a whole.

Many of Derrida's shorter pieces were published in more than one place. This list indicates which particular edition I am working with. I have occasionally consulted the French originals. But including all of those references here would be cumbersome and unnecessary. I am largely relying on the work of Derrida's translators. What I provide here is only a key to the works that, in the course of my argument, I happen to have quoted directly. A fuller list of all the texts by Derrida mentioned, referenced and discussed is provided in the bibliography at the end of the book.

AL   *Adieu to Emmanuel Levinas*, trans. P.-A. Brault and M. Naas, Stanford: Stanford University Press, 1999.

AR   *Acts of Religion*, ed. G. Anidjar, New York: Routledge, 2002.

BS1   *The Beast and the Sovereign, Volume 1*, trans. G. Bennington, Chicago: University of Chicago Press.

BS2   *The Beast and the Sovereign, Volume 2*, trans. G. Bennington, Chicago: University of Chicago Press.

'D'   '*Demeure*: Fiction and Testimony', in M. Blanchot and J. Derrida, *The Instant of My Death / Demeure: Fiction and Testimony*, trans. E. Rottenberg, Stanford: Stanford University Press, 2000.

DIS   *Dissemination*, trans. B. Johnson, Chicago: University of Chicago Press, 1981.

GD   *The Gift of Death* and *Literature in Secret*, trans. D. Wills, Chicago: University of Chicago Press, 2008.

'HAS'   'How to Avoid Speaking: Denials', trans. K. Frieden and E. Rottenberg, in H. Coward and T. Foshay (eds), *Derrida and Negative Theology*, Albany: State University of New York Press, 1992.

'LS'   'Literature in Secret', in *The Gift of Death* and *Literature in Secret*, trans. D. Wills, Chicago: University of Chicago Press, 2008.

MO   *Monolingualism of the Other, or, The Prosthesis of Origin*, trans. P. Mensah, Stanford: Stanford University Press, 1998.

MP   *Margins of Philosophy*, trans. A. Bass, Chicago: University of Chicago Press, 1982.

OG   *Of Grammatology*, trans. G. Spivak, Baltimore: Johns Hopkins University Press, 1976.

OS   *Of Spirit: Heidegger and the Question*, trans. G. Bennington and R. Bowlby, Chicago: Chicago University Press, 1991.

'P'   'Passions: "An Oblique Offering"', trans. D. Wood, in D. Wood (ed.), *Derrida: A Critical Reader*, London: Wiley-Blackwell, 1991.

'PT'   'The Purveyor of Truth', trans. W. Domingo, J. Hulbert and M. Ron, in *Yale French Studies*, 52 (1975): 31–113.

R   *Rogues: Two Essays on Reason*, trans. P.-A. Brault and M. Naas, Stanford: Stanford University Press, 2005.

SM   *Specters of Marx: The State of the Debt, the Work of Mourning, and the New International*, trans. P. Kamuf, New York: Routledge, 1994.

SQ   *Sovereignties in Question: The Poetics of Paul Celan*, ed. T. Dutoit and O. Pasanen, New York: Fordham University Press, 2005.

'UG'   'Ulysses Gramophone: Hear Say Yes in Joyce', trans. T. Kendall, in *Acts of Literature*, ed. D. Attridge, London: Routledge.

WA   *Without Alibi*, ed. and trans. P. Kamuf, Stanford: Stanford University Press, 2002.

Introduction: *Cavernosis Anfractibus*

The Myth of Gyges

Some time before we arrive at the famous Allegory of the Cave, a passage to which *The Republic* is perhaps too often reduced, Plato tells the story of another cave – one in which the main character goes down into the earth, rather than emerging from it, and becomes, not transparent and visible, or awash in the penetrating light of the sun, but invisible, concealed, or hidden from the realm of phenomena and appearance. The story in question is sometimes called the Myth of Gyges, or the story of the Ring of Gyges, and it is recounted by Glaucon in Book Two. And while it is obviously well known, or at least familiar to anyone interested in philosophy and ideas, it rarely receives the attention I think it merits or deserves.

The myth forms part of the discussion of justice, and it goes something like this: Gyges of Lydia is a shepherd. One day, while in the mountains tending to his flock, an earthquake and a deluge tear open a rift in the ground, revealing a hidden cavern. Gyges enters the cavern, to find that it is an underground tomb. Buried there is the skeleton of a giant, sitting on top of a giant horse. Gyges notices a ring on the giant's finger, and decides to pilfer it. When he puts the ring on his own finger, he realises that, when manipulated in a certain fashion, it makes him invisible. He then uses this power to gain access to the royal court, seduce the Queen, and, with her assistance, murder the King and usurp his throne.[1]

The Myth of Gyges is typically read as a bit of counterfactual ethical speculation or moral philosophy. Glaucon himself uses it to propose that there might be no substantive difference between the just and the unjust – that what we call justice is merely our awareness of other people's opinion of us, and that any person in Gyges' position would do the same thing, or abandon justice and pursue naked self-interest instead. Socrates does not really refute Glaucon's argument at this stage. But later he will propose that justice concerns the happy soul (*eudaimonia*) – one that is not a slave to its passions, as Gyges clearly is, but rather takes care of itself, or that justice involves less the judgement of others than the care of the self.[2]

This, of course, is all fine and well, and it is probably what I would teach anyone reading *The Republic* for the first time. It is entirely uncontroversial. But here, and for reasons that I hope will become clear throughout the course of both this Introduction and this book as a whole, I want to place the emphasis in a different spot – not, for example, on the problem of justice, or the question of what modern thinkers would come to call 'human nature', and not on Socrates' promulgation of an ethics of the self, but instead on the strange theme of secrecy and concealment, darkness and seduction, that we find at work in this text. And I want to propose that, if we come at the Myth of Gyges from this direction, we might begin to discern a different approach, not only to *The Republic* (which would undoubtedly be an enormous task on its own), but also to much of the philosophical tradition that follows in its considerable if not overwhelming wake, up to and including today.

As I have already insinuated, it is surely relevant that the Myth of Gyges mirrors the Allegory of the Cave, or that, on his way down into the earth, Gyges crosses paths, as it were, with the philosopher on her way back out. And it is surely relevant that, by going down into the earth, or the realm of the dead, and burglarising a crypt, Gyges discovers the power of invisibility. And I would not be the first to make either of these points. But, to narrow the focus, and perhaps say one small unique thing about this philosophical monument called *The Republic*, it seems to me that the most intriguing detail of the story (intriguing in the sense of unusual and even inconsistent) is the notion that Gyges could use his power of invisibility to seduce a Queen. For while it is certainly conceivable that this power might allow a shepherd to enter the court and murder the King, it is not entirely clear (on first glance at least) how it would assist in a practice of seduction.

Does the Queen fall for Gyges simply because he is invisible? Does she accept his advances merely because she cannot see from whence they came? It would be an odd fetish if she did, and, as Glaucon tells it at any rate, the story does not even hint at such a thing. Nor does it say that Gyges rapes or forcibly assaults the Queen, yet another thing that the power of invisibility would likely help facilitate. No, both Plato and Glaucon tell us that Gyges uses his power to seduce the Queen. This, I would propose, is the mystery of this story about mysteries, or the mystery hidden in the mysterious itself. It is the secret at the heart of this story about secrets.

When hermeneuts come up against a mystery, an *aporia*, or a secret, it is sometimes necessary to change terrain, or look outside the text for help. They sometimes need to move on the diagonal, or make a 'knight's move' (move sideways in order to move forward) as Gilbert Ryle might have said.[3] Thankfully, and as any classicist would know, Plato was not the only ancient writer to consider the story of Gyges of Lydia. Indeed, Gyges was a real historical figure, and all accounts suggest that he did become King of Lydia by way of some act of deception. Thus it will come as no surprise, perhaps, that, alongside Plato, the other great canonical author to tell the story of Gyges, and of his curious method of ascending to power, was Herodotus. And the differences between the two accounts (that of the philosopher and that of the historian) might shed light on the mystery or secret noted a moment ago.

In Herodotus, the story of Gyges appears quite early in the First Book of *The Histories.* Importantly, it is void of the kind of mythological tropes that we find in Plato. Indeed, this is a feature of Herodotus' approach to the story of Gyges that has often been used to commend him over Plato, and thus the historian over the philosopher in general. In Herodotus, unlike in Plato, there are no magic rings, no tombs revealed by earthquakes, and no dead giants on giant horses. In fact, there is no mythology or *muthos* whatsoever. But, as Herodotus tells it, the story still concerns the question of secrecy, as well as that of the visible and its opposite. So it is not completely unjust to proceed by comparing the two.

Herodotus begins his version, not with Gyges himself, but with King Candaules, for whom Gyges is a bodyguard. Owing to the particular desire that has since acquired his name (that is, Candaulism) Candaules asks Gyges to hide in his bedchamber, and spy on his wife while she is undressing. At first Gyges rebuffs the suggestion, but the King presses the matter, until it becomes impossible to refuse. Gyges hides in the appointed place, and watches the Queen disrobe. But, crucially, and unbeknownst to him at the time, the Queen notices Gyges, and is thus aware of his presence throughout the entire episode. The next day, the Queen springs her trap. She calls Gyges to her chambers, and tells him that she knows what he has done. She insists that, as punishment, he must either kill himself, or kill the King and take his place. Gyges sensibly accepts the second option, and thus becomes the progenitor of a long line of Lydian Kings.[4]

An important detail in Herodotus's account of the story of Gyges, a detail that modern archaeologists have since verified as accurate and correct, is that, once he ascended to the throne, Gyges became the first King in history to stamp metal coins with his image, and distribute them as legal tender.[5] That is to say, Gyges – the real historical Gyges – could be said to have invented money. And inasmuch as money is a visible representation of an invisible concept (namely value) one could surely draw a line between the story of how Gyges became the King, and that of his greatest, indeed world historical, governmental accomplishment. In fact, this problem of economics, and its relation to the theme of visibility and invisibility, could easily fill an entire book, if not a library. Here, however, in the name of parsimony, while reading Plato's account alongside that of Herodotus, I want to keep the emphasis on the question of seduction, and I mention economics only to note that the two issues are rarely that far apart (if they can really be separated at all), and that this is undoubtedly something Herodotus knew as well.

On the question of seduction, and all its attendant practices of revelation and concealment, secrecy and disclosure, there is really no comparison between the version of the story of Gyges that we find in Plato and the one that we find in Herodotus. The latter provides an infinitely more complicated analysis of desire, and of everything that goes along with it (which is to say, almost everything full stop). Instead of simply giving Gyges the power of invisibility, and asserting, without explanation, that this power somehow allows a shepherd to seduce a Queen, Herodotus puts into play a whole series of very sophisticated and erotic substitutions and displacements. In watching his wife undress, for example, Gyges takes the place of the King. He becomes, in the precise French meaning of the word, the King's lieutenant. But then, while Gyges thinks that he is the one who sees the Queen without being seen, in fact it is the Queen who sees him without him noticing. So, in some sense, she takes his place as well. And, politically speaking, it all adds up to the Queen engineering yet another substitution, and thus a new King who must know from the beginning that, as a condition of his being King, he is always already substitutable.

But perhaps the central issue here, the one that cuts through both Plato's and Herodotus' texts (or at least the one that I want to highlight or amplify) is the whole problem of seeing without being seen, or noticing without being noticed – in short, the problem of invisibility. Because what is at stake, it seems to me, is not simply a moral issue, or a bit of moral philosophy, as the traditional (or at any rate, most obvious) reading of the Platonic text might suggest. If we focus on Herodotus' account for a moment, and especially the point when Gyges is in the Queen's bedchamber, something rather surprising begins to emerge. For at that point in the narrative, Gyges clearly sees the Queen. He sees her naked body, exposed and in the flesh. But he does not see that she sees him. He does not know that she has noticed him – made a mental note of his presence, if you will, or become aware of something in a place that Gyges could not possibly intuit or discern, namely the hidden, interior world of her own consciousness, psyche, or mind. What is hidden from Gyges, what remains absolutely invisible to him, no matter how naked the Queen becomes, or how many veils she removes, is what is hidden from all of us, or what no one of us can ever know about another, and not only at moments of seduction or deception, but at any moment whatsoever, in any context, anywhere, ever.

This, I think, is also how we should approach the story of Gyges as it is found in Plato, and how we should begin to locate that story in both Plato's *Republic* and the philosophical tradition that it more or less set in motion. As a bit of moral philosophy, the myth of Gyges is, no doubt, not especially compelling. Or, at any rate, the kinds of questions that it raises have been rehearsed now for many hundreds of years, and it would be hard for me to justify offering yet another exploration of them. But, if we take the story of Gyges, or the myth of Gyges in Plato's rendering, as something like an allegory for consciousness (or, to use a phrase each element of which our analysis will have to dismantle at a later point, the inner world of the soul) then we can begin to work with it in new ways, or draw it into alignment with new kinds of investigations. For the power of invisibility is not something only afforded those who come out of caves wearing pilfered rings. It is also a power that all of us have – a power that may even be the definitive feature of what we call consciousness and what we call a self, namely, the ability to keep secrets, or to keep things to ourselves. And this power is manifest (or rather latent, or paradoxically manifest in its latency), not only when we are engaged in significant activities like, say, seducing a Queen or usurping a King, but in every interaction we have with one another, or indeed with anything other, every time we interact in any manner whatsoever.

Here, then, is the basic idea animating this book: what I will call secrecy (or if you prefer, following Plato, invisibility), is a condition of our relations with others, or a condition of interaction, and we can only reveal ourselves to one another, and indeed to anything other (including all of those things we call both subjects and objects), in so far as, at the exact same moment, we conceal as well. Or, to borrow some language from one of the figures who will return more than once in this book, namely the great German sociologist Georg Simmel, secrecy is not simply one kind of social interaction among many, or one way that we might decide to engage with others and the world (although it is certainly that); it is also a general 'form of sociation [*Vergesellschaftung*]'.[6] It is something that structures all of our engagements and all of our relations with everything. Indeed (and this may be one of the points at which what I have to say will start to sound strange, or perhaps just plain absurd) secrecy even structures our relationship with ourselves. There is always some secret. Everywhere, in every instance, no matter what. And, as I hope to show throughout the course of this book, this simple fact or assertion has some rather significant consequences for many of the questions that philosophers, and perhaps especially political philosophers or political theorists, have been asking themselves at least since the time of Plato's *Republic*.

The Clapper Defence

While appearing before the Senate Intelligence Committee on 12 March 2012, the then Director of National Intelligence of the United States of America James R. Clapper was asked (while under oath) whether or not the American government was secretly collecting intelligence information on millions of American citizens. Without the slightest hesitation or qualification, Clapper immediately answered 'no'. Thanks to the Snowden revelations, which began to appear about a year later, it soon became clear that what Clapper had said was false – that, in point of fact, the American government was collecting intelligence on a colossal number of its own citizens, and a colossal number of individuals all around the globe. As a result, many (including the journalist Glenn Greenwald, who had been instrumental in breaking the Snowden story) began to wonder out loud (or on Twitter) whether or not Clapper would be charged with perjury – a charge that the Obama administration had been rather quick to level in other, appreciably less serious instances.

To the disillusionment of some, and the vindicated cynicism of others, Clapper avoided the charge by issuing an absurdly flimsy excuse. He said that, while his statement before the Senate Intelligence Committee had undeniably been false, it was not a lie, and he had not committed perjury because, at the time he had answered the question, he did not understand what he was being asked. That is to say, the Director of National Intelligence of the United States of America avoided a perjury charge by insisting that he was not a liar, only an idiot – not someone capable of deliberately deceiving the American people, only someone *in*capable of understanding a simple interrogative sentence.

One way to make sense of this episode would be to treat it as an example of the now very familiar concept of the sovereign exception. On this account, what I am calling the Clapper defence would constitute little more than an ideological smokescreen (and not a very good one at that) for the fact that, as a powerful (and perhaps the most powerful) figure in the American security apparatus, James R. Clapper was essentially above the law. Republican constitution notwithstanding, the United States of America is not really governed by a universally applicable rule of law. Rather, in the wake of 11 September 2001, and with the justification of a potentially endless war on terror, it exists in a permanent, if also undeclared, state of emergency. Or, more precisely, the executive branch of the American government can choose, more or less at its whim, to operate as if it were in a state of emergency, and thus suspend or break the law in the name of preserving or protecting it.

No doubt there is something to this interpretation. At the same time, the issue is complex, as the Obama administration also tried quite deliberately to set itself apart from the notorious exceptionalism of its predecessors by inserting various juridical, legal or quasi-legal processes into their security-related decision making – notably, and most controversially, via their use of the Foreign Intelligence Surveillance Court or FISA, which was certainly a secret court, but something like a court nonetheless. Rather than seeing the Clapper episode and dozens of others like it in terms of a state of exception in any simple sense, or merely an executive suspension of the law, it would probably be more instructive to borrow a phrase that Giorgio Agamben borrows from Gershom Scholem. Here law does not disappear but, as Agamben and Scholem might say, remains 'in force without significance'.[7]

Beyond the question of sovereignty and the exception, one element of the whole Snowden Affair worth emphasising is the particular paucity of the kinds of debates and positions that it generated. It was a scandal, no doubt, but, as far as I am aware, it did not produce a great deal of new intellectual activity, or new ways of thinking. Indeed, most of the commentary that followed, and that continues up to today, has broken down into two basic positions: a defence of privacy, on the one side; and of security, on the other. And as the cultural theorist Clare Birchall points out in a recent article, these are not really two separate positions at all, but two elements within one ideological arena or frame – namely, liberalism.[8]

Now, if we want to avoid this trap, or the trap of liberalism, it would be necessary, I think, to go in at a much deeper level, or to begin by asking very fundamental kinds of questions – ontological questions such as 'what is a secret?' or 'what is a lie?', or political-ontological questions such as 'what is the relationship between the state and the secret?' and 'to what extent is our current conception of both the political and the social, or the public and the private, bound up with a particular, limited understanding of the secret?' And here I want to suggest that we can attempt to explore those kinds of issues if we approach the Clapper defence from a slightly different direction, or on a different angle.

I will begin by stating very clearly that I, for one, do not doubt for a moment that, on 12 March 2012, Clapper lied – that he committed perjury, broke the law, and knowingly misled the American Senate. At the same time, his defence points to a paradox or a problem at the heart of the concept of perjury in particular, and perhaps mendacity as such. For while I can hardly doubt that he lied, I also know that neither I nor anyone else will ever be able to *prove* that he did so. Indeed, to push the point further, or generalise the issue, no one will ever be able to prove that anyone has committed perjury, or even lied without being under oath, in any situation or any context anywhere ever. The lie, whatever else it might be, exceeds the order of proof.

To understand this claim, we must try to pin down exactly what we mean by a lie. Here it is helpful to consider a distinction that goes back at least as far as Saint Augustine's seminal treatise '*De Mendacio*' or 'On Lying', namely the distinction between a falsehood and a lie. 'Not everyone who says a false thing lies', Augustine maintains, so long as they 'believe' or 'opine' that what they say is true.[9] That is to say, a falsehood concerns something in the external, objective world, and can thus be shown to be incorrect; a lie, on the other hand, concerns, not the external world, but the internal one – not what *is* the case, but what the liar herself *believes to be* the case.

As Augustine puts it, the liar possesses a 'double thought' or a 'double heart'; she 'has one thing in mind [*animo*] and utters another in words [*urbis*]'.[10] And, as we saw in our analysis of the story of Gyges in the previous section, we cannot know what another person has in their mind. It is not available to our senses or intuition. Thus, no matter how suspicious we might be, we can never verify or be certain whether someone else has lied, or whether they were simply mistaken. Every perjurer and every liar everywhere can always have recourse to what I am calling the Clapper defence. They can always say, 'yes, while what I said was demonstrably false, nevertheless, at the time I said it, I genuinely believed it to be true. And therefore I did not lie, I only made a mistake.' And no one will ever be able to prove otherwise.

This is a point that the philosopher Jacques Derrida also made, and made repeatedly, throughout what is typically called his later work. In the background of this point is a more general claim about consciousness and the other – a claim or a whole cluster of problems that, in his work *The Gift of Death*, Derrida tried to sum up with the untranslatable phrase '*tout autre est tout autre*', or 'every other is every bit other' (*GD* 83). Matters here can, and in this book will, get far more complicated and involved. But for our purposes now, the basic insight concerns what we could call the opacity of the other, or the fact that we cannot see inside one another's heads. As a result, the possibility of deception, or of an undetected and undetectable secret, conditions or haunts every single relation we have with one another. And, as Derrida notes on many occasions as well, for the same reason, this means that every relation and every interaction, even the most minimal mode of communication or exchange, relies on an act of faith, or an ungrounded and ultimately ungroundable belief or trust in the other. We could not understand a single word anyone said, and thus have any relation at all, unless, on some level, we allowed ourselves to trust them.

I suspect that, at first glance, the point I am making here, or the point I am using the Clapper defence to make, will appear a little obvious, and even banal. We cannot see inside one another's heads, so we are compelled on some level to trust one another. Ho-bloody-hum. But, in this book, I want to contend that this deceptively simple point opens onto a whole array of extremely difficult problems: for law, no doubt, and what we mean by perjury; for politics which, while obviously having to do with the public realm (the *res publica*, as one tradition puts it), is also, and has always been, conditioned by secrecy and deception; for the study of literature and language; for psychology, if we want to call it that, or the definition of the self, as well as sociology, or the relationship between the self and others; perhaps for the relationship between the singular or the particular and the universal more generally; for the way we understand conscious- ness, and thus the way we have always tended to characterise the ostensible difference between humans and animals, even humans and the world, objects, or existence as such; and thus, ultimately, for the very concept of truth, and of the perpetual interplay of revelation and concealment that makes up what we perhaps too blithely like to call our experience.

Of course, no single book, or even collection of books, is going to do justice to all of these issues, or begin to open them up completely. Here we will have to content ourselves with a broad sketch, and with only occasional dips into the deeper problems, the choice of which will be justified by little more than my own personal interests and preoccupations. But if there is one thing that I hope to accomplish with my consideration of the question of the secret in this book, or one thing that I hope will come out of it for readers, it would be to begin the process of thinking this question beyond or outside of the moribund liberal notion of privacy, of the ostensible right to privacy, or of the liberal opposition or tension between privacy on the one side and security on the other. For, I believe, there will be no understanding of the significance of things like the Clapper defence and the Snowden Affair, not to mention countless other related and adjacent phenomena and events that have increasingly come to define our age, if we remain within that essentially liberal framework. Or, at any rate, there will be no understanding of them that changes anything about the context that makes them possible, and in which they inevitably take shape.

Derrida's Secret

In the opening section of 'On Lying', Augustine makes another point that is relevant to our discussion here. He notes, in essence, that the problem of deception is itself a deceptive problem – that what seems obvious at first becomes infinitely more complicated as we move towards it, as if, each time we solved one of its mysteries or puzzles, it suddenly locked itself up even tighter. Thus Augustine starts out by issuing a warning, or perhaps reading a warning sign above the door of a cave. The topic he is about to address, he cautions, is 'full of dark corners, with many cavern-like windings [*cavernosis anfractibus*] . . . so that at one moment what we found seems to slip out of our hands, and anon comes to light again, and then is once more lost to sight'.[11] This claim, and even this image, are intriguingly echoed throughout the history of philosophical considerations of mendacity or the lie, up to an including the ones that Derrida developed in his later writings. Thus, in his 'History of the Lie: Prolegomena', a paper from which I have tacitly borrowed much of what I have said so far, Derrida maintains that the problem of deception is 'overdetermined to infinity', and that it consists of 'a labyrinth where one can take a wrong step at every turn' (*WA* 35).

In the previous section of this book, we have already seen how something like this is the case. We entered in through the narrow opening of the proceedings of the Senate Intelligence Committee on one day in March 2012, and what I called the Clapper defence. But, as soon as we were inside, so to speak, we found ourselves faced with a formidable array of political and philosophical problems or concerns: the nature of consciousness; the definition of the self; the relation between the self and others; the relation between humans and animals or humans and objects; and so on. Now that we are in this labyrinth, I think, we need to find a way to orient ourselves, or keep our bearings in the dark. It is a difficult problem. But in this book, I would like to suggest we do so by laying down a thread of sorts, or by holding close to, and repeatedly returning to, one particular thinker – the one thinker (or at least the one recent thinker) who, in my estimation, applied himself to the question of the secret with the most rigour and the most sophistication, namely Derrida himself.

The great goddess of fortune (or rather fashion) does not shine well on those of us who want to write about Derrida today. If the mere mention of his name once got you in the door of many exclusive events, now the mood has changed. People are more interested in problems that he is supposed to have ignored, or even barred from consideration. The fascination with language that dominated the previous century, and with which Derrida is frequently aligned, has been eclipsed by a new concern with objects and ontology, mathematics and things. Derrida, it is said, was, for all of his efforts to be radical and unique, part of a critical tradition that extends back at least as far as Kant (and perhaps to Berkeley), and that basically makes it impossible to engage with the world beyond our linguistic framing or our specifically human arrangement of that world. Kant did not effect a Copernican turn in the history of thought, or decentre the human, and place it in the orbit of something else, this argument continues; no, he effected something more like a Ptolemaic turn. By insisting that knowledge is structured by the forms of the intuition and the categories of the understanding, he placed the human back at the centre of the universe. Or, at any rate, he took away our capacity to say meaningful things about the world itself, or what he called noumena, and reduced philosophy and thought to the question of the 'correlation' between humans and the world. And, whether they want to admit it or not, anyone (including, on this line of thought, Derrida) who emphasises the question of language, or the way that language mediates our experience, is ultimately a 'correlationist'. They are stuck in a Kantian paradigm that today's philosophy must endeavour at every point to smash or escape.[12]

My summary here of the Speculative Realist critique of Derrida is admittedly a little simplistic. Or rather, I am summarising the more simplistic version of the critique. This version of the critique tends to be organised around that old canard 'there is nothing outside of the text' (OG 158–9), a mistranslation of one sentence in Derrida's *Of Grammatology* (which, in French, reads '*il n'y a pas de hors-texte*' or 'there is no outside text') that resulted in a great deal of confusion – confusion that, moreover, Derrida attempted to redress during his lifetime on more than one occasion. A more complicated challenge is developed by Quentin Meillassoux, in his book *After Finitude: An Essay on the Necessity of Contingency*, which he has elaborated on more recently in his 'Iteration, Reiteration, Repetition: A Speculative Analysis of the Sign Devoid of Meaning'. Beginning with Bishop Berkeley's correlationist idealism, Meillassoux traces a complex genealogy of the argument that we cannot have knowledge of the outside world or what Kant called the 'thing-in-itself' without articulating that knowledge in the form of human reason or understanding (typically language), and therefore framing it with some mode of human reason or understanding.

But here, and by way of introduction, I do not want to engage in a polemic with the Speculative Realists. This is, in any case, something that I think others (and especially the philosopher Peter Gratton and the literary critic Christopher Peterson), have already done better than I ever could.[13] Rather, and in an entirely different mode, I want to keep the focus on Derrida, and to present what I think is a relatively new approach to his work. More precisely, I want to try to seduce some of my readers back to a consideration of Derrida (and perhaps even to something like 'correlationism', although I will have to qualify that point considerably a little later) by, in a sense, turning my back on the way I think he is too often written and talked about, or by drawing on an aspect of his thought that, in my estimation, has too often been lost, missed, or set aside, perhaps especially among some of his most fervent acolytes and followers. More precisely, whether or not I effectively face the Speculative Realist challenge, I would like to suggest that Derrida has a great deal to say about the real world, and that his main arguments need not be clouded in obscurantism or mystery, but can be presented in lucid and even logical terms. If there is one thing that the Speculative Realists have done very well, I believe, it is return philosophy to the ideal of rationality – and this is something that, whether or not I agree with all of their arguments, I nevertheless applaud and want to follow.

With this in mind, I want to begin by noting that, in my reading, I have always associated Derrida with the phenomenological tradition, not only in the sense that he starts out with Husserl and Heidegger (and perhaps the former even more than the latter, although this is something that not many have noticed), but also, and more importantly, in the sense that his arguments often proceed by way of first-person phenomenological descriptions or accounts of experience. This, I think, is a point worth highlighting, and drawing out of his text as much as we can. For there has always been a tendency among Derrida's readers to emphasise his treatment of, let us say, the philosophical tradition, or how he relates to a rarefied notion like 'the history of metaphysics' (or, if we prefer the more Heideggerian articulation, 'the history of Being'). Now I do not disagree with taking the latter approach. It has generated an enormous amount of important work, to be certain.[14] But as a point of departure, I will note that, as often as I possibly can, I intend to focus on the former, or on those places in his works where

Derrida simply describes experiences or things. And when I say 'Derrida's Secret', I am being a little ironic. His secret is not the hermetic, puzzling and obscure thought with which he is so frequently associated. On the contrary, it is his approach to the most ordinary, quotidian events and experiences imaginable. In a certain sense, or at least in one sense, Derrida's secret is that he has no secret.

Along with this point about phenomenology, then, or about the phenomenological description, I must note and emphasise that, while Derrida will remain central throughout (the thread that we lay down and follow in the cavern), this book is not really, or not entirely, a work of Derrida commentary. I think that Derrida's texts are and always have been both completely open to interpretation, but also completely closed. That is to say, there are many places in Derrida's work where he invites engagement and exchange. In fact, he does so at more or less every point. But, at the same time, his work almost systematically refuses to be systematised. You cannot reduce Derrida to a slogan or a phrase, although (as I suggested just a moment ago) that is exactly what many of his enemies (and, we have to admit, many of his friends as well) try to do. So commentary in the sense of engaging with Derrida's thought to help organise or orient my own – that seems entirely legitimate, and it is what I will do here. But commentary in the sense of trying to circumscribe Derrida's position, to set it apart from other positions, or ultimately to have the final word on him and his work – that seems entirely impossible, and it is what I will try to avoid.[15]

All of that said, it is still necessary to attempt a little bit of the impossible, or to say a few very general things about Derrida's career or his body of work – not in an effort to contain or comprehend them, but simply in order to make it easier to understand how I will draw on them as my arguments and ideas unfold. And if I have one crucial point to make here, or one contribution to the Derrida literature, it is this: in Derrida, or at any rate in the later Derrida, which is where we will be spending most of our time in this book, the problem of the secret is not one problem among many; rather, it is integral to nearly everything he has to say, or every topic he discusses. To date, I think, the importance of the problem of the secret has been overlooked by most of Derrida's readers.[16] And, if we can put it this way, that is in part because the problem of the secret secretly informs everything else Derrida does. It remains a little closed off or hidden from view. Some element of this might have been deliberate or intentional on Derrida's part – one of those performative gestures that he loved to make, such that his discussion of the secret would itself remain somewhat secretive, and thus operate as an example of what it states. But, to come back to the ground, the somewhat secretive status of Derrida's discussion of the secret is more likely an effect of more obviously empirical concerns, or simply the way Derrida found himself working in the later part of his career, and the current state of his corpus, archive, or body of work.

I will try to explain what I mean. Very schematically, and while acknowledging that any such arrangement conceals as much if not more than it reveals, I think we can break Derrida's career down into three periods or stages. In the first, which would include the early writings on Husserl, the essays collected in both *Writing and Difference* and *Margins of Philosophy*, and, perhaps most importantly, *Of Grammatology*, Derrida was concerned with elaborating on what he called deconstruction, and especially the deconstruction of the metaphysics of presence. As we have already noted, this work is a little preoccupied with the problem of language, writing and the text. Or, at any rate, that is the element that has attracted the most attention. But as I will try to argue at a number of different places in this book, I think Derrida's more important contribution in this period is his treatment of the problem of time. In particular, and despite many misunderstandings, he does not, I think, deny the possibility of experiencing something like presence, or suggest that all of what we call experience is mediated by language or text, and thus secondary and derived. Rather, and far more complexly, he suggests that every experience of presence is constitutively split by something that he calls 'the trace', and by 'spacing', or 'the becoming-space of time' and 'the becoming-time of space' (*MP* 13). This is a point that I think Martin Hägglund makes extremely well.[17]

The second broad period in Derrida's career would then be the more experimental, and often more literary and obscure, texts that came after these early philosophical investigations. Here I am thinking of works like *Glas*, *The Postcard* and *Truth in Painting*, as well as others of the same sort. During this period, it seems clear that Derrida was trying to put into action (practice, or perhaps more precisely, perform) some of the ideas about language, writing and texts that he had developed in the earlier deconstructive essays and engagements. *Glas* in particular seems like an effort to dismantle or undo the concept of the philosophical treatise, and all of the system-building assumptions that can be attached to it, from the inside out. The same goes for some of the collaborative works that Derrida began to help produce around this time, including, most famously perhaps, his 'Circumfession', which consisted of a running commentary on Geoffrey Bennington's introductory (taxonomic and synoptic) commentary on him.[18] Perhaps here we could also include that slightly vicious little book *Limited Inc.*, in which Derrida basically runs philosophical circles around poor John Searle, who, in taking issue with Derrida's critique of J. L. Austin, had made the considerable error of leaping into a tank battle wielding a kitchen knife.[19]

But my focus in this book is on what I will call the third and final period, or what, once again, has often been referred to as the later Derrida. Here, in approximately the last fifteen years of his life, it would be easy, and maybe not unjustifiable, to maintain that Derrida became a victim of his own success, and that, in some sense, there is no later Derrida, or no clear body of work from which we might depart. For much if not all of what Derrida published during this period were not finished books exactly, but rather transcripts of papers, presentations, lectures, plenary addresses, and speeches that he gave, typically at academic conferences where he had been invited to say something, and often in the United States. In other words, on face value, Derrida's third period can appear very fragmented and inchoate. Rather than a consistent and developed research project, we seem to get responses to calls. Derrida appears to become, less of a solitary scholar working in a recognisable field, and more of a respondent or correspondent, notably with what is sometimes called the English-speaking world. Indeed, some of Derrida's books from this period were published in English translation before they appeared in French. And many of the books that appeared in English (the language in which Derrida arguably had the largest following and the greatest influence) consisted of fragmented rearrangements of bits and pieces of the French originals.

That would be the easy criticism of the later Derrida. On the other hand, even while what I have said here is true of the material Derrida published during this period, it seems to me that Derrida's former students, and especially the ones working on the 'Derrida Seminar Project' (who have the extraordinarily ambitious plan to publish all of Derrida's seminar transcripts, which span no less than forty years of his teaching career) are showing that it is not the case.[20] That is to say, it is becoming increasingly clear that there is a consistent and extensive research project operating in the later Derrida, but that it is to be found, less in the published works than in the seminars. Even going by the little glimpses that we have had of the seminars so far, we can see very directly that, during this period, Derrida worked by preparing and delivering his seminars, and then drawing on them almost entirely for the speeches and addresses he was asked to present – the same speeches and addresses that typically went on to become his published texts. So, without wanting to press the point too hard, or place too much emphasis on the seminars, it seems plausible that the published material is in some sense epiphenomenal, or a kind of outward and public expression of a much more (not private, but) intimate engagement.

If we turn our attention to the seminars, or to what has been made available or known about them, we can see rather quickly that, while for most of his career he presented on a different topic each year, during the period we are referring to as his later work, Derrida presented a ten-year-long series of linked seminars under the heading '*Questions du Responsabilité*'. It is here that we find all of the familiar themes that we associate with Derrida's later work: witnessing and testimony, for example; or perjury and the promise; or hospitality and cosmopolitanism; as well as the death penalty (the first part of which is the only one of these seminars to have appeared in print to date). And it is also this period that is typically associated with Derrida's so-called 'turn', or rather his many supposed and often commented on turns – towards politics, or ethics, or religion, or whatever. But, significantly, and in a way that we should, I think, reflect upon, the first of this ten-year-long series of seminars is called '*Questions de Responsabilité I: Le Secret*'. So that is where Derrida begins his long exploration of responsibility. And thus, it would come as no surprise if we were to discover that that concept has an, if not foundational, at least heavily determinate, influence on everything that follows. This is what I mean when I say the secret is Derrida's secret preoccupation. At least during this period, and perhaps in others as well, it secretly informs everything else that he has to say.

I am aware that using this kind of language about Derrida will make some people bristle. Surely we cannot reduce Derrida, of all people, to one single concept. And surely we cannot carve up his career in such a cavalier manner, or propose that one part (the seminars, for example) contain the truth or the essence of another (the publications). Of course, I absolutely agree with these comments. And I would further add that I sympathise with the situation of Derrida's literary executors, who have to try to deal with the archive of a thinker who so thoroughly and consistently dismantled or deconstructed the concept of the archive, not to mention the *arche* or the original, and all of the attendant notions of authorial intention, concealed truth or discursive essences that tend to go along with the way we treat a dead writer's corpus or body of work.[21] In this instance, my only defence is to say that my schematisation of Derrida's career is designed, not to reveal its essential truth, but to put it to work, or to start making it work for me, as I begin to work on this problem of the secret. It is a weak defence, no doubt. But I absolutely promise you, with a sincerity that you will never be able to verify or know, that it is not a lie.

A Synoptic View

This book is broken down into four chapters. Each of the first three relate Derrida's treatment of the secret to a particular discipline – sociology, literature and philosophy respectively. Each also takes up a different component or element of Derrida's approach to the secret. In the first, I focus largely on what he has to say about the oath; in the second, I turn my attention to his consideration of testimony; in the third, the central concern is what he says about deception, or rather consciousness and deception. At the same time, and despite these general divisions, there is a great deal of overlap between the chapters, and perhaps even repetition. While here, and for analytic purposes, I will provide a sketch of each independent chapter, in practice, matters are much more complex. In fact, and to invoke Augustine's metaphor once again, we are now entering into a labyrinth or a cave. And things that come to light will invariably fade out too, and have to be brought back into focus later on from another direction. Unlike the first three, my fourth and final chapter is not really organised around a discipline or a concept. Rather, it consists of a meditation on Derrida's final seminars, and on the questions of death and solitude that he explores there. These too, however, will be understood from the perspective of the secret, and of Derrida's examination of that question.

The first chapter, then, begins with a discussion of the oath – a concept that, I maintain, while integral to Derrida's later work, has yet to receive a great deal of critical or scholarly attention.[22] The basic argument concerns the relationship between the oath, faith, or belief, and what I call the social bond, or simply society and social relations in general. In essence, I try to show that, for Derrida, every social relation or interaction relies on a (typically silent or implicit, but nonetheless effective) promise, pact or sworn agreement to say what one believes, and to believe that the other is doing the same. Indeed, here pushing a little beyond the letter of Derrida's text, and putting it into conversation with Simmel's (also often forgotten or misunderstood) work on the secret, I propose that what we mean by society is nothing other than this exchange of belief or, as I call it, 'act of faith'. Moreover, and as Simmel asserts quite explicitly, such acts of faith become more (in fact, exponentially more) frequent and required in modernity – a fact that avers against the secularisation hypothesis that, under the influence of Max Weber in particular, became so prominent in twentieth-century social theory.[23] We are creatures of faith. But this is the case, not because we believe in god, or because only a god can save us, as someone once said. No, it is the case because, in order to engage at all, we must believe in each other.

But the point of this first chapter is not only to establish the intimate relationship between the oath and the social bond. Rather, and somewhat more radically I hope, my intention is to show how a close and rigorous examination of this relationship also has the effect of dissolving both sides, or both the oath and the social as such. In the first case, I look closely at Derrida's reading of Emmanuel Levinas, and try to show how, on Derrida's account, any fidelity to or faith in the other is shot through with its opposite, or infidelity and faithlessness. There can be no pure relation to the absolute alterity of the other. Every relation we have is, as I put it, contaminated. And this contamination is also the condition of what Derrida means by ethics. In the second case, or the dissolution of the social, I look closely at Simmel's work, and try to show how, for him, the distinguishing feature of the human, or of human consciousness or what Simmel calls the 'inner world', is the ability to keep secrets, or to conceal itself from others. However, and as a direct logical consequence, if this is the case, if consciousness or the inner world is defined by its capacity to conceal itself, then, and by definition, we can never know whether or not we are encountering it. And thus there is no good reason to limit it to the human being, or to those creatures we assume make up the social. The first chapter ends, then, by opening up Derrida's discussions of the animal, and especially his challenge to what he takes to be an implicit or disavowed humanism organising the thought of Jacques Lacan.

If the first chapter of this book focuses on society or the social bond, and ultimately winds up dissolving that concept, or showing how it invariably dissolves itself, the second chapter focuses on literature, and perhaps does something similar with respect to it. I begin (a little off centre) by opening up some of the specifically or more directly political stakes of my consideration of the secret – by which I mean the contemporary expansion of the surveillance state, and all of the political questions that fall out from or can be organised around the Snowden Affair, and Edward Snowden's revelation of the extent of state spying practices today. My basic claim here is that the contemporary state attempts to establish a monopoly, not only on violence, which has always been one of its functions, but also on secrecy, and that this is a dangerous fantasy, one that has the potential to destroy, not so much liberal privacy and freedom, but the social bond itself, or the way that we share what divides us, and can only be held together by also being held apart.

Those political concerns having been placed on the table, the gamble or gambit of the second chapter is to suggest that we might shed new light on our current situation by way of a reconsideration of a very old, and in many ways waning, in-stitution – the institution of literature. Along with Derrida, I maintain that there is an inextricable link or association between what we call literature and the question of the secret. To draw out this link, I begin with a consideration of Edgar Allan Poe's 'The Purloined Letter', and of Derrida's fairly well-known critique, or deconstruction, of Lacan's treatment of that story in his 'Seminar of "The Purloined Letter"'. My argument here is that literature entails a paradox. It is always both absolutely public or exposed, and absolutely hidden or concealed. This then binds literature to what, throughout his later work, Derrida referred to as testimony or avowal. Literature becomes a kind of paradigmatic case, or an example *par excellence*, of a very average speech act – a speech act, in fact, that Derrida takes to be a condition of all speech, all interaction, and perhaps even experience in the broadest possible sense.

The central text in the second chapter is an essay that Derrida wrote on Maurice Blanchot called '*Demeure*: Fiction and Testimony'. On face value, this essay consists of an extended commentary on a very short, and apparently autobiographical, story that Blanchot wrote towards the end of his life called 'The Instant of My Death'. But out of this meticulously close and detailed analysis of one text, Derrida derives a whole series of general statements about consciousness, language, the self, the relation to the other, and arguably existence as such. This gesture, I maintain, operates as a performative enactment of a concept that, I believe, is crucial to Derrida's later work, and to his understanding of the secret in particular – namely, the singular universal, or the particular, discrete and indivisible instant that nevertheless constitutes an example or an instance. At the end of the chapter, I take some issue with Derrida's treatment (or defence really) of literature as an institution, or as a particularly fragile legal fiction that takes shape in the nineteenth century and that must be associated with a certain conception of democracy and legal rights. But I hold to and try to preserve literature as an experience of what I am calling here the secret and the singular universal.

In the third chapter, I turn my attention towards philosophy. I attempt, in an ecumenical rather than polemical fashion, to span the gap that typically separates Continental and Analytic or Anglo-American philosophy. I thus bring Derrida's approach to the secret into conversation with a handful of paradoxes or problems that have, particularly in recent years, tended to vex his Analytic counterparts. More precisely, I seek to show, in an explicitly modest and exploratory fashion, how Derrida's work might inform three philosophical debates. First, there is the paradox of self-deception or the self-lie. This is in some sense a subset of the famous Liar's Paradox, or the notion that one who admits to lying may by lying in that very admission. Except here it is a question of whether or not a single and unified self can deliberately deceive itself, or hide something from itself. In short, how can the agent of deception also be the target of deception? Second, there is a debate concerning the nature of consciousness, and especially what the Australian philosopher of mind David Chalmers has dubbed 'the hard problem' (that is, how we account, not merely for the function, but also for the experience of consciousness). And finally, there is the long-standing debate within Analytic philosophy over 'the problem of other minds', or how or whether we can know or ascertain the inner experience of another.

While the bulk of this chapter is devoted to explaining Derrida's work, and how it contributes to debates from which Derrida and his followers are frequently excluded, I also make some effort to address the criticisms of the Speculative Realists, already mentioned above. Again, here my project is not to develop a systematic defence of Derrida, or to respond to the criticisms point by point. Indeed, at the end of the day, my aim is to displace the issue a little, or to suggest that Derrida and the Speculative Realists (and here I am mostly concerned with Quinten Meillassoux) are simply interested in different kinds of questions. But the crux of my response is to say that, while the Speculative Realists are interested in descriptions of the world, or what Meillassoux calls 'the great outdoors',[24] Derrida is as interested (along with describing the world) in the performative act of engaging with the world. This perhaps makes him a 'correlationist' in Meillassoux's terms. But it also compels us to put the emphasis of that word in a slightly different place.

The fourth chapter of this book deals largely with Derrida's seminars, or with the seminars that have been made available in print and translation so far, specifically the two volumes of *The Beast and the Sovereign* (which Derrida originally delivered in 2001–2 and 2002–3 respectively), and the first volume of *The Death Penalty* (which he delivered in 1999–2000). While remaining focused on the question of the secret, here I take up three other topics or themes that appear to have organised much of Derrida's very last work — namely solitude, death and time. Perhaps the central problem here has to do with Derrida's suggestion (which he makes in a number of places, but notably in an essay on Hans-Georg Gadamer called 'Rams: Uninterrupted Dialogue, Between Two Solitudes – the Poem') that each and every death of a unique living creature constitutes the end, not merely of a particular world, but of the one and only world. This assertion, I claim, whilst impossibly hyperbolic, also provides a key to understanding Derrida's extremely complex conception of time – a conception that, as I try to show, he works out in conversation with many other authors, but perhaps most especially with the poet Paul Celan. Thus, along with providing a reading of Derrida's last seminars, this chapter also pays close attention to his study of Celan, and particularly Celan's prose work 'The Meridian'.

One point I want to make in this chapter about Derrida's approach to solitude, death and time (which is also a point that Derrida makes about Celan's work) is that we cannot really telegraph what Derrida has to say without missing too much. That is to say, we cannot really do what I am obliged to do here, in an introductory synopsis of the chapters of my book. In a sense, we must come at the issue patiently, by circling around, or tracking back and forth like a wolf stalking its prey. If we try to make the point directly, we risk missing it entirely, or rendering it as a trite slogan, rather than a sophisticated and imbricated thought. Nevertheless, and having established that disclaimer, I will risk fulfilling my obligation here. Particularly in *The Death Penalty, Volume 1*, but also in the two volumes of *The Beast and the Sovereign*, Derrida sets out, among many other things, to deconstruct the concept of death. He shows how all philosophies organised around this concept (and the notable example here is Heidegger) presuppose that they already know what death is, and when it occurs – even if, as in the case of Heidegger, they then go on to rely on its uncertainty or unknowability. For Derrida, on the other hand, nothing is less certain than what constitutes the moment of death. We cannot speak of life and death, then, as though their separation were self-evident. We can only speak of what I call life-death, or what Derrida calls 'living death' and '*survivance*'.

The Conclusion of this book – which I have titled 'Secretions' – attempts to situate the consideration of Derrida and the secret in a number of larger contexts, and in relation to a number of other thinkers who explore or have explored the same concept. I attempt, in other words, to show how Derrida's work on the secret secretes, or spills out of itself, and into other contexts. I begin with a consideration of Deleuze's and Guattari's approach to the secret in *A Thousand Plateaus*, and to try show how Derrida would both connect with and separate from it in important ways. Turning my attention to more explicitly political matters, I then show how Carl Schmitt, Hannah Arendt and Georges Bataille all (albeit in very different fashions) link the concept of the secret to that of sovereignty. I maintain that, for Derrida, while each of these thinkers touches on something essential, there remains a secret that exceeds the order of the sovereign. Finally, and in an admittedly cursory fashion, I offer some comments on the relationship between Giorgio Agamben and Derrida, especially with respect to their related but also distinct understanding of the oath.

Particularly in his later work, Derrida often begins his texts with a single sentence, or even sentence fragment or phrase, almost always gnomic and ambiguous, that he then proceeds to analyse in microscopic detail, as if spinning a gem between his fingers to suss out its quality, or look for imperfections. In *Specters of Marx*, for example, there is Hamlet's famous pronouncement 'the time is out of joint' (*SM* 1), which Derrida effectively explodes into a complete theory of time, messianism and the contemporary political scene. In *The Beast and the Sovereign, Volume 2*, it is simply the phrase 'I am alone' (*BS2* 1), which then becomes the basis for an elaborate and detailed examination of solitude, temporality, sovereignty and death. Here I will follow Derrida, and propose that this book also, if a little less explicitly, consists of a protracted meditation on one phrase – specifically the ultimately untranslatable words, found in Derrida's *The Gift of Death*, '*tout autre est tout autre*' (GD 83). We could render this phrase in English as 'every other is every bit' or 'completely' or 'entirely other'. And some version of this is what Derrida's translator David Wills typically opts for. In this case, the emphasis would be placed on what is usually called Derrida's ethics, or his ethics of the relation to the other. But we could also render the phrase '*tout autre est tout autre*' a little more directly, and still correctly, as 'every other is every other'. Here I think the emphasis would be placed in a more obviously political place. For it would invoke a particular brand of political universalism that Derrida takes up in his later work – a political universalism that is closely related to the notion, or the paradox or enigma, of the singular universal.

It is fair to say that, in this book, I am critical of the ethical and the theological or religious readings of Derrida, and more interested in politics. In particular, one of my aims is to distance Derrida from Levinas, and to amplify the places where Derrida disagrees with Levinas. Or perhaps disagreement is not the right word. I think, more often than not, Derrida challenges Levinas by showing how experiences he takes to involve the infinite, the absolute, or the divine, can in fact be grounded in far more quotidian matters and concerns. The so-called alterity of the other is a good example here. For Derrida, the other is not 'infinitely other' because she stands in for or somehow manifests the alterity of god or the divine. No, far less mysteriously, Derrida begins his understanding of the alterity of the other with the simple insight, mentioned numerous times already, that we cannot really see inside one another's heads, and that, while I can hear what you say, and try to make sense of the words, I can never know or prove or be certain of what you believe, and must take it on faith that the two – what you say and what you believe – are the same. From my perspective, this kind of claim has nothing to do with theology, negative or otherwise. It is, instead, part of a very rigorous and convincing phenomenological account of the world.

No one is going to set out to write a book about secrets without desiring, at the same time, to keep some of their own. The challenge I am setting myself in this book, and the intended irony of its title, is something like this: I want, as much as possible, to write plainly, directly and lucidly about Derrida. And I want to suggest that what Derrida has to say is far plainer and more lucid than many of his enemies recognise or allow. As mentioned earlier, part of the joke here is to suggest that Derrida's secret is that he has no secret – that the one who is so often ridiculed for being hermetic and obtuse is actually a very clear thinker of everyday experience, and of our everyday exchanges with others. Or, to put the point from another direction, I want to suggest that, whatever else he might be, Derrida is a profound observer of human behaviour. He is not a hideously abstract, pretentious and out of touch Parisian academic, but a student of our most quotidian engagements with one another and with our world – even if, at every moment, he shows us how those engagements, while extraordinarily familiar, are also entirely unfamiliar or, to employ the German word the double sense of which Derrida liked to remind us of, *unheimlich*. The most familiar is also the most unfamiliar, Derrida says. The most obvious is simultaneously the most obtuse. And that, in a nutshell, is probably what Derrida means by the secret. It is, in other words, Derrida's secret.

Notes

1 Plato, *Republic*, 359a–360d.

2 Plato, *Republic*, 612b.

3 Ryle, 'Thinking and Self-Teaching', 217.

4 Herodotus, *The Histories*, 1.7–13.

5 The authoritative study of the issue is undoubtedly Marc Shell's *The Economy of Literature*, the first chapter of which is devoted to the story of Gyges.

6 'Form of sociation' is Kurt H. Wolff's older translation of Simmel's neologism *Vergesellschaftung*. He adopted this translation in *The Sociology of Georg Simmel*, a collection of Simmel's work that Wolff also selected and edited, including selections from Simmel's masterwork, *Sociology*. The translators of the more recent, complete two-volume edition of Simmel's *Sociology* do not preserve Wolff's translation. They prefer to render *Vergesellschaftung* differently each time, depending on the context in which it is used. Here, even though I am working largely with the more recent, more complete edition of Simmel's *Sociology*, I will still occasionally use Wolff's phrase, as it emphasises that it consists of a single, developed concept from Simmel's work.

7 Agamben, *Homo Sacer*, 68.

8 Birchall, 'Aesthetics of the Secret', 27.

9 Augustine, 'On Lying', 457.

10 Augustine, 'On Lying', 457.

11 Augustine, 'On Lying', 457.

12 The basic parameters of the Speculative Realist approach to Derrida, and the essential critique of that approach, are set out in Peter Gratton, 'Post-Deconstructive Realism: It's About Time'. This position is expanded and developed in Gratton's *Speculative Realism: Problems and Prospects*.

13 See Gratton, 'Post-Deconstructive Realism' and *Speculations*. See also Christopher Peterson's 'The *Gravity* of *Melancholia*: A Critique of Speculative Realism'.

14 The first work in English to approach Derrida from a discretely philosophical (as opposed to literary) perspective was probably Rodolphe Gasché's *The Tain of the Mirror: Derrida and the Philosophy of Reflection*. Here we might also note the work of David Wood and Robert Bernasconi; for example, the essays collected in their edited volume, *Derrida and Différance*. See also John Sallis (ed.), *Deconstruction and Philosophy*. More recently, the chief philosophical reader of Derrida has arguably been Michael Naas; see,

for example, his *Taking on the Tradition: Jacques Derrida and the Legacies of Deconstruction*. Perhaps more than anyone else, Leonard Lawlor has done the work of locating Derrida's thought against and within the phenomenological tradition. See for instance his *Derrida and Husserl: The Basic Problem of Phenomenology*. A more creative, but still recognisably philosophical approach to Derrida can be found in David Wills's *Matchbook: Essays in Deconstruction*.

15 Martin Hägglund, whose work I will follow in many ways, does in some sense over-emphasise the systematic nature of Derrida's argument. For a critique of this tendency, see: Gregg Lambert's *Return Statements: The Return of Religion in Contemporary Philosophy*.

16 Essays on Derrida and the secret are surprisingly rare, especially given the apparent prominence of the concept in his later work. The field is covered primarily by theologians. See, for example: Ian Almond's 'Derrida and the Secret of the Non-Secret: On Respiritualizing the Profane'. Roughly, in this book I will argue the opposite – namely that Derrida's work on the secret does far more to profane the spiritual, or that we should approach it from that direction. John D. Caputo devotes a section of one of his books to the issue. See his *The Prayers and Tears of Jacques Derrida: Religion Without Religion*, 108–12. I will address some of this reading later, in Chapter 4. Alongside this slim volume of references to Derrida and the secret, there has been some critical discussion of Derrida and the lie, particularly with reference to his essay 'History of the Lie: Prolegomena', and his relationship with Hannah Arendt. See, for example: Marguerite La Caze, 'It's Easier to Lie if You Believe it Yourself: Derrida, Arendt, and the Modern Lie'; Martin Jay, 'Pseudology: Derrida and Arendt on Lying in Politics'; Charles Barbour, 'The Acts of Faith: On Witnessing in Derrida and Arendt'.

17 Hägglund, *Radical Atheism: Derrida on the Time of Life*.

18 Bennington and Derrida, *Jacques Derrida*.

19 Searle was replying to Derrida's reading of Austin in 'Signature, Event, Context'. There Derrida had suggested that Austin's treatment of the 'speech act' or 'performative' remained too bound up with a fairly simple notion of 'intention' – one that, thought through to its inevitable conclusions, Austin's own theory of speech acts and performatives would properly put to the test. See Austin, *How to Do Things with Words*; Searle, 'Reiterating the Differences: A Reply to Derrida'. Derrida's reply to Searle in *Limited Inc.* also includes a pre-emptive reply to many of the criticisms developed by the Speculative Realists today.

20 See 'Derrida Seminar Translation Project', at http://derridaseminars.org.

21 The crucial text here is Derrida's *Archive Fever: A Freudian Impression*. Derrida takes as his point of departure a consideration of the Freud archive. But the arguments he makes could be applied to any archive.

22 As far as I can tell, the only article on the topic to appear to date is my own: 'The Hazard of Truth: Perjury and Oath in Derrida's Later Work'.

23 The canonical statement of the secularisation thesis is Max Weber's *The Protestant Ethic and the Spirit of Capitalism*.

24 Meillassoux, *After Finitude*, 26.

1

Under Oath: Secrecy, Perjury and the Social Bond

The Work of Deception

This chapter explores the relationship between secrecy and the social bond, or secrecy and society. The overall argument is derived from a reading of a number of Derrida's later works on secrecy and deception, perjury and the oath, and it can, I think, be stated in fairly plain terms. In short, secrecy or concealment are not only things that distinguish or separate us from others; they are also an integral part of what relates us to others, or keeps us within one another's orbit. The basic idea here has already been stated in the Introduction, but I will rehearse it again for the sake of clarity. We all have the capacity to hide our thoughts from one another. This is part of what Derrida means when he says 'every other is every bit other' (*GD* 84). So, in some fundamental sense, the other is always opaque to me. They are separate from me – an enigma, a mystery, a secret. And yet, for that very same reason, every time I interact with someone else, every time I exchange a word or even just a glance, I must enter into a kind of silent pact, oath, or bond. I must have already agreed to trust them, to have faith, and to believe that what they

38

are telling me is also what they genuinely believe. Otherwise no communication, no language or sign, would be possible at all.

This exchange of faith, or ungrounded and ungroundable belief, is, I would contend, constituent of any social relationship and any interaction whatsoever. Later, borrowing from Simmel, and from his important but often overlooked or misunderstood treatments of the secret, I will even go so far as to say that this belief is basic to what we mean by society – that, not only are there secret societies, or societies that try to conceal themselves from others, but that all society is structured or formed by the secret, and thus by the possibility of concealment and mendacity, prevarication and deceit. As mentioned above, in Simmel's terminology, secrecy is not only a type of association, it is a 'form of sociation [*Vergesellschaftung*]'.[1] Here, however, I simply want to point out the broad strokes of the argument that I will make in this chapter: We can hide from one another, I will claim or maintain, and therefore we must already be together. We share what divides us. We are held together by the very thing that holds us apart.

To begin opening up this line of thought, or to begin to provide a sense of what I think it entails, I want to develop a reading of a literary text – partly because, as we will see more explicitly in the next chapter, Derrida links this entire issue of the secret and the social to what we call literature, and especially literary fiction; but partly because I think this particular text captures much of what I am about to say in a uniquely effective manner. The text I have in mind is not one that especially preoccupied Derrida himself. But, in my opinion, it is the great canonical work of deception (with both meanings of that double genitive being intentional and significant). I am referring, as you might have guessed, to Shakespeare's *Othello*, a tragedy that is all about the failure of the kind of oath or bond I have just described, or the failure of faith. And here the issue is not only Othello's tragic inability to trust or have faith in Desdemona (or rather, the tragic way that Iago destroys that trust or faith). It is also about the tragic way that he places his faith in Iago, or in the one who is ultimately deceiving him. In fact, it might even be about *our* relationship with Iago, or the way we in the audience are strangely compelled to trust him as he tells us about his terrifying plans. But we will come back to this in a moment. First let us set the scene.

Shakespeare almost always introduces all of his major themes in the first act of his plays. In the case of *Othello*, it seems to me, the principal theme is revealed in the very first word. You will recall that Iago comes on stage with poor gullible Roderigo, the wealthy man whose foolish love for Desdemona becomes a key tool in Iago's plot. We do not know this yet, but we soon discover that Iago has just told Roderigo that Desdemona has eloped with Othello. We imagine that Iago has twisted the knife a little, or embellished his story with lewd details. At any rate, that is something he will take every opportunity to do as the play unfolds. Distraught, torn apart, Roderigo demands that Iago retract what he has just said: 'Tush never tell me! I take it most unkindly / That thou, Iago, who hast had my purse / As if the strings were thine, shouldst know of this.'[2] Tush, then, be quiet: do not tell me what you have already told me; perform the impossible task of recovering the secret you have just divulged; repay the debt you owe me by taking away from me something you have already given; extract me out of the fraternity of deception in which you have so viciously included me. From this moment forward, we in the audience are cued to the fact that the play will deal with secrecy and deception, including all of the cruelty involved in keeping secrets, but also, and perhaps more importantly, all of the cruelty involved in not keeping or telling them as well.

As we move into the play, along with becoming aware of the theme of secrecy, we also start to realise that this is not quite like Shakespeare's other great tragedies. For in every other case (Lear, Hamlet, Macbeth), the tragic hero either is the sovereign, or is immediately in line to become the sovereign, or battles his way to that position. This, however, will not be a play about political sovereignty. Othello is not and never will be the King. Although, in a sense, it will be a play about the sovereignty of the self, or the way that each of us, or some element of each of us, remains hidden from all others, or withdrawn in sovereign isolation. Indeed, in this respect, it seems very important that Othello is not a sovereign but a general. For he is a military general, to be sure; but, compared to Shakespeare's other tragic heroes, he is also quite general in the other sense of the word – average, quotidian, more like one of us. Even more precisely, Othello is a Moor, he is black, and this obviously marks him off from the other characters on the stage. But he is also general, or a kind of universal representation of anyone at all. Thus Othello is, paradoxically, the singular universal – a notion I will come back to a number of times throughout my argument in this book.

However, beyond the question of Othello's sovereignty, or his non-sovereign sovereignty, or singular universality, the character who really configures what I have called the opacity of the other, or the sense in which we all have an inner world, and thus a fundamental capacity to deceive, is, transparently, Iago. And there is a long history of interpretation, particularly prominent among the Romantics, which suggests that he is the more intriguing figure on the stage – that, in fact, in his diabolical nature, in the carnage he is able so calmly to effect, and the complexity of the plot he employs to do so, he is really Shakespeare's greatest creation.[3] Or, to put the point more dramatically, to the extent that he plots and stages the destruction of Othello, Iago mirrors the author himself. Iago *is* Shakespeare; he is the playwright, or the one who plots and stages. As a Spinozist might say, he is the creation that is also the creator.

Whether or not we accept this interpretation of the play, and of the relative status of Iago and Othello in Shakespeare's universe, there is one aspect of the Romantic consideration of Iago that I want to highlight here, or put to use for my own purposes. I am referring to Samuel Taylor Coleridge's well-known notion of Iago's 'motiveless malignity' – or, more elaborately, Coleridge's description of Iago's soliloquies as 'the motive searching of motiveless malignity'.[4] The idea here seems quite straightforward. In his soliloquies, or *parabases*, Iago often explains to us what he is about to do, and why he is about to do it. In fact, the dramatic tension of the play relies on this device. And, just as Roderigo is somehow drawn into Iago's secret from the first words of the play, so too are we in the audience always aware of what is happening behind the scenes, as it were. Iago confides in us. He tells us and only us his darkest secret. And this is an odd and frustrating experience, because it makes us tacitly complicit (everyone knows the notorious story of an enraged nineteenth-century audience member jumping up on stage and stabbing the actor playing Iago to death).

But, as Coleridge understood as well, despite all this divulging of secrets, the reasons that Iago gives for his actions (that he hates the Moor, that he hates all Moors, that he is also in love with Desdemona, that he heard a rumour that Othello has slept with his wife Emilia) account for neither the horror he sets in motion, nor the apparent glee with which he does so. We never really understand why Iago does what he does. And when he is finally caught, and Othello demands that he explain himself, Iago's response to Othello, and his last words in the play, might just as well be directed to us in the audience: 'Demand of me nothing, what you know, you know: / From this time forth I never will speak word.'[5]

On one reading, this notion that Iago lacked motivation could be said to point to his diabolical nature. It might signify the sense in which evil has no purpose, or issues from nowhere, and is directed towards nothing, and is thus akin to a natural or even ontological phenomenon or fact. This is a fascinating line of thought. But here I would like to suggest something entirely different – namely that, just like Othello, Iago is general, and the opacity of his inner world, the fact that his motivations or ideas remain hidden from us, configures, not evil *per se*, but our relations with any other in any situation whatsoever. We are all opaque to one another. Or, to refer to the famous cliché derived from Iago's first soliloquy in the play, no one can really wear their heart on their sleeve – although those who, like Othello, do not quite understand the human capacity to deceive, or, more accurately, operate with a sense of revelation and concealment that those around them do not share, are eminently vulnerable to the kind of plots that Iago ('Honest Iago', as Othello and others repeatedly call him) knits together, or spins like webs.

Another way to put this point would be to use an idiom that, not long ago, was very common, but today, has fallen out of favour – the idiom of semiotics. It is hardly an accident that Iago is Othello's ensign, or the one whose job it is to carry his sign or his banner when going into battle. It is also (and to recall a French etymology I mentioned in passing in the Introduction) hardly accidental that Cassio (or the figure who gets unjustly promoted above Iago, and who Iago also destroys by making it appear as though he has been sleeping with Desdemona) is Othello's lieutenant, or the one granted the authority to stand in for him, or take his place when he is absent (a meaning that Iago somehow finds a way to shift from the battlefield to the bedroom, which also advances his plan). Here signs are obviously very significant. But, to employ the language of semiotics, the richest and most powerful signifier in the play is, of course, Desdemona's handkerchief – an object that becomes the central engine, as it were, of Iago's machinations.

Because Iago the ensign understands the basic principle of semiotics (that the signifier has no natural relationship with the signified, and that its meaning is determined, not by its referent, but by the context in which it is put to use, and its difference from other signifiers), he proves to be particularly adept at manipulating the handkerchief, and manipulating Othello by way of this manipulation. Like any signifier, the handkerchief floats through the play, never having a specific or determinate meaning of its own, but, as it were, sponging up meaning from the world around it. For Othello, at any rate, if it were in Desdemona's possession, it would signify her fidelity. But if it is in Cassio's bedchamber (which, of course, is where Iago is able to have it placed, with the help of Emilia), it signifies the exact opposite. That one object might mean two diametrically opposed things is a knowledge that Iago the ensign brings into the action or the battle. And it is a knowledge that allows him repeatedly to trick those who do not share it.

But Othello is also deceptive about the meaning, or rather the origin, of the handkerchief. Despite Iago's insistence that he is honest to a fault, or has 'a constant, loving, noble nature',[6] and is thus particularly vulnerable to the kind of deception Iago intends to perform, Othello is not entirely innocent, it would appear, or entirely unfamiliar with the art of deception. Thus, and as many other commentators have noticed, in the course of the play, he tells two inconsistent stories about the handkerchief. First, after having already been shown by Iago that the handkerchief is in Cassio's possession, and been convinced that this must mean that Desdemona has been unfaithful, Othello confronts Desdemona, asks her to produce the object he already knows she does not have, and tells her that it was given to his mother by 'an Egyptian' magician or 'charmer' – one who, significantly, 'could almost read / The thoughts of people'.[7] The question of whether we can read one another's thoughts is, of course, what the scene, and indeed the play, is all about. But then later, after he has committed the unthinkable crime at the centre of the plot, he tries to explain himself, or explain how he was manipulated and deceived, to Grattiano. 'It was a handkerchief', he says, 'an antique token / My father gave my mother.'[8]

And it does not matter which of these versions is true. It matters that, with the possible exception of Egyptian charmers, no one will ever know which is true. In fact, no one will ever know which one Shakespeare believed to be true, or whether, in having his character tell two different and inconsistent stories about the handkerchief, he simply made a mistake. And now, finally, with this point in the background, we can hone in on the central issue in the play, or in my reading of the play – what I take to be Othello's crucial and tragic flaw, namely his enraged demand for 'ocular proof' of Desdemona's infidelity. In the famous Temptation Scene,[9] the moment Othello demands such proof is also the moment that Iago knows he has won. For, as Iago the great deceiver knows better than anyone else, 'ocular proof' of the faith or infidelity of another ('ocular proof' of their honesty or dishonesty) is something that no one can ever have, anywhere, at any time, in any situation whatsoever. In order to engage or interact in even the most minimal sense, we are compelled to trust the other, or to believe that what they say is also what they believe. And a lie is not just a falsehood about the external world. It is not a falsehood about, for example, what a handkerchief might mean, where it came from, or where it might be found. No, a lie is a deliberate manipulation of this absolutely necessary inter-subjective act of faith.

The Acts of Faith

Perhaps the most influential recent book on Derrida (or at least, the most celebrated and discussed one) is Martin Hägglund's *Radical Atheism*. It is a rich and sophisticated work, but its basic mission is stated very clearly at the outset. In sum, Hägglund wants to wrest Derrida from the tight embrace of the theologians who have laid claim to his inheritance, notably John D. Caputo and Kevin Hart, but many others as well. 'This book presents a sustained attempt to reassess the entire trajectory of Derrida's work', Hägglund announces with confidence. 'Refuting the notion that there was an ethical or religious "turn" in Derrida's thinking, I demonstrate that a radical atheism informs his writing from beginning to end.'[10] The argument from there gets complex, but it essentially involves an attempt to clarify Derrida's conception of time ('the becoming-space of time' and 'the becoming-time of space', as Derrida puts it, or the concept of 'spacing' more generally [*MP* 13]), and to show that he was consistently against any theological notion of what he called 'the unscathed [*l'indemne*]' (*AR* 85n31). Thus, and despite his frequent use of religious terminology, especially in the later work, for Derrida, there is no god – neither a positive one nor a negative one, neither a *deus absconditus* nor, to refer to Richard Kearney's hopeful phrases, a non-metaphysical 'god of the possible' or 'god who may be'.[11] There is only this world; there is no other or next.

While I am not willing to pledge my total commitment, and in fact agree with some of the reservations expressed by Michael Naas in his masterful work *Miracle and Machine* (which, I must point out, I believe to be the very best piece of Derrida scholarship to appear in a long time, and the standard by which we will have to judge all future efforts), I am nonetheless partial to this line of thought, or this attempt to ground Derrida in this world. But at the same time, anyone who wants to read Derrida in this fashion is going to have to account for his frequent use of explicitly religious terminology (faith, belief, the sacred, the holy, and so on), and provide some indication of how these parts of his thought are trying to say something other than what, on face value, they appear to mean.

The next few sections of this book are dedicated to that task. I will begin by trying to explain Derrida's use of one particularly important religious concept – specifically, the concept of the oath. This is an aspect of his later thought that, while hard to overlook when reading him, has received noticeably little attention in the secondary literature. But it is, I think, at the basis of much of what he is doing in his apparently religious works, or the works that, as Hägglund notes, so many have mistaken for an ethical and religious turn in his thought. Thus, and after having explained what I think Derrida means by the oath, and grounded it in this world, I will attempt to show how this concept has a bearing on larger elements of his project, and especially his understanding of the individual or the self, and its relationship with others, or the social. Ultimately my aim here is to show that, in Derrida, religious terms are not speculative claims about the absolute or the divine, but something more like phenomenological descriptions of rather average and everyday human and non-human interactions, most of which are articulated in that phrase that I will reference over and over: 'every other is every bit other' (*GD* 84).

The theme of the oath is persistent throughout Derrida's later work, and it can even be found in some very unlikely places. To take just one example as a point of departure, Derrida's *Specters of Marx* (perhaps his most widely read later text, or the one that generated the most commentary) is framed by a reflection on the oath, and on the way that it is constituent of any social or political bond. Thus Derrida's epigraph to the first chapter, 'Injunctions of Marx', comes from Act 1, Scene 5, of *Hamlet*, a play that Derrida uses as a kind of leitmotif in the book, and to which he repeatedly returns. As you will recall, having just encountered the ghost of King Hamlet, and agreed to take revenge on his murderer, Hamlet, his friends and the ghost all swear a pact of secrecy, at the end of which Hamlet utters the famous lines (also lines to which Derrida repeatedly returns in *Specters of Marx*, and reads in a completely overdetermined fashion), 'The time is out of joint: Oh cursed spite, / That ever I was born to set it right' (*SM* 3).

Now a great deal has been said about Derrida's appeal to the messianic, or the messianic promise, in *Specters of Marx* – the way that Marx's work promises, not this or that particular future, but some futurity, or some future yet to come. And a great deal has been said about his curious notion of a 'messianicity without messianism' and 'democracy to come' (probably, as I will explain later, my least favourite of Derrida's locutions or commitments) (*SM* 65). But as far as I can tell, in the considerable literature that has grown up around Derrida and Marx, and *Specters of Marx* in particular,[12] almost nothing has been said about this other religious concept – the concept of the oath, or the act of swearing to god. But I think if we can figure this out, we will have gone a long way towards understanding what Derrida wanted to say about both religion, on the one hand, and politics and society, on the other.

Derrida's treatment of the oath is closely bound up with another theme that we see developing in his later work, particularly in the wake of so many attempts to cast both Derrida and deconstruction as nihilistic, believing in nothing other than the endless play of signifiers and texts – specifically, the theme of 'affirmation', which Derrida gestures towards in his readings of Joyce's *Ulysses*, and especially of the climactic 'yes, yes' of Molly Bloom's final monologue ('UG' 296), but then develops more programmatically, I think, in his work on Heidegger and the question, *Of Spirit*. Thus, in a frequently cited footnote to that text, Derrida recalls Heidegger's privileging of the question – the forgotten 'question of Being', for example, or the sense in which *Dasein* is the 'being for whom Being is a question',[13] or the notion that 'questioning is the piety of thought',[14] and so forth.

But, Derrida continues, at another marginal or understated moment in his work, Heidegger admits that such questioning relies on a prior or more fundamental affirmation of language, or, if we can put it this way, of its promise. 'Language', Derrida writes, here parsing Heidegger, 'is already there, in advance of the moment at which any question can arise about it. In this it exceeds the question.' 'This advance', Derrida continues, 'is before any contract, a sort of promise or originary allegiance to which we must have in some sense already acquiesced, already said yes, given a pledge, whatever may be the negativity or problematicity of the discourse which may follow.' Importantly, what Derrida calls this promise or pledge implied *by* language need not be made *in* language. It need not be spoken explicitly as it is, in a sense, the prior condition of all speech. Thus, Derrida concludes, 'before the word, there is this sometimes wordless word which we name the "yes". A sort of preorginary pledge which precedes any other engagement in language or action' (*OS* 129n5).

If we had to articulate these claims in simple terms, we could say that, for Derrida, all language presupposes a belief in what it says. That is, on Derrida's account, whether or not they make this explicit (and obviously they usually do not), in order for language to function in any manner whatsoever, anyone who says anything at all to anyone else, or who uses any sign, implicitly prefaces it with a 'believe me when I say this', or a 'believe that this is also what I believe'. Conversely, and on the other side, anyone who hears anything, anyone who is the target or the object of any address, must (merely in order to recognise it as an address, and before trying either to question or to judge it) have already allowed that it is believable, or that the other person is being sincere. Moreover, Derrida maintains, even when this exchange of belief is betrayed (even when the speaker is lying or endeavouring to deceive, or even when the addressee is rebarbative or refuses to listen), it must already in some sense be in place, as a kind of background condition for the possibility of language or signification as such. We affirm, then, we say 'yes', we pledge to mean what we say and to believe what we hear, before we say or hear anything at all. We must believe, in other words, before we can doubt.

Of the many places in his later work where Derrida develops the themes of affirmation, promise and belief, here, and by way of example, I will point to just two: Derrida's autobiographical book (which is also a book about autobiography and testimony) *Monolingualism of the Other*, and a short but instructive essay that he wrote on Paul Celan called 'Poetics and Politics of Witnessing'. I will return to Derrida's interest in the concept of autobiography and testimony in my third chapter, especially when discussing his long consideration of Maurice Blanchot in '*Demeure*'. And I will explore his relationship with Celan in more detail in my fourth chapter, especially when considering *The Beast and the Sovereign, Volume 1*, to which Celan is integral. Here, however, I am primarily interested in sketching in broad terms how these two texts – *Monolingualism of the Other* and 'Poetics and Politics of Witnessing' – help us link Derrida's concern with affirmation, promise and belief, to the problem of the oath and the social bond.

As mentioned, *Monolingualism of the Other* is, in part, a work of autobiography (Derrida recounts his formative years growing up in Algeria, and his, as it were, fractured or split sense of identity). But it also a work about autobiography as such, or the act of testifying or speaking one's own unique truth. In a sense, Derrida proposes that, in so far as it issues from some particular subject, all language involves something like testimony, or an individual claiming to say what they genuinely believe, and what no one else can possibly know. In this manner, Derrida claims, 'an immanent structure of promise or desire, an expectation without horizon of expectation, informs all speech' (*MO* 21). Or, put differently, 'one can testify only to the unbelievable' or 'to what can, at any rate, only be believed' (20). And this is so because the referent or content of testimony (namely what the one who testifies genuinely believes) remains indiscernible to its audience or addressee. In this sense, testimony 'lies beyond the limit of proof, indication, certified acknowledgment [*le constat*] and knowledge'. And, Derrida concludes, we can only understand testimony (which means, ultimately, any language or sign whatsoever) in so far as we have 'faith' in the one who testifies. In every instance, testimony constitutes something of a 'miracle' (20) – the simple, everyday miracle of speaking and being believed.

A little later in the text, Derrida returns to and elaborates on this theme, now emphasising the concept of the promise. 'Each time I open my mouth', he writes, 'each time I speak or write, I *promise*' (*MO* 67). Invoking the work of J. L. Austin on performatives or speech acts, he maintains that 'the performative of the promise is not one speech act among others'; rather, 'it is implied by any other performative, and this promise heralds the uniqueness of a language to come' (67). That is to say, to speak or indeed engage with another at all is already to have promised to say something that only the speaker can know – something, as Derrida says, 'unique'. 'It is not possible to speak outside this promise', he continues. 'There can be no question of getting outside of this *uniqueness without unity*. It is not to be opposed to the other, nor even distinguished from the other. It is', Derrida maintains, here giving some indication of the meaning of his title, 'the monolanguage *of* the other' (68). Put differently, on Derrida's account, to speak at all is to have already promised to tell *my* truth – my unique and singular truth which the other can never fully verify or ascertain, but only affirm or believe.

In 'Poetics and Politics of Witnessing', not to mention many other places in Derrida's later work, this religious or theological idiom (testimony, faith, miracle, belief and so forth) gets amplified and expanded. Thus, in this short text, Derrida explicitly associates the affirmation implied by language with a 'belief', and even with what he calls a 'sacred trust', that is neither optional nor voluntary, but necessary and irreducible. 'We believe', Derrida says, 'as soon as we enter into relationship with the other' (*SQ* 77). 'As soon as you open your mouth, as soon as you exchange a look, even silently, a "believe me" is already involved, which echoes in the other' (84). Using even more conspicuously religious or theological language, Derrida refers to this a priori trust or belief as 'a holy or sacred space in the relationship to the other' (83). Even those who seek to lie, bear false witness, or commit perjury must assume the existence of this 'sacred space' or 'sacred trust' – this unspoken agreement or oath – in order to do so. Thus, in Derrida's words, perjury 'presupposes the sworn word, which it betrays' (79). It 'implies . . . sacrilisation in sacrilege'. And the perjurer 'commits perjury as such only insofar as he keeps in mind the sacredness of the oath'. He 'sacrifices', Derrida says, 'to the very thing he is betraying' (83).

These are undoubtedly the kinds of moments when it becomes tempting to associate Derrida's later work with religion and theology, to claim it took a 'religious turn', or to try to derive a theology from it – to characterise him, as Caputo has it, as a 'weak' theist,[15] or, to repeat Kearney's language, a 'post-metaphysical' one.[16] It is also, I think, the moment at which we should be cautious of doing so. For while it might seem like, in speaking about the 'holy and sacred space' of our relationships with one another, Derrida wants to situate human interaction within something like a religious frame (not, as Kearney says, to reaffirm 'the old god of metaphysics', but to invoke, again, 'the god who may be' or 'the god of the possible'),[17] one could just as well argue that what Derrida wants to reveal here is something far less mysterious, far less secretive, and far less obscure – something I will try to sketch in terms of two basic insights or claims:

First, for Derrida, the problem of belief, the sacred, the holy and what he calls the oath has to do, not with some fundamental mystery, but with the opacity of the other – the fact, once again, that we cannot know what another person is thinking. That is to say, for Derrida, the realm of thought (what we have provisionally been calling the inner world or interiority, and what our intellectual and spiritual tradition calls the soul) is something that no other person can see or know. It exceeds or is impenetrable to the interrogative gaze. And, if you will permit me to point this out yet again, this means that, while we might be able to verify whether or not something that the other person says accords with the external world of facts, we will never be able to verify whether it accords with their own inner convictions or beliefs. And that is why, each time anyone says anything to anyone else, they must implicitly preface it with a kind of sacred oath – a 'believe me when I say this', or a 'believe that this is what I believe is true'.

Second, and for related reasons, on Derrida's account, this sacred oath or, as he puts it, 'sacred trust' that structures all language and all interaction, is inseparable from perjury, betrayal and deceit. And it is inseparable in at least two ways, the second of which is more important, and more radical, than the first: In one sense, and obviously, every promise includes the possibility or the potential that it will not be kept. It relies on the uncertainty of the future, or what Derrida would call the 'to come'. There would be no promise, or no need to promise or to exchange an act of faith, if this were not the case. But in another sense, and beyond perjury as a future possibility, every promise (every oath, every act of swearing, whether explicit or implicit) includes, as part of that very act, an act of perjury as well. For Derrida, in other words, to swear is also, and at the same time, or in the same breath, to betray.

In the next section, then, I would like to elaborate on these two points by grounding them more directly in Derrida's texts, and especially in two texts in which he explicitly takes up the theme of perjury and the oath – namely, his *Adieu to Emmanuel Levinas*, on the one hand, and the essays and lectures collected together by Peggy Kamuf as *Without Alibi*, on the other. As I implied in the Introduction above, the difficulty with this procedure is the fact that, while these documents give us a great deal to work with, they are probably secondary in relation to the as yet unpublished seminars, particularly the seminar for 1997–8, which Derrida named *Questions de Responsabilité VII: Le Parjure et le Pardon*. At the same time, while it might be a little dodgy, I do not think it is a complete dodge (an abdication of responsibility or an alibi) to say that what we know of Derrida's theory of perjury justifies us in referring to, precisely, only what we know, or what is available at the moment. For while it might illuminate a great deal, the publication of the seminars, or even of a much larger and as yet unheard of *Nachlass* or literary remains, will not overcome what I have dubbed the opacity of the other, or the inseparability of perjury and the oath. It will not overcome the structural limits to knowledge. And to sacrifice saying something to the possibility that, in the future, something else might be shown to be the case is to sacrifice saying anything at all.

The Contaminating Third

Those who want to suggest that Derrida's work is amenable to theism, or that, at some point in his career, he took a 'religious turn', invariably emphasise his engagements with Levinas. And it would be difficult to deny either the rigour of this school of Derrida scholarship or the mutual respect that Derrida and Levinas clearly shared. At the same time, and as is also well known, Derrida was not uncritical of Levinas, or simply a proponent of his work. Indeed, from the time of his early essay 'Violence and Metaphysics', he issued a very serious challenge to Levinas, and to his central concept of ethics – a challenge that, depending on whose reading we accept, Levinas may or may not have spent the rest of his career trying to deflect. In this section, rather than rehearsing all of the debates over the relationship between Levinas and Derrida, I want to take up Hägglund's suggestion that, for Derrida, all theology, no matter how 'weak' or 'post-metaphysical', relies on a fantasy of purity, or a space or a realm of (as Derrida puts it and as Hägglund repeats), 'the unscathed [*l'indemne*]' (*AR* 85n31). Drawing on this approach, I want to show how, in the case of Levinas or Levinasian theology, this space or realm of 'the unscathed' is ethics itself, or the ethical relation or encounter with the other. Finally, I want to propose that, in his readings of Levinas, and perhaps especially in *Adieu*, Derrida reveals how this supposedly 'unscathed' ethics is, in fact, deeply scathed – impure, contaminated and corrupt. Indeed, for Derrida I think, ethics could not be ethical if this were not the case.

We can begin by recalling the broad parameters of Levinas's project, or the elements of it that are the most significant here. According to Levinas, of course, ethics is 'first philosophy'. It precedes ontology in the Heideggerian sense, or the realm of being as such, and justice, or the realm of politics and law. And it essentially entails a relation, or more accurately an encounter, between two people – an 'I' and a 'Thou', as Martin Buber puts it, or a 'me' and a 'you'. In contrast to liberal notions of tolerance and consensus, as well as the more Hegelian and communitarian theories of recognition, Levinas's ethical relation or encounter is not a dialogue, a conversation, or an attempt to achieve mutual understanding. On the contrary, Levinas argues that every attempt to achieve understanding in this fashion conceals a reduction of the other to the logic of the same – a comprehension or containment of the other that Levinas equates with violence. For Levinas, the ethical encounter must be an encounter with the other that remains other. It must be an encounter with absolute alterity or difference, an alterity or difference that Levinas configures in terms of 'the face'.[18]

On Levinas's account, then, ethics is a 'face-to-face'. It is an 'epiphany',[19] as he sometimes says, or a non-dialectical relation without relation in which I do not come to know the other, but experience a sense of infinite responsibility for them. Justice, on the other hand, is something rather different. While it is always marked by its 'trace', as Levinas says, justice can only follow or come after ethics. It is, in a word or two, secondary, derivative. And, unlike ethics, justice does involve an attempt to achieve mutual understanding. It also involves antagonisms and struggles, confrontations and debates. And, most significantly, it begins to take shape as soon as the primordial ethical 'face-to-face', or encounter between two people, is interrupted by that Levinas calls 'the third'[20] – another other, as it were, whose appearance ruptures or breaks the ethical relation and precipitates the juridical and political order of agreements and contracts, antagonisms and laws.

In *Adieu*, Derrida does not exactly critique this treatment of ethics, or attempt to reveal what it excludes or overlooks. Rather, he seeks to be both faithful and unfaithful to it. Or, more precisely, he seeks to show how one can only be faithful while being unfaithful at the same time. And, moreover, this faithful-unfaithfulness, this mixture of fidelity and its opposite, operates as a performance or enactment of the argument Derrida wants to make. That is to say, along with being faithful and unfaithful in his encounter with Levinas, Derrida wants to show how, on Levinas's own terms, every ethical encounter, or every encounter with the other, must be both faithful and unfaithful. It must both respect the absolute alterity of the other and betray this respect, or allow for the interruption of the third. Thus, and like many of Derrida's texts, *Adieu* can be read as a speech act, of sorts. It stages, enacts, or performs the logic that it describes.

In direct terms, Derrida shows how, according to what he calls Levinas's own 'axioms', the effort to separate the ethical 'face-to-face' from the juridical and political 'third' is untenable, and that neither can exist without presupposing the other. 'The third does not wait', Derrida maintains. 'His illeity [a Levinasian neologism intended to nominalize the French '*il y a*' or 'there is', and suggesting the sheer givenness of the other, or the sense in which the other subject is not constituted by me, like objects, but simply there] calls from the moment of the . . . face-to-face' (*AL* 33). And this is so, Derrida continues, because 'the absence of the third party would threaten with violence the purity of the ethical in the absolute immediacy of the face-to-face with the unique'. That is to say, while the presence of the third introduces one mode or manifestation of violence, namely that of comprehension, or the reduction of the alterity of the other to the same, the absence of the third leaves open the possibility for another, ultimately indistinguishable violence – what Derrida calls 'the violence of a pure and immediate ethics in the face-to-face of the face', one that entails 'the impossibility of discerning good from evil, love from hatred, giving from taking, desire for life and death drive, hospitable welcome from selfish or narcissistic enclosure'. And in this sense, Derrida concludes, 'the third party . . . protect[s] against the vertigo of ethical violence itself' (33).

The simple (but by no means false) way to understand this set of claims would be to say that, for Derrida, there is no opposition between ethical non-violence, on the one hand, and juridical or political violence, on the other. Rather, there are various modes and distributions of violence – modes and distributions that we are always seeking to negotiate, calculate and adjudicate. A more complicated approach would be to say that, on Derrida's account, ethics and justice are both separate and inseparable. Or more precisely, if also paradoxically, Derrida proposes that, if ethics and justice are separate in the way that Levinas describes (if they must be separated because the latter entails a violence that destroys the former), then ethics and justice cannot be separate in the way that Levinas describes (then they cannot be separated because the latter is the only thing that prevents the same violence in the former). Despite his effort to avoid this outcome by placing one before the other, or characterising one as 'first philosophy', Levinas's reflections on ethics and justice constitute what Derrida often refers to as a 'double bind'.

It is at this moment in his reading of Levinas that Derrida begins to introduce the themes of secrecy and deception. Or, more precisely, at this moment he begins to reflect on the concepts of perjury and the oath. And, in essence, he proposes that, if the ethical 'face-to-face' or the relation between two people is necessarily contaminated or compromised by the third and the realm of justice in general, then every relation is structured by a faithlessness or infidelity. Every ethical person is an infidel, we might say. Thus, while acknowledging that Levinas does not really use this language, Derrida suggests that the 'face-to-face' – which, again, is not about mutual understanding, and might even be said to precede language in the communicative sense – can be characterised as 'a sort of oath [*serment*] before the letter', or 'a promise of respect or unconditional fidelity' that comes before any particular agreement or exchange (*AL* 68). But, Derrida continues, if the ethical encounter is always already compromised or contaminated by the third, then that promise of fidelity (that 'oath before the letter', as Derrida calls it) is compromised and contaminated as well. Put simply, my implied promise of fidelity to you, my oath to you, is inseparable from my equally compelling promise of fidelity to another. Or, as Derrida writes, I am always forced to decide 'between betrayal and betrayal, always more than one betrayal' (68). Thus, for Derrida, every encounter involves, if we can put it this way, a failure to keep the word (that has not been spoken) even before it has (not) been spoken.

Moving away from his engagement with Levinas now, it is significant, I think, that Derrida develops a number of similar themes in *The Gift of Death* – the book from which we have taken our watchword, or 'every other is every bit other', but also a text that has attracted rather theistic readings. At the centre of *The Gift of Death* is a discussion of Kierkegaard, and especially Kierkegaard's treatment of the story of Abraham in *Fear and Trembling*, or what Derrida calls the 'nocturnal mystery' of Abraham's silent obedience in the face of God's command that he sacrifice his son (his silent affirmation of a higher, singular, or particular law that exceeds the universal law of ethics). But as I have been stressing throughout, what appears rather elevated at first, is actually quite quotidian and down to earth, and Derrida goes out of his way to point this out, relating the story of Abraham sacrificing his son to 'the most common everyday experience of responsibility' (*GD* 68). For, Derrida says, here still echoing or silently invoking Levinas, 'what binds me in my singularity to the absolute singularity of the other propels me into the space or risk of absolute sacrifice' (68). In other words, to be responsible to one other is to be irresponsible towards infinitely more. 'I can respond to the one (or to the One), that is to say to the other, only by sacrificing to that one the other', Derrida writes. 'I am responsible to anyone (that is to say to the other) only by failing in my responsibility to all others' (71). And in this sense, Derrida concludes, once again demystifying what many of his readers want to mystify, 'what can be said about Abraham's relation to God can be said about my relation without relation to *every other (one) as every (bit) other* [*tout autre comme tout autre*]' (78).

To return briefly to the text with which we began, or *Othello*, you will recall that, on my reading, there is a sense in which we are all in the same position as, or could be substituted for, both Othello (in that he is the general, or more like one of us) and Iago (in that his opacity, or his ability to hide his inner world, configures the opacity of everyone, or each and every one of us). Here however, and given what we have just said about perjury, the oath and the necessity of betrayal, we might add that we are also all in the same position as Desdemona as well, or the Desdemona who, when asked by her father Brabantio to whom she owes her 'obedience', Othello or himself, replies: 'My noble father, / I do perceive here a divided duty.'[21] It is indeed part of the essential nature of every duty (or, if you prefer, every responsibility, ethics, or oath) to be divided, and thus contaminated, not only by a possible future betrayal, or what may or may not come to pass, but by the betrayal that is built into the very act of promising, swearing or agreeing (whether tacitly or openly, as part of the structure of language or as part of a formal procedure) with one another to be faithful. From the very beginning, then, in every instance, and without exception, we have always already betrayed the one we love most, simply by pretending we can love just one, or love anything most. From the very beginning, we have always already failed to keep our word. And that, in fact, would be a condition of giving it in the first place.

Perjury Squared

The story of Abraham provides Derrida with a powerful example of the manner in which we are never outside of or prior to the realm of betrayal and perjury, and, contra Levinas, especially not when we are called upon to be ethical. It is an example of the sense in which we are always compelled to decide between betrayals – the sense in which 'there is always more than one betrayal'. But we must also ask, as Derrida asks, exactly how we should characterise Abraham's betrayal of the ethical (in the sense of the universal, as Kierkegaard would say) in favour of faith (or his singular faith in God). For, when commanded to take Isaac and travel to Mount Moriah, Abraham does not tell Sarah, his wife, what God has asked him to do. Rather, he remains silent – he paradoxically betrays her with his silence. What, Derrida wonders throughout *The Gift of Death*, is the status of this silence? Can we call it a lie? Is it really an intentional act of deception? Can we call it a perjury, or a betrayal of a sworn oath? The problem is compounded by the fact that, in the story, Abraham is not told why he must sacrifice Isaac on Mount Moriah, although he is told to keep it a secret. So in a sense, the secret he must keep is a secret to which he himself is not privy. In a sense he is silent, not about something that he knows, but precisely about what he does not know. Can *that* kind of silence constitute a lie? Can it constitute a perjury?

In this section I will consider the way Derrida explores these conundrums and others like them, not in *The Gift of Death* (which is a text that I will return to in other parts of this book), but in the collection of essays and lectures called *Without Alibi* (material that, as far as I can tell, has received less attention in the secondary literature, or at any rate, far less than it merits). I want to begin by explicating a distinction that Derrida makes between a lie and a perjury, and the way that, for Derrida, and contrary to our conventional understanding, perjury is not a species of lying, but lying is a species of perjury – the way that, on Derrida's account, while every lie is a perjury, or breaks the at least implied oath that we have already discussed, not every perjury is a lie. I will then try to draw out some of the consequences for this inversion of what we might call common sense – consequences which are, I hope to show, formidable and profound. For essentially Derrida maintains that a lie is an intentional act, or the act of a self-conscious subject, while perjury is not, or does not need to be. That is to say, while I can only lie in so far as I know that I am lying, I can commit perjury in far less conscious and intentional ways. Indeed, for Derrida, and in a very unusual sense, it may even be possible for someone else to commit perjury on my behalf.

With this last statement in mind, it is perhaps helpful to begin our interpretation of *Without Alibi* by recalling some of the details of its production and publication. As intimated above, while it has his name on the cover, there is a sense in which *Without Alibi* was not written by Derrida, or a sense in which it both was and was not. For it consists of essays and lectures that Peggy Kamuf translated, edited and collected together in a volume that has no French equivalent or original, but that, as Kamuf tells us in her 'Preface', was first devised while she was working on a translation of Derrida's '"*La Parjure*", *Perhaps*: Storytelling and Lying'.[22] Thus we might say that, just as *Adieu* is an example of what it states, in that it is a faithfully-unfaithful reading of Levinas about the faithfully-unfaithful nature of all relationships, so too, and in a more radical way, is *Without Alibi*, in that it *is* a kind of perjury, on the one hand, and it is *about* all kinds of perjury, on the other. In some sense, that is to say, and to invoke a scenario the significance of which will soon become apparent, in constructing Derrida in this fashion, Kamuf tries to speak his truth for him – to provide a confession, as it were, or to ventriloquise his inner, hidden, secret convictions.

After a series of prefaces and introductions, the first chapter of *Without Alibi* is 'History of the Lie: Prolegomena', a piece mentioned in my Introduction above, and one based on a lecture that Derrida gave at the New School of Social Research in memory of Hannah Arendt. The most programmatic piece in the volume, it is also the one that has been commented on most extensively.[23] But at the same time, as it is positioned in the volume as a whole (which, again, was not Derrida's devising), it operates as a way of clearing ground – of, as we said, establishing the distinction between the perjury and the lie, and showing how the former is a subset of the latter. For, as Derrida insists, and as we have already noted in other places, what characterises a lie is not the error or falsehood of the statement, but that the liar intends to deceive.

The lie is, as Derrida puts it, here following Augustine to the letter, 'an *intentional* act' (*WA* 34). It relies on what Augustine calls 'the explicit will to deceive (*fallendi cupiditas, voluntas fallendi*)' (35). It therefore relies on a self that is capable of, or even defined by, intention and will – a self-present or self-identical self, one that is entirely in control of its will and its desire. Thus Derrida ultimately concludes that, while we can never really do away with what he calls 'the *frank concept* of the lie' (36), while 'no ethics, no law or right, [and] no politics could long withstand . . . its pure and simple disappearance' (37), nevertheless, in a post-psychoanalytic and post-Heideggerian scene, where concepts like intention, will and self-presence have been so thoroughly realigned, we must acknowledge it limits as well.

It is at this point that Kamuf has Derrida turn to the question of perjury, and of perjury as opposed to (or as other or more than) lying. Thus the next two chapters of the book deal with the work of Paul de Man, and invoke, in one way or another, the notorious events surrounding the so-called 'De Man Affair'. To recall: shortly after his death, Derrida's friend and intellectual companion was revealed to have published as a young man a number of essays and articles in collaborationist journals during the Nazi occupation of Belgium and France – articles that, moreover, he never acknowledged having written, and seems to have wanted to hide or conceal. In 'Typewriter Ribbon: Limited Inc (2)' and (even more so, or more explicitly at least), in '"*La Parjure*", *Perhaps*: Storytelling and Lying', Derrida explores this context, as well as the curious experience of having been involved in publishing and commenting on the articles in question as soon as they had been exposed, and thus the experience of, in a sense, confessing for de Man, or being asked or expected to do so. And Derrida does all of this by way of a reading of a number of literary and philosophical confessions: the *Confessions* of Augustine and Rousseau in the first case; and a novel by Henri Thomas called *La Parjure* (which, significantly, could be translated as either 'The Perjury' or 'The Perjurer') in the second.

The reference to these three texts (Augustine's *Confessions*, Rousseau's *Confessions*, and Thomas's *La Parjure*) is particularly relevant, given that all three of them explicitly cross back and forth across the boundaries between literature and truth. That is to say, all three call on us to consider the truth of the literary statement, or what it might mean to tell the truth in writing. Or, to put it differently, they call on us to consider the extent to which the truth is inseparable from literature and fiction, and the sense in which it is always inflected by something like perjury, or betrayal of an implicit promise to 'tell the whole truth and nothing but the truth', as one familiar locution has it. Those issues aside for a moment, here I merely want to point out that, while the first two confessions Derrida discusses (Augustine and Rousseau) are well known, in fact canonical, the third, or Thomas's *La Parjure* (a work that was first published in French in 1964, and that has yet to be translated into English) is not. And yet, in the context of the theory of perjury developed in these essays, Derrida's reading of *La Parjure* can probably be given privilege over his reading of Augustine and Rousseau.

As Derrida notes, *La Parjure* is presented as a novel. That, at any rate, is what it says on its cover. But at the same time, Derrida also notes that, 'toward the end of the Seventies' de Man informed him that the main character in the novel (Stéphane Chalier) was loosely based on him (*WA* 170). So, like most fictions, it is partly fictional and partly real. It does and it does not hook into the so-called 'real' world. In the novel (as in real life, or the real life of someone named de Man), Chalier emigrates from Belgium to America, leaving behind him a wife and a child; then, after becoming a successful academic in America, he marries another woman, thus committing perjury, or lying under oath. Significantly, the story is not told by Chalier, but by a friend and acolyte, who is also the narrator. When agents of the law finally catch up to Chalier, the friend–acolyte–narrator attempts to intervene on his behalf. But because of this intervention, the committee investigating the case demand that Chalier confess his crime. Chalier in turn demands that the friend-acolyte-narrator himself write the confession, on the grounds that he is in some respect responsible for the committee having demanded it.

The issue, then, if we can put it this way, is what it might mean to write, or rather to ghost write, the confession of a perjurer, and thus become a perjurer as well. Can I confess for another? Is that not the precise opposite of confession, inasmuch as confession entails the singular individual revealing their own inner convictions? At the same time, and on the other hand, is not every confession also a kind of confession for another, inasmuch as, when I confess, I do so about things that I did in the past, or I claim to speak as the person I was in the past – and I today am not entirely the same I who I was yesterday or then? Moreover, and as Derrida points out as well, is there not a sense in which the novel itself, or the words of the narrator in the novel, constitute the confession that Chalier requested? Is there not, in other words, a sense in which the novel itself is 'the perjury' named in its title? And does this not compel us to wonder if all narrative fiction, and perhaps all literature, involves something like perjury, or even a kind of double or triple perjury – betraying the law by betraying someone else's act of betrayal?

As I will discuss in the next chapter, many of these ideas return in Derrida's later writings on secrecy and literature – paradigmatically, I think, but not exclusively, in an essay called '*Demeure*', which deals with a short story by Maurice Blanchot called 'The Instant of My Death'. In that piece Derrida explores in considerable detail the enigmatic notion of the singular universal, already hinted at in my consideration of the character of Othello above (Othello the singular black character on stage, but also Othello the general, or the one who could be substituted by anyone). But for our purposes here, in this consideration of Derrida's reading of Thomas's *La Parjure*, I will focus primarily on the second aspect of this paradox, or what I will call 'the substitutability of the "I"' – the notion that the 'I' or the self cannot be undivided, self-identical or unique, but is in some manner constitutionally doubled or split, and receives its meaning from this split.

That is to say, what interests Derrida in his analysis of perjury and confession is not only the sense in which every 'I' can be substituted for or by someone else, or some other 'I' (as, for example, when we authorise someone else to speak in our name, or name someone else as the executor of our inheritance or remains), but the more radical sense in which there is no 'I' without such substitutions – the sense in which the 'I', while singular, is also the effect of an illimitable chain of substitutions, and thus plural, even up to the point of being universal. Or, put crudely, each 'I', each supposed in-dividual, takes shape only in relation to the other, and is thus divided from the beginning.

In Levinas, for example, and as we have seen, this fundamental relation to the other, and thus this internal division, constitutes the basis for ethics, or for a kind of hospitality or openness to the other that does not collapse into a totalising embrace, or a reduction of the alterity of the other to the same. On this point, Derrida kind of agrees. But he also, and in equal measure, disagrees. For he proposes that, at the exact same moment, or in the exact same experience or act, this relation to the other also requires, necessitates, and even itself constitutes a perjury, a betrayal, or an absolute infidelity. It ensures the impossibility of being entirely true, as well as the impossibility of ever really communicating or confessing one's own unique truth. It opens me up to the other by simultaneously closing me off. It relates me to the other by separating me from her. It leaves all of us forever in the midst of what, in her considerable wisdom, Desdemona calls a 'divided duty'.

The Secret Society

A. The Point and the Whole

In 1906, the then fledgling *American Journal of Sociology* (now the major organ of empirical sociology in the United States and probably throughout the world) published an article by Georg Simmel (in the English translation of the journal's founding editor Albion Small) called 'The Sociology of Secrecy and of Secret Societies'. A slightly different version of the German 'original' appeared two years later, as '*Das Geheimnis und die geheime Gesellschaft*', the fifth chapter of Simmel's masterwork *Soziologie: Untersuchungen über die Formen der Vergesellschaftung*. Simmel's *Soziology* (the entirety of which was translated for the first time into English only very recently as *Sociology: Inquiries into the Construction of Social Forms*) consists of a compendium, of sorts, of Simmel's earlier studies and investigations – a cobbling together and rearticulation of previous research projects and lines of thought. So we must conclude that, in 1906, Albion Small was translating from a manuscript that Simmel had lent to him, or given him a copy of, and that Simmel would later rework (in minor but nevertheless interesting ways), and insert into his larger book.

I mention this history, in part to keep the record as straight as it can be, and in part because, by means of an accident of publication, this text on secrets is itself a little secretive. In being published first in English translation, and later in the German 'original', it conceals its origin, in some sense, or plays a sleight of hand with the very concept of origins, as well as that of the author, authority and intentionality. And, as I point out elsewhere,[24] there are some intriguing differences, not only between Small's original English translation and Simmel's original German original, but also between the original English translation and the more recent English translation of the original German original – that is, the fifth chapter of *Sociology: Inquiries into the Construction of Social Forms*. But rather than getting lost in the maze that is the publication and translation history of this text (a maze that, I would contend, and if I had more time, try to prove, merely configures in a stark manner the production and publication history of any text anywhere), perhaps I should start by setting out its basic claims, and explaining how it helps illuminate the point I am trying to make in this chapter.

On face value, Simmel's 'Sociology of Secrecy and of Secret Societies' looks like a prolegomenon to a much larger study, or an attempt to open up an entire field of research. It looks, that is, something like the sociology of the secret society. And, to the extent that it has received attention among professional sociologists, that is how it is typically put to use. Simmel sets out a number of very broad theoretical parameters, or some speculations about the general structure and function of secret societies, and then goes on to say a few things about a handful of specific examples: the Illuminati; the Pythagoreans; the Gallic druids; the Freemasons; the Omladina and Carbonari; and so forth. But this approach to the text, while very fruitful no doubt, in some sense misses Simmel's main point, a point that he makes in nearly all of his more empirical investigations of particular social phenomena – namely that the secret is not only one social object (or, to employ his own terminology, one particular 'content') among many, but also, and at the same time, a general 'form of sociation [*Vergesellschaftung*]',[25] or something that structures and gives shape to social relations as such. To understand this point, we should probably begin by saying something very quickly about Simmel's method (or what he dubbed 'sociological aesthetics',[26] which is also the title of one of his more important early essays), and his principal concept (namely, what he called 'interaction [*Wechselwirkung*]').[27]

In his essay 'Sociological Aesthetics' (published in 1896, on the cusp of his most creative period), Simmel proposes not simply that society can be treated or studied as though it were analogous to a work of art, but rather that society operates exactly like a work of art, even that society *is* a work of art, in that each particular element is reflective of, or makes sense in relation to, the totality or the universal whole. The essay is organised around a dialectic (or an opposition or dynamic tension) between what Simmel calls symmetry and asymmetry. 'The origin of all aesthetic themes is found in symmetry', Simmel maintains. 'Thus the first aesthetic step leads beyond the mere acceptance of the meaninglessness of things to a will to transform them symmetrically.' However, he continues, 'as aesthetic values are refined and deepened, human beings return to the irregular and asymmetrical'.[28] But this dialectic or tension (which appears to be modelled on the distinction, in Kant's *Critique of Judgment*, between the beautiful and the sublime) does not quite capture or exhaust the thrust of Simmel's argument.

For Simmel, it is not simply a question of an opposition between the discrete charm of a model where parts make sense in relation to the whole, on the one hand, and that of a model in which they do not, on the other. Rather, society is a work of art because each particular element can be treated or represented as the universal structure of the whole; each singular content can be conceived of as a general form. Thus, in a crucial passage, Simmel writes: 'For us the essence of aesthetic observation and interpretation lies in the fact that the typical is to be found in what is unique, the law-like in what is fortuitous, the essence and significance of things in the superficial and transitory . . . Every point', he goes on, 'conceals the possibility of being released into absolute aesthetic significance. To the adequately trained eye, the total beauty, the total meaning of the world as a whole radiates from every single point.'[29] In other words, there is no direct opposition between particular and universal, element and whole, or content and form. Rather, for Simmel, every single element can, when analysed by a 'trained eye', or in microscopic detail, be made to stand in for the general form.

Simmel employs this method, or this 'sociological aesthetics', in many of his writings, as when he considers, for instance, the city, the stranger, fashion, or simply the place settings at a dinner table. But perhaps the most extensive example (an example, that is, of Simmel's approach to exemplarity in general) can be found in his crucial book-length study *The Philosophy of Money*. Here again, it would be a mistake to think of this book exclusively as an empirical and historical discussion of one social phenomena (although, here again, it is surely that as well). Simmel's more profound claim is that this thing that we typically think of as, at best, a secondary representation of something else (like value), or, at worst, a fetishistic and mystifying tool of economic oppression, can actually be shown to configure, or, more dramatically, to *constitute*, the general form of all social relations, or all interactions. As seen in the passage from 'Sociological Aesthetics' cited a moment ago, what appears to be completely 'superficial and transitory' actually contains 'the total meaning of the world'. Thus Simmel begins his discussion of money by insisting that 'not a single line of these investigations is meant to be a statement about economics'. Rather, he says, 'money is simply a means, a material or an example for the presentation of relations that exist between the most superficial, "realistic" and fortuitous phenomena and the most idealized powers of existence'. His point, then, is less to study money itself, than to 'derive from the surface level of economic affairs a guideline that leads to the ultimate values and things of importance in all that is human'.[30] And money is his chosen example, not because it is somehow fundamental to the human condition, but precisely because it is not.

But what exactly does Simmel mean when he proposes that money can be treated as the general form of all relations or inter-actions? It is a difficult question to answer in brief, because, for reasons you might already be able to intuit, Simmel was a thinker of the detail, and of the infinite significance of the infinitely small. But broadly, he meant that money holds us together while holding us apart, or that it operates as a way of relating us to one another while at the same time separating us from one another. It is an object or a concept that comes in-between us, representing the trust we must have for one another precisely because we cannot collapse into one another, or become fully socialised and void of our discrete identity. To elaborate, it might be helpful to note that Simmel makes the same sort of argument in his essay 'The Sociology of the Meal', where he develops a reading of the table at a dinner party, and shows how, not only the table, but all of the different place settings and cutlery, ornaments and linen, not to mention gestures and manners, etiquette and norms, come in-between the guests, relating them to one another by simultaneously separating them from one another.[31] Indeed, if it were an exaggeration, it would not be much of one to say that, on Simmel's account, society consists of nothing but an infinite number of such acts or moments of relation and separation, identity and difference, revelation and concealment.

This, then, is what Simmel means by 'interaction', which he defines quite clearly in a subsection of the opening chapter of his *Sociology* called 'How is Society Possible?' An older translation of this passage is more eloquent, although the new one, in the most recent full English edition of the *Sociology* mentioned above, is more accurate. So I will provide them both. 'The fact that in certain respects the individual is not an element of society constitutes the positive condition for the possibility that in other respects he is', Simmel writes; 'the way in which he is sociated is determined or co-determined by the way in which he is not'.[32] Or again, in the more recent translation, with some of the original German interspersed for guidance: 'What kind a person's socialized being [*Vergesellschaft-Seins*] is, is determined or co-determined by the kind of one's unsocialized being [*Nicht-Vergesellschaft-Seins*].'[33] In other words, our social existence is correlative with our unsocial existence, or what Simmel sometimes calls 'psychology' or the 'inner world'. To engage with others in a public space, or in the clear light of day, is also, and in the exact same moment, to build, compose, or carve out an interior realm that others cannot access or see – an inward darkness that remains impenetrable to the light. To be public is simultaneously to be secretive.

B. *The Human and Its Other*

With this basic understanding of Simmel's method (sociological aesthetics) and principal concept (interaction) in the background, then, we can perhaps begin to understand why, for him, the problem of the secret was not just one problem among many, or one particularly intriguing social arrangement. For Simmel, our capacity to be social at all is intimately bound up with our capacity to keep secrets, or to hide things from others in a place they will never be able to access or know. Thus Simmel begins his essay (or chapter, depending on where we decide to start, and which version we decide to read) on secrets and secret societies with some very broad claims about what we might call social epistemology, or the way that what we know about other people is premised on, and in fact relies on, an infinitely larger amount that we do not know. And this premising of knowledge on ignorance is not something we can overcome, Simmel maintains. On the contrary, it is an absolute law of social interaction, or the unshakable condition for the possibility of any engagement whatsoever.

This is obviously the case for everyday encounters, where we must engage with one another, not as complete human beings, but as particular social functions or roles. If the barista says, 'how are you today?' the answer is never how you actually are today

('I am terrible, I had a fight with my father, my car broke down, everyone I love is avoiding me'). No, it is, and it must always be, 'fine', or something along those lines – something parsimonious and, to put the matter bluntly, false. Otherwise the line-up at the coffee shop would eternally be a block long, and every conversation would entail a potentially endless mutual spilling of thoughts and affect, with neither function nor uptake on the part of any other person. But, on Simmel's account, the same principle applies even to relations of absolute intimacy, such as love. We are always compelled to hold back or stay silent about infinitely more than we could ever give up or say. Society (all society, from the order of the smallest exchange to the order of the entire world) requires this capacity for silence and reserve. It must include and even foster these colossal, pitch chambers of the unspoken that each of us carries around within ourselves, everywhere we go, whenever we go there.

As Simmel puts it in a passage that, intriguingly, we do not find in the English original of 'The Sociology of Secrecy and of Secret Societies', the one translated by Albion Small, but only in Simmel's original German, which was, once again, published later (and, to confuse matters even more, a passage that Simmel appears to have lifted from an even earlier, and as yet untranslated 1899 essay called '*Zur Psychologie un Soziologie der Lüge*'):[34] 'All' of what 'we share with another in words or perhaps in some other way, even the most subjective, the most impulsive, the most intimate [*Vertrausteste*], is a selection from the actual mental totality.' We only ever disclose what Simmel calls 'fragments [*Bruchstücke*] of our actual inner life', and keep the vast majority of it to ourselves. 'With an instinct that automatically excludes its opposite, we show nobody the purely causal real course of our mental processes, wholly incoherent and irrational from the standpoint of logic, factuality, and meaningfulness', Simmel writes, 'but always only extract from them stylised by selection and arrangement, and there is no other interaction [*Verkehr*] and no other society [*Gesellschaft*] at all thinkable than that resting on this teleologically determined ignorance of one for the other.'[35]

Simmel's point, then, is not merely that humans have the capacity to keep things to themselves, or remain silent rather than speaking. No, far more dramatically, his point is that humans can only engage with one another *because* they have this capacity. In fact, even more radically, Simmel's point is that each and every social interaction both requires and actively constitutes or creates this silent interiority, or this inward void of the self. And finally, he concludes, this principle holds for relations of 'sincere self-revelation [*aufrichtige Uns-Offenbaren*]' just as much as it does for those of 'deceptive self-concealment [*lügenhafte Uns-Verbergen*]'.[36]

Now again, these kinds of claims, while found in his essay or chapter on secrets and secret societies, are not reducible to that one study, but form components of his much greater and ever shifting theoretical programme or architecture. In particular, they are related to two of his larger projects or lines of investigation: first, and as we have already mentioned, his work on money; and second, and perhaps more interestingly, his sociology of religion. In the case of money, Simmel makes the connection explicitly in 'The Sociology of Secrecy and of Secret Societies' when he says that, because humans have this particular capacity to conceal, and thus potentially to deceive, all relations involve an element of trust, faith or belief. Every society can be understood in terms of what Simmel calls 'a *credit-economy*',[37] or an exchange of credit without any guarantee of a genuine return. And these assertions, of course, are very similar to the ones we saw Derrida making in the earlier sections of this chapter. Money configures all social relations, first of all, because it relates and separates us at the same time, and second, because it involves an enormous, collective and completely ungrounded and ungroundable act of faith.[38]

And this brings us to the second larger line of investigation in Simmel's work that the theory of the secret helps illuminate, namely Simmel's sociology of religion. This element of his thought is very complex, and I will not attempt to do justice to even a single part of it here in one paragraph. Nevertheless, the central claim, or the one that I want to emphasise at least, is relatively clear: Just as, in Durkheim, the religious concept of God emerges as a way to make sense of the social fact, or the immaterial, unseen, but still compelling force of society,[39] so too, for Simmel, does the religious notion of faith emerge as a way of configuring, or giving form to, the innumerable acts of faith in one another that make up all of our relations.[40] So religion has a kind of epiphenomenal status. And it is also mistaken (or at least not quite accurate) to think that secularisation diminishes the power of religion in modernity. In fact, on the contrary, while in what Simmel would call a 'traditional society' people had a fairly good sense of all of the other people with whom they might interact on any given day, and thus did not really have to extend a great deal of credit to trust or mistrust them, in modernity, and especially in urban modernity, we are relentlessly being asked to trust forces and individuals that or who we know exactly nothing about. In other words, from Simmel's point of view, or from a Simmelian one at any rate, modernity is the great age of faith.

But the point in Simmel's treatment of the secret that I want to highlight (and I guess deconstruct, if I can be granted just one use of that terribly overused word) comes from a slightly different direction or place. Specifically, I would like to point out that, when Simmel speaks about the secret, he speaks about it as something specifically human. In fact, he goes so far as to say that the ability to keep secrets is the defining feature of the human, or what other thinkers might have called the human essence. The key passage appears relatively early in 'The Sociology of the Secret and of Secret Societies', where Simmel is setting up his discussion of what we have already dubbed social epistemology. He begins by noting, in a fashion that is very reminiscent of phenomenology, that all of our experience or relations with other beings involve both blindness and insight, ignorance and knowledge. But, he proposes, our relations with other *human* beings involve something more or something else as well. 'Our knowledge of the whole of being [*Gesamtdasein*] on which our actions are grounded is marked by characteristic limitations and diversions', Simmel explains. We 'preserve only so much truth' and 'so much ignorance' or 'error as is useful for our practical actions'.[41] At the same time, he continues, while all beings might be hidden from us in various ways and to varying degrees, only the human being hides itself intentionally or deliberately. More accurately, only the human being possesses an interior or inner world that it can actively (and indefinitely) conceal.

As Simmel puts it: 'There is inside the sphere of objects for truth and illusion [*Warheit und Täuschung*] a certain portion in which both can take on a character that occurs nowhere else: the interior [*das Innere*] of the person before us, who can either intentionally [*mit Willen*] reveal to us the truth about oneself or deceive us with a lie or concealment [*Lüge und Verheimlichung*] about it.' In fact, Simmel contends, 'no other object can explain itself to us or hide itself from us in this way as a person can, because no other modifies its behaviour through consideration of its becoming known'.[42] Thus, on Simmel's account, while the human or the person is clearly one being among many, what makes it unique, what makes it a specifically *human* being, is not only the fact that it possesses an 'inner world', or what is sometimes called consciousness, but, and perhaps more importantly, the fact that it can conceal this world from others – or, in simple terms, lie. In short, the human is human because the human can deceive. And consciousness more or less is the capacity to hide itself from others, or to keep itself to itself.

Now this is a very powerful notion, and it is not a new one. As we will see in a later section of this book, it is also a notion that interests Derrida, particularly in an essay on negative theology called 'How to Avoid Speaking: Denials'. But, without wanting to take pot shots at a fairly venerable idea, it does seem to invite a rather quick riposte. For if the very nature of consciousness or the inner world is the capacity to hide itself, or keep itself to itself, then how can we ever know whether or not we are encountering it? And more importantly, how can we humans deny this capacity to other beings, or pretend that, somehow, we are the only ones who possess it?

To be clear, I am speaking here in strictly logical terms. I am not speculating wildly, or suggesting, for example, that animals, or objects, or simply existence as such could possess what we call consciousness. I am simply saying that, if we define consciousness as the ability to conceal itself, then that definition gives us no good reason to limit it to human beings; indeed, and in the opposite sense, it would appear to give us many good reasons to suggest that it is *not* something only possessed by human beings. In fact, if the goal of the definition of consciousness or the inner world is to delimit what is unique about the human, if that is the purpose of this particular intellectual manoeuvre, then one could hardly think of a worse definition. For it basically tells us that we can never really know. It bars us from knowing what it pretends to expose. And thus, to put the matter frankly, it seems to me that, along with opening up a whole array of fascinating problems, Simmel's treatment of the secret almost compels us to dismantle the humanist assumptions on which both it and many other theories like it (in fact, an entire tradition of them) are based, or that they take as their completely unjustified point of departure.

In the next, and last, section of this chapter, then, I would like to begin do just that – or rather, begin the process of dismantling what I will call the humanist conception of the secret, by returning to Derrida. In particular, I would like to consider a moment in Derrida's work where he criticises Jacques Lacan for making an argument that sounds a great deal like the one we have just seen Simmel deploy, namely the argument that, while animals and other beings may be able to conceal themselves or even distort their appearance, only the human has the capacity to lie, to deceive, or deliberately and intentionally to hide its deliberations and intentions. As we will see, this line of thought might even result in the unravelling of the concept we have been circling around throughout this chapter – the concept of society or the social. Or, to put the point differently, this line of thought may reveal the spot at which the concept of society (at least in so far as we assume that it applies to a discrete or even universal collection of that being that calls itself the human being) unravels itself, or collapses in on itself, exposing its barren foundation.

Feint Trace

We have been speaking, then, of a social bond, and of a bond that is paradoxically reliant on what appears to stand outside of it, namely, the secret. We have been speaking about an oath that we all must take, implicitly or explicitly, each and every time we engage with one another in any manner whatsoever – an oath, moreover, that is structurally broken from the instant we take it, or that we can only honour in so far as, at the exact same moment, or in the exact same breath, we dishonour or betray it. And, particularly in our reading of Simmel, we have been trying to argue that this always already taken and always already broken oath or pledge is in some sense what we mean by society, or the stuff we try to capture when we use that particular word. But we have also arrived at a curious impasse or block. If we follow Simmel's logic, we have discovered, or the logic of this line of thought in general, to what appears to be its inevitable conclusion, then we seem to lose the meaning of what we are trying to define, or lose the meaning of the social as such. More accurately, we have discovered that, if we accept the notion that secrecy is a condition of the social, or that we are held together in so far as we are held apart, then it becomes difficult to set boundaries on the social. And we certainly cannot limit it to something called the human being.

Does this mean, I wonder, that we must abandon the concept of the social altogether? At this point, does it liquefy, and slip through our fingers? I am not certain, nor will I take a position on that topic one way or another, at least not at this point. Rather, in this final section of my chapter I will turn my attention back to Derrida, and particularly (and as mentioned) to one of his key engagements with Lacan. Like Simmel's 'The Sociology of Secrecy and of Secret Societies', the text I have in mind also has a rather complicated production and publication history, one that it is worth trying to explain before we begin to approach it. Its original source is a ten-hour long seminar that Derrida presented at a conference in Cerisy in 1997 called *'L'animal autobiographique'*. He published part of that seminar in the conference proceedings under the title *'l'Animal que donc je suis (ti suivre)'*. Later, after his death, in 2006, some of Derrida's literary executors collected together a number of his texts on the animal, and published them under the general title *L'animal que donc je suis*. Along with *'l'Animal que donc je suis (ti suivre)'* these included a piece called *'Et si l'animal répondait'*, which was also one component of that ten-hour long seminar. In the meantime, however, Derrida had reused the same text as the 'Fourth Session' of his 2001–2 seminars. And those seminars have subsequently been published and translated as *The Beast and the Sovereign, Volume 1*. So we have a document that has taken many forms, one that Derrida himself repeated in more than one context, and thus one for which he must have had some affection.

For our purposes, I am going to work with the version of the text found in the 'Fourth Session' of *The Beast and the Sovereign, Volume 1*. I am doing so, primarily to avoid confusion, but also because it situates the thought within the context of a larger research agenda on sovereignty, which will be important in this book. Derrida begins the session by putting some decidedly clear limits on his approach to Lacan – limits that, to my mind, almost disqualify the piece as a serious engagement with Lacan's work. Effectively, Derrida says he will focus exclusively on the early Lacan, or the Lacan of the *Écrits*, and brushes aside a whole history of debates over how or whether Lacan's thought changes and develops in the seminars that follow. With this limitation established, the point here is not to determine whether Derrida's reading of Lacan is accurate or fair, but to explore how it might help us understand the cluster of issues we are examining – specifically, the question of the relationship between the secret and the social, and the, as we now know, connected question of the relationship between the human and the non-human, or in this case, the animal. And to telegraph my point: basically, Derrida has Lacan argue that the robust difference between the human and the animal consists of the ability to lie, and that, against his own explicit intentions, this compels Lacan to reinscribe a very traditional concept of the sovereign, self-legislating human subject. And this is a conception of the subject that the Freudian or psychoanalytic notion of the unconscious destroys. As a result, Derrida concludes, we should adopt his idiom of what he calls the trace rather than Lacan's idiom of the signifier or the sign.

The text that Derrida emphasises in his analysis is Lacan's 'The Subversion of the Subject and the Dialectic of Desire in the Freudian Unconscious', which is the transcript of an address that Lacan gave to a philosophical colloquium on 'Dialectic' in Royaumont in 1960.[43] Derrida draws our attention to a handful of remarks in that text on the topic of the animal. As Derrida explains, Lacan begins by describing the difference between the animal and the human in terms of a fairly classical distinction between 'reacting' and 'responding'. While the animal can only react to external stimuli or to the other in general, the human can effectively respond, or engage the other in spontaneous and unpredictable conversation or exchange. To put it differently, while animal language is generally reducible to signification in the simplest sense, with each signifier designating a clearly defined signified, human language entails a gap between the signifier and the signified, and thus the possibility of both misunderstanding and understanding. To react is to know immediately what something means, and thus not to have any real sense of 'meaning' as humans experience it. To respond, on the other hand, is not to know immediately, and thus to be afflicted with the desire for meaning that human language sets in motion.

In Lacanian terms, and again as Derrida explains, this means that the animal remains 'captured' within the 'imaginary' stage, wherein they relate to themselves and not to the other. The human, however, is able to graduate, as it were, into the 'symbolic' realm, or the realm of what Lacan calls Speech and Truth — the realm, that is to say, of genuine language and of relations with others. Thus, as Lacan puts it, while the animal might use some rudimentary form of signification, only the human is 'the subject of the signifier'. To be slightly more precise, while certain animals (roughly, from bees to apes) use something like language to communicate, and thus to relate to one another, only humans use language in a way that is ambiguous, uncertain, or impossible to pin down, and thus to relate to what Lacan calls the Other.

But the trick here has to do with trickery itself. For Lacan's point is not only that animals live in a meaningless world while humans live in one teeming and pulsating with meaning. Rather, and more complexly, his point is that the world of meaning in which we humans live is opened up by the possibility of deception, or a fundamental lack that is inscribed in every human relationship, and that is not there in animal ones. More accurately (and this qualification is crucial to the whole discussion), on Lacan's account, only the human experiences meaning, or enters into the symbolic order of language, Speech and Truth, because only the human can lie.

Lacan elaborates on this paradox by way of a distinction between what he calls 'feint' and 'trickery'. While the animal can 'feign', he says, or deceive in any number of ways, it cannot, like the human, 'feign feigning', or deceive by pretending to deceive. On this account, the animal can, for example, use camouflage to avoid being detected by either predators or prey, or it can exaggerate one feature or another in order to attract a mate. It can even seek to elude a pursuer by first moving in one direction and then suddenly bolting in a different one. But it cannot do these things in such a way as to make the other believe that it is trying or intending to deceive them so as to deceive them, as it were, from another direction or on another level. It cannot engage in what, parsing Lacan, Derrida calls 'second degree feint' (*BS1* 122). To put it differently again, while animal 'feint' involves hiding an objective truth behind a simulation or false display, human 'trickery' entails playing a game of truth, or toying with or manipulating, as it were, *both* the other's expectation that I will tell the truth, or reveal to them what I genuinely believe (what, above, we referred to as the oath), *and* their knowledge that I might not (the betrayal that is built into the oath).

Here it is helpful to recall the classic definition of the lie, derived from Augustine, and outlined in my Introduction above. The lie, we remember, is not the same as the falsehood or the mistake. 'Not everyone who says a false thing lies', as Augustine says, so long as they 'believe' or 'opine' that what they say is true.[44] The liar, in other words, does not need to say something objectively false, although they often do that as well. Rather, what characterises a lie, and what distinguishes it from an error or a mistake, is that the liar says something that they themselves do not believe – something that is, if we can put it this way, subjectively false. More accurately (and this is another important qualification), what characterises a lie is that the liar *tries* or *intends* to make another believe that they believe something other than what they genuinely believe. In fact, that will be our formal definition of the lie: I lie when I intentionally set out to make *you* believe that *I* believe something *other* than what I *genuinely* believe. A lie, in other words, is not necessarily objectively false; and it is not even subjectively false. Rather, and as I already intimated above, towards the end of my discussion of *Othello*, a lie is inter-subjectively false. It is an attempt to take advantage of the faith that inter-subjective (or simply social) relations require and entail.

Thus, and to elaborate, it is more than possible to lie while saying something that is objectively true (for example, when I am trying to deceive another concerning something about which I myself am mistaken, and mistakenly tell the objective truth). Moreover, it is even possible to lie while saying something subjectively true, or what I genuinely believe (for example, when I know that the one I want to deceive is likely not to believe me, or when I am operating in a context in which I know that I will be perceived as a prevaricator or a fool). The lie, then, is not merely about concealing the truth, whether objective or subjective. Rather (and this is the crucial part for Lacan, and for his effort to use the lie to distinguish between the human and the animal), it can only take shape in a symbolic realm or inter-subjective world where truth is the effect of an illimitable set of expectations, conventions, presuppositions, background assumptions, prior arrangements and so on – the vast majority of which remain unspoken and even unconscious. And this, overall, is the experience that Lacan wants to deny the animal. It is, for him, the essentially human experience. To put it in pithy terms, for Lacan, or for Derrida's Lacan at any rate, we are capable of Truth because we are capable of lying.

Now, as if matters were not complex enough, Derrida's response (or reaction) to this line of thought is more suggestive than definitive. He moves, as he says early in the seminar series, like a wolf, tracking back and forth across the texts he reads, almost eternally preparing – '*à pas de loup*', as he puts it (*BS1* 9). However, if we had to cut to the chase, and articulate his claims directly, we could probably do worse than to say that Derrida asks Lacan two questions: First, can we really be so certain that the animal, or rather all animals (and throughout *The Beast and the Sovereign, Volume 1* Derrida constantly reminds us that 'the' animal does not exist, and that the concept of 'animal' is almost absurdly totalising, with no clear boundaries or internal consistency), do not engage in something like trickery? And second, and conversely, can we really be so certain that the human does?

In the first instance, Derrida refers us to his own much earlier work on psychoanalysis, specifically the essay 'Freud and the Scene of Writing' (a reference that, as an aside, suggests an incredible amount of consistency in Derrida's career, or an incredibly long and connected engagement with psychoanalysis). As you might recall, in 'Freud and the Scene of Writing' Derrida reads Freud's metapsychology though the lens of Freud's brief 'Note on the "Mystic Writing Pad"', in which Freud compares memory to a children's toy made up of a carbon block covered by translucent plastic, thus allowing one to write on the plastic with any blunt object and to erase what is written by lifting it up, while at the same time leaving traces of what was written on the block underneath. In this earlier work, Derrida says, he therefore 'substituted the concept of the trace for that of the signifier' (*BS1* 130). He also did so, he suggests, because, while we can at least conceive of the signifier in terms of its immediate reference or connection to a signified, 'the concept of the trace presupposes that *to trace* comes down to *effacing a trace* as much as imprinting it' (130). We cannot think of the trace, in other words, without thinking of its effacement. And for Derrida, this suggests that even the most rudimentary signs, or the most rudimentary acts of 'feigning', whether those of humans or animals, are already acts of 'trickery' or 'feigning feint'. Or, to put it differently, the unconscious is already implied in the concept of the trace, and thus already there, as soon as there is anything like a trace.

In the second instance, or the question of whether we can be so certain that, in contradistinction to animals, the human can 'feign feigning' (that is, lie), Derrida reminds us of what we can only call the most basic Freudian or psychoanalytic insight or concept – namely, of course, that the ego is not the master of the self, and that we are driven by unconscious compulsions and desires that we cannot consciously or fully control. Thus, while it is certainly possible to lie in the conventional sense, or to conceal our thoughts behind the veil of our expressions, it is not entirely clear that anyone could ever do so in a *fully* wilful, intentional or conscious manner. It is not entirely clear, that is to say (indeed, from a psychoanalytic perspective, it is entirely unlikely), that one can do so without leaving behind all kinds of symptomatic traces, not only of what one is hiding, but also of one's both conscious and unconscious reasons for trying to hide it. As Derrida says, 'this does not come down to saying that the trace cannot be effaced'; rather, it suggests that 'it is in the nature of the trace that it always effaces itself'. As a result, Derrida maintains, nobody, whether it is 'God, man, or beast', is a 'master or sovereign subject', or has 'the power to efface *its* trace' entirely 'at its disposal'. On the contrary, Derrida concludes, 'in this respect man has no more sovereign *power* to efface his traces than the so-called "animal"' (*BS1* 131).

We can try to put these claims in formulaic terms: For Derrida, before any individual subject wills it or intends it to be so, and before any inter-subjective community or symbolic order of language and exchange opens up the possibility for it to be so, the trace (or if it helps to stay with the more familiar language, the sign) is itself tricky, or entails a kind of trickery. To repeat Derrida's words, 'the trace . . . always effaces itself'. Yes, both individuals and collectives or groups can trick one another. They can intentionally and wilfully keep all kinds of secrets and tell all kinds of lies. However, no individual and no collective, not even the collective we call humanity, can contain or control trickery as such. No sovereign can master it, or surround it with a wall to limit its motion. It is always already operative on a level that precedes or subtends sovereign authority, as soon as there is any trace or any sign whatsoever. Before there is an 'I' or a 'we', I or we might say, there is the possibility of trickery. And this, finally, is the insight that Derrida derives from the Freudian or psychoanalytic notion of the unconscious, and the one that, inasmuch as he insists on the distinction between the animal and the human, or reaction and response, eludes Lacan.

But where does this leave us with respect to our consideration of the secret and the social bond? Where does it leave us with respect to the problem of the always taken and always broken oath that conditions every relation and exchange? Are we dismantling the concept of the social altogether, or attempting to expand and develop it in new and previously unheard of ways? Again, I do not have a direct or simple answer to these kinds of questions. Rather, or for now at least, they will have to remain questions or provocations – efforts to open issues up rather than finish or resolve them. But we can say that, in his discussion of the animal, Derrida has clearly expanded the stakes of these matters considerably. After Derrida, if we are going to speak about society, we must already be speaking about a multitude of things that have never even once been considered under that rubric or term, the iceberg tip of which would be 'animals', whatever that word is supposed to mean. In the next two chapters, I want to continue to explore these issues: first, by way of a detour, as it were, through the question of literature, and the related notion of testimony or avowal; and then, more directly, and more philosophically, through a consideration of what Derrida has to say about consciousness, or consciousness and ontology.

Notes

1 See note 6 to the Introduction (p. 35).

2 Shakespeare, *Othello*, 1.1.1–3.

3 The critic who placed the most emphasis on Iago was undoubtedly Samuel Taylor Coleridge. We will analyse his famous notion of Iago's 'motiveless malignity' in a moment. In the nineteenth century, the counter-argument to Coleridge's was presented by William Hazlitt. But it only amplifies the significance of Iago. 'Iago is to be sure an extreme instance of this kind; that is to say, of diseased intellectual activity, with the most perfect indifference to moral good or evil, or rather a decided preference for the latter . . . He is quite nearly as indifferent to his own fate as he is to that of others; he runs all risks for a trifling and doubtful advantage' (Hazlitt, *Characters of Shakespeare's Plays*, 55). That is to say, for Hazlitt, Iago appears to be motivated by neither moral concerns nor crass self-interest. Rather, he is diabolically evil. That is, he pursues evil for evil's sake.

4 Coleridge, *Coleridge's Criticism of Shakespeare*, 113.

5 Shakespeare, *Othello*, 5.3.300–1.

6 Shakespeare, *Othello*, 1.2.280.

7 Shakespeare, *Othello*, 3.4.56–8.

8 Shakespeare, *Othello*, 5.2.215–16.

9 Shakespeare, *Othello*, 3.2.

10 Hägglund, *Radical Atheism*, 1.

11 Kearney, *The God Who May Be*, 2.

12 Selecting here from a considerably larger literature, see: Sprinker (ed.), *Ghostly Demarcations: A Symposium on Jacques Derrida's Specters of Marx;*

Guerlac and Cheah (eds), *Derrida and the Time of the Political*; Bennington, 'Derrida and Politics'; Leitch, 'Late Derrida: The Politics of Sovereignty'. For a rather recent exploration of the issue that takes a similar approach to reading Derrida as I do (that is, that endeavours at every step to render his thought in lucid terms and relate it to the 'real world'), see Lüdelmann, *Politics of Deconstruction: A New Introduction to Jacques Derrida*.

13 Heidegger, *Being and Time*, 6–7.
14 Heidegger, 'The Question Concerning Technology', 341.
15 Caputo, *The Weakness of God: A Theology of the Event*.
16 Kearney, *God Who*, 64.
17 Kearney, *God Who*, 2.
18 Levinas, *Totality and Infinity*, 79–81.
19 Levinas, *Otherwise than Being*, 212–13.
20 Levinas, *Otherwise than Being*, 16, 81–2; see also Simons, 'The Third: Levinas's Theoretical Move from An-Archical Ethics to the Realm of Justice and Politics'.
21 Shakespeare, *Othello*, 1.3.179.
22 Kamuf, 'Preface: Toward the Event', in Derrida, *Without Alibi*.
23 See Introduction, note 16, above.
24 Barbour, 'The Maker of Lies: Simmel, Mendacity and the Economy of Faith'.
25 See Introduction, note 6, above.
26 Simmel, 'Sociological Aesthetics', in *The Conflict of Modern Culture and Other Essays*.
27 For a discussion of Simmel's crucial concept of 'interaction', see Nedelmann, 'The Continuing Relevance of Georg Simmel: Staking Out Anew the Field of Sociology'.
28 Simmel, 'Sociological Aesthetics', 69.
29 Simmel, 'Sociological Aesthetics', 69.
30 Simmel, *The Philosophy of Money*, 6.
31 Simmel, 'Sociology of the Meal', in *Simmel on Culture: Selected Writings*.
32 Simmel, 'How is Society Possible?', 18.
33 Simmel, *Sociology*, 45.
34 Simmel, '*Zur Psychologie un Soziologie der Lüge*', in *Georg Simmel: Gesamtausgabe in 24 Bänden: Band 5*.
35 Simmel, *Sociology*, 311.
36 Simmel, *Sociology*, 311.
37 Simmel, 'Secrecy and Secret Societies', 445.
38 At a number of moments in this book, I brush up against the question of

economics. We have already seen, for example, how, along with being the great mythological and historical figure of secrecy and invisibility, Gyges of Lydia also played an instrumental role in the invention and development of money, or a system of exchanging value through representations that themselves have no intrinsic value. Here we have just touched on Simmel's notion that, far from being an illusion or a fetish (as a Marxist might say), money is a paradigm or a privileged example of social interaction in general. It configures what we are always doing whenever we relate to one another, or even to the world, in any way whatsoever. If I had more space, and if it did not take me too far away from the central theme of secrecy, I would be inclined to associate this line of thought with Derrida's comments on money, and on the work of Charles Baudelaire, in *Given Time: I. Counterfeit Money*. On this topic, see Jennifer Bajorek's *Counterfeit Capital: Poetic Labour and Revolutionary Irony*.

39 Durkheim, *Elementary Forms of Religious Life*.
40 See Simmel, 'A Contribution to the Sociology of Religion' and 'Religion', both in *Essays on Religion*.
41 Simmel, *Sociology*, 309.
42 Simmel, *Sociology*, 310.
43 Lacan, 'The Subversion of the Subject and the Dialectic of Desire in the Freudian Unconscious', in *Écrits: The First Complete English Edition*.
44 Augustine, 'On Lying', 457.

2

Open Secrets: Literature, Politics and Testimonial Truth

Paper Screen

We concluded the last chapter by discussing Derrida's treatment of Lacan, and especially the 'Fourth Session' of *The Beast and the Sovereign, Volume 1* – a text that, as we mentioned as well, has also been published separately, under the name 'And Say the Animal Responded'. The impetus behind our interpretation of this text was the unravelling, as it were, of the concept of society we had spun together throughout the course of the earlier argument, and perhaps an unravelling of the concept of society full stop. If society consists of our relations with others, or, paradoxically, with that aspect of the other that remains hidden from us (the part that is, in Derrida's words, 'every bit other'), then, we noted, there is no reason to limit what we mean by the other to the other human being, or even the other living creature. And at that point, and at the risk of sounding completely speculative, even bizarre, we had to admit that what we mean by society might just as well dissolve into something more like ecology, perhaps even ontology, or existence in the broadest possible sense of the word. Society thus becomes a concept with no boundaries, and thus no concept at all.

At the same time, while this dissolution of society or the social was underway, some of the more conventionally political implications of our investigation of the secret began to appear as well, albeit in an understated and less than explicit manner. For, as we saw, in replacing the idiom of the sign with that of the trace, Derrida was trying to get at a definition of the secret that subtends or exceeds any notion of the sovereign subject, or simply the sovereign as such. In Derrida's words, which we quoted above, 'it is in the nature of the trace that it effaces itself', and 'man has no more sovereign power to efface his traces than the so-called "animal"' (*BS1* 131). This reference to sovereignty, or to the political in general, is part of the reason why I chose to use the 'Fourth Session' of *The Beast and the Sovereign, Volume 1* as my point of departure, rather than the piece published separately as 'And Say the Animal Responded'. For doing so implicitly locates Derrida's reflections on the animal within the context of a larger or parallel research agenda on the problem of the sovereign.

For Derrida, then, the trace (which operates by effacing itself) is something that can never be fully mastered or controlled by a sovereign, or by any localised or centralised authority. In more directly political terms, we might say that, on this account, there is always some secret that exceeds the order of the sovereign – some secret, then, that exceeds every political or juridical order, as well as every *res publica*, every institution, and every public sphere or realm. As I suggested in my Introduction, however, the mistake would be to reduce this secret to the liberal conception of privacy, or the dialectic between privacy, on the one side, and security, on the other. Indeed, such a reduction would only reinstate the concept of sovereignty that, along with Derrida, we are trying to dismantle or get in underneath.

We will have to circle around some more before we get a clearer picture of what, exactly, we mean by a secret that exceeds the sovereign, or that cannot be mastered by it. But here one fairly straightforward implication can be sketched at the outset. If it is the case that secrecy is somehow greater or more than sovereignty, or that some secret remains beyond its control, then the surveillance state that is currently in the process of being forged (the emerging state that the Snowden revelations began to expose) is not only an affront to privacy in the liberal sense, but is also based on a particularly dangerous fantasy scenario, namely the fantasy of full exposure, complete illumination, or absolute transparency.[1]

Here the state appears to seek a monopoly, not so much on violence, as one familiar conception has it, as on the secret. It claims, as it were, a secret right to expose all secrets, and to do so in secret. And this is a dangerous fantasy, I want to propose, not in so far as it threatens to collapse the distinction between the public and the private, thus trammelling liberal freedom, but in so far as it makes an attempt to eliminate the secrecy on which all of our relations and engagements with one another rely. In other words, the fantasy of full transparency is not simply an affront to the sovereign individual or liberal subject, isolated from others and equipped with her rights (although it might be that as well). No, more radically, and more destructively perhaps, it is an affront to the social, to the very fabric of our being-together (our *Mitsein*, as Heidegger would say), or to that which, to repeat my own expression, holds us together by holding us apart.

In recent years, some very interesting work on secrecy and politics has been pursued by the English scholar and author Clare Birchall. In an article called 'The Aesthetics of the Secret', for example, Birchall sets out explicitly to politicise the question of the secret, and to do so in a new way. She argues, as I have here, that, while the Snowden revelations were crucial, the Snowden Affair, or the debate that took place as a result, was meagre at best. Its participants, Birchall notes, broke down into two basic groups: those who defended Snowden as a champion of liberal privacy and freedom ('#Patriot', as she sharply puts it); and those who attacked him as a threat to American national security ('#Traitor').[2] In an attempt to avoid this deadlock, or what I have presented as the deadlock of liberalism, Birchall introduces the concept of what she calls 'the datatariat', and turns our attention to the theoretical work of Jacques Rancière.

On Birchall's account, the 'datatariat' is organised by a demand for a politics that 'puts first not privacy but rather a secrecy that interferes with the dominant order', or (and here the influence of Rancière becomes manifest) the dominant 'distribution of the sensible'. To this end, Birchall proposes a distinction between what she calls a 'hermeneutics' and an 'aesthetics of the sensible'.[3] If the first treats the secret as essentially a problem to be overcome, a mystery to be solved, or a code to be broken, or if it treats secrets in strictly cognitive or intellectual terms, with the ultimate telos or goal being total transparency or truth, the second treats the secret, again, in terms of a 'distribution of the sensible' – a distribution, as it were, of the said and the unsaid, the seen and the unseen, the heard and the unheard, and so forth. And again following Rancière, Birchall suggests that it cannot be a question of getting rid of all state secrets (rendering the state 'transparent') or defending privacy rights. Rather, the issue is, how to distinguish between a distribution of the sensible (or the secret) that supports inequality (which is what the Snowden revelations exposed) and one that supports equality (which is what Birchall's 'datatariat' is intended to build).

This approach to the secret has the virtue of inserting the question into a number of larger conversations going on right now around the question of data – having to do, for example, with what Davida Panagia calls 'data-politik',[4] or what Lilliana Bounegru calls 'data publics'.[5] Behind much of this work, I think, in one way or another, is Gilles Deleuze's influential 'Postscript on the Societies of Control', in which Deleuze challenged Foucault's continued use of notions like the subject and the body, and suggested that, in a post-disciplinary society, power operates on a much more micrological level, one having to do with the organisation or control, not of knowledge, but of bits of information, or what today we call data. I think this is all extremely interesting and promising. However, my concern with it (which is not a robust concern, and perhaps more a question of temperament than one of tactics) is its tendency towards a teleo-logical conception of history, especially the recent past, and a deterministic conception of technology – its tendency, that is to say, to suggest that recent technological developments necessitate a complete break with all previous modes of investigation, and constitute the advent of an entirely new political scene or age.

In my last chapter, I will briefly touch upon a somewhat different approach to the problems of time and technology, one informed by Derrida's conception of time (which, as mentioned in my Introduction, I take to be the most significant contribu-tion of his early work, or his deconstruction of the metaphysics of presence) and by his notions of prosthetics and originary technics.[6] Here, however, I want to turn my attention to a question that many, I suspect, will think of as moribund, or at least a little quaint and antique – namely, the question of litera-ture. No doubt we will discover that, as we saw in the previous chapter with respect to the concept of society, upon close inspection, the concept of literature will unravel, or buckle, as it were, under its own weight. And no doubt the once powerful and formidable tradition or institution called 'literature' is under considerable stress today, and often for very good reasons. But it is the claim, or perhaps the gamble, of this chapter that an engagement with this tradition or institution can shed important light on the question of the secret, and the way this question has increasingly come to define our age.

To begin this consideration of literature, then, I would like to return to a much earlier piece in which Derrida sought to engage with the work of Lacan – specifically, the essay 'The Purveyor of Truth', where Derrida took issue with Lacan's reading of Edgar Allan Poe's short story 'The Purloined Letter' in his 'Seminar of "The Purloined Letter"'. Here as above, in my reading of the 'Fourth Session', my concern will not be to determine whether or not Derrida got Lacan right, or how Lacan might have reacted or responded. It will not even be, hermeneutically, to try to unlock the essential meaning of Derrida's extremely sophisticated piece.[7] Rather, I will endeavour to use Derrida's discussion of Lacan and Poe to open up a problem that will concern me throughout the rest of this chapter – the same problem that we began to glimpse earlier, when considering Othello's status as both a Moor and a general, namely the problem of the singular universal. Once this problem or issue has been sketched, I will turn most of my attention to Derrida's later engagements with Maurice Blanchot, and especially an important essay called '*Demeure*: Fiction and Testimony'. This, I think, is the essay in which Derrida parcels together the questions of literature, politics and secrecy most explicitly. And our consideration of it will also begin to prepare us for the topic that will be at the centre of the final chapter of this book: the question of time.

But before we go any further into this particular labyrinth, let me be very clear that, as we move ahead, things are not going to become very clear. That is to say, we are going to have to come at the question of politics and the secret a little obliquely – not head on, but on the diagonal or via the peripheral. The reasons for this approach will emerge, I hope, as it develops and takes shape. But if I had to put the matter directly (but also a little crudely, for the purposes of introduction), I would say that, since we are talking about something we cannot really ever talk about (that is, a secret), it will never be possible to put the matter directly. For some, then, it will be a frustrating experience. It will seem like we are circling around indefinitely, without ever putting our foot down on a definitive assertion or claim. Or, to use Derrida's image once again, it will seem like we are tracking back and forth across something's trail, eternally preparing, '*à pas de loup*' (*BS1* 9). It will seem, perhaps, like we are putting something off, or deferring a moment of confrontation, or holding something in abeyance, out into a future yet to come, or suggesting, in Kantian terms, that it has a regulative but not a constative status. But that is not at all what we will be doing; and it is not at all what Derrida suggests either. And this question, too, will return in the final chapter.

Open Secrets

As we saw with *Othello* above, 'The Purloined Letter' seems to announce its major concern, or the theme of secrecy and deception, straight away, in its opening words. First, following the title, we have an epigraph – a passage in Latin, attributed to Seneca. The number of readers who happen to speak Latin will, of course, be limited. And so, we have a passage, one that leads into the text by way of an arcane and hermetic language, in fact the language of the arcane and hermetic *par excellence*. What does the passage say? '*Nil sapientiæ odiosus acumine nimio*',[8] which can be roughly translated as 'nothing is more odious to knowledge (or more harmful) than too much (or acute) wisdom (or cleverness)'. Do not be too clever, in other words. Do not be irritatingly smart. But if we were too clever or smart (if we were a Smart Alec, as the English idiom has it), and we took our meagre knowledge of Latin, and we returned to our Seneca (or if we simply Googled it all, as any Smart Alec worthy of the name surely would), we would soon discover that this passage is not to be found in Seneca, but comes instead from Petrarch's '*De Remedis Utriusque Fortunæ*'. Was Poe, then, deceiving us? Or was he simply mistaken? Did he have a comprehensive knowledge of classical literature and languages? Or did he merely pinch the quotation from another source (Samuel Warren's novel *Ten Thousand a Year*, for instance). In both and in fact all similar cases, the truth is, while evidence might point very strongly in one direction or another, for all of the reasons discussed in the previous chapter, we will never know or prove for certain what the truth is. And that impossibility of knowing for certain what another person thinks (and perhaps especially an author, or the writer of a text) is precisely what is at stake in Poe's story 'The Purloined Letter'.

After the epigraph, then, Poe sets the scene. 'In Paris, just after dark one gusty evening in the autumn of 18——'. A precise place and time, then: Paris after dark. But also an imprecise time: the autumn of some unspecified year in the nineteenth century. The story will repeat this gesture, or this mingling together of precision and imprecision, revelation and concealment (we might say the mathematical and the poetic) over and over again as well. 'I was enjoying the twofold luxury of meditation and meershaum, in the company of my friend C. August Dupin'. The narrator introduces his hero, then. But he also introduces himself. Or rather, he introduces himself by not introducing himself, or by withholding his proper name, referring to himself only as 'I', and thus remaining anonymous (and, as you may know, but as I will discuss later one way or the other, this present but anonymous narrator becomes crucial to the way Derrida tackles Lacan's interpretation of the text). But, the sentence continues: 'in a little back library or book-closet, *au troisieme, No. 33, Rue Dunot, Faubourg St. Germain.*'[9] Precision, therefore, once again. But this time, in a foreign language, namely French, so imprecision, or at least obscurity, as well. But what is the scene? A dark, smoke-filled book-closet or personal library. Mystery. Uncertainty. Arcane knowledge. The unknown.

'For one hour', our narrator continues, 'we had maintained a profound silence, while each, to any casual observer, might have seemed intently and exclusively occupied with the eddies of smoke that oppressed the atmosphere of the chamber.' Silence, then, and apparent lethargy or inactivity. But actually, a different kind of activity – that is, mental activity, and particularly memory. Thus the narrator continues: 'For myself, however, I was mentally discussing certain topics which had formed matter for conversation between us at an earlier period of the evening.'[10] What our narrator is referring to is what, in the last chapter, especially in our consideration of Simmel, we called the inner world or interiority, a psychological space that itself might be compared to a dark, smoke-filled book-closet, or personal library. But what is happening in his inner world, or inside his head? He is not alone there. He is discussing something, with himself, or rather, with a kind of projection or prosthetic double of his interlocutor and companion, our hero, Mister C. August Dupin. This problem of the inner world or interiority has a considerable bearing on Derrida's later work, and I will return to it as well, primarily in the next chapter. But here it is enough to point out that Poe is arranging for us a number of topics, or potential lines of interpretation: the questions of the secret and the mysterious, to be sure; but also, and in a way that Poe will soon relate, the question of interiority, or the inside and the outside; as well as solitude, and how solitude relates to the other.

The rest of the story is well known, but I will offer a synopsis, so we can keep our bearings as we analyse both it and Derrida's interpretation of it. In the sentence that follows what we have just recounted, our narrator tells us that the Prefect of the police barges into the quiet scene, and then he narrates a story: The Queen is in her bedchamber. She is holding a letter. Suddenly, the King and the Minister enter (invading her solitude just as the Prefect has just invaded the narrator's and Dupin's — there will be countless of these kinds of self-referential doublings throughout the text, and we will not be able to keep track of them all in this brief summary, but I mention one by way of example). The Queen puts the letter down on a table, pretending it is not important, so as not to raise the suspicion of the King. That is to say, she hides it in the open. But the Minister watches her perform this little conjuring trick. Recognising a potential for advantage, he purloins the letter. And, he knows, it does not matter if the Queen watches him do so, because if she were to ask for it back in front of the King, that would only draw the King's attention to it, which is the last thing that she wants. The Minister takes the letter. The Prefect knows he has hidden it somewhere in his apartment. He has had his police break in numerous times while the Minister is out, and search for it. They have looked everywhere, but they are stumped. The purloined letter cannot be found.

We now turn to the second part of the text, or what Lacan will call the 'second scene' – namely, Dupin's narration of how he found the letter. This scene or narration includes two important excurses. The first excursus concerns the relationship between what Dupin calls 'mathematical' and 'poetic' thinking, in which he explains that the Prefect and the police rely too heavily on the first to catch a person like the Minister, who himself combines both, but relies on the second. The second concerns the children's game odds and evens, and the way one child learned to win this game by mimicking the facial expressions of his opponent, and thereby reading their mind, or knowing exactly what they were thinking. So again we have the question of the inner world, or of the relationship between the inside and the outside. But at any rate, the upshot is that Dupin realises that the Minister has repeated the Queen's trick himself, and hidden the letter in the open. With this knowledge in his possession, Dupin visits the Minister. He finds the letter – or rather, sees it where it has obviously been placed. And he purloins it in turn. But, unlike when the Minister took the letter from the Queen, Dupin cannot let the Minister know what he is doing. So he takes it while the Minister is otherwise occupied for a moment, and replaces it with a double that he has prepared – a double the contains a cryptic message, a message that, Dupin tells us, refers to an earlier and unrelated episode in which the Minister slighted Dupin in some unspecified manner: '*Un dessein si funeste, S'il n'est digne d'Atrée, est digne de Thyeste.*'[11] Such a cruel plan is unworthy of Atreus, but entirely worth of Thyestes.

In his 'Seminar of "The Purloined Letter"', Lacan approaches this story as a way of understanding what Freud, in *Beyond the Pleasure Principle*, calls the 'compulsion to repeat', or the tendency we have to repeat traumatic experiences, in a manner that would seem to deny Freud's earlier supposition that the mind is primarily driven to seek equilibrium, and thus pleasure. But it is also, for Lacan, a kind of elaborate allegory for the process of analysis itself, and the relationship between the analyst and the analysand. So, as mentioned, Lacan breaks the story down into two essential scenes: what he calls the 'primal scene', in which the Minister purloins the letter belonging to the Queen; and its 'repetition', in which Dupin purloins the letter from the Minister's apartment. He then breaks each of these scenes down into three subject positions (or 'glances', in his words), each one of which is occupied by a different character in each of the two scenes: the one who sees nothing (the King, the police); the one who sees the first seeing nothing but 'deceives itself as to the secrecy of what it hides', or mistakenly believes that it can operate without being seen (the Queen, the Minister); and finally, the one who sees the second endeavour to trick the first by leaving what should be hidden in the open (the Minister, Dupin).[12] The key here is the vulnerability of the second position, or the one who possesses the letter, and believes they are, as it were, invisible, or can see without being seen.

We have only sketched Lacan's extremely complex interpretation of the story. But again, we are not concerned here with the hermeneutic effort accurately to represent Lacan. To get where we want to go, we need to turn to Derrida's approach. In 'The Purveyor of Truth' Derrida commends Lacan for revolutionising the psychoanalytic approach to literature by placing the emphasis, not on the psyche of the author or the characters, but on the text, and the on function of the signifier within it – namely, in this case, the letter itself. But he also challenges Lacan's division of the story into two basic scenes, and his effort to understand it in terms of profoundly Oedipal triads, or as two sets of three subject positions, each of which would translate into child, mother and father. Instead of two scenes, Derrida maintains, we have two narrations, the first one narrated by the Prefect, and the second one by Dupin. Moreover, both of these narrations are, in a sense, supra-narrated by the unnamed narrator, or the 'I' who I drew your attention to a moment ago. This, I think, is the thrust of Derrida's challenge to Lacan's reading of Poe. The narrator (the fourth that supplements the Oedipal triad, and that configures the analyst herself, or perhaps Lacan himself) cannot be ignored, because the narrator is both above or outside of the text and within it at once. The narrator is the frame, as it were, that is also part of the framed content. As Derrida puts it, 'the narrator does not fade away [*s'effacer*]'. Rather, and more complexly, 'in making himself fade away into homogeneous generality, he moves forward as a uniquely singular character in the narrated narration' or 'the framed' ('PT' 54).

Again, while recognising that a great deal more is at stake here than I could possibly capture in a few paragraphs, these would seem to be Derrida's central claims in 'The Purveyor of Truth': that Lacan fails to attend to the specifically literary elements of 'The Purloined Letter'; that he is too concerned to use it as a screen for projecting certain claims about psycho-analysis; and that, if we do pay attention to its literary elements, or its status as text rather than speech, we find, not Oedipal triads, but a whole series of doublings (the kind of doublings that characterise the analytic session, when an analysand sits down with her analyst), the crucial one being the narrator who simultaneously withdraws into abstract generality or universality and gets inserted into his own narrative as a particular or singular subject. This kind of doubling, or what we are calling here the singular universal, generates a number of philosophical paradoxes that I think Derrida is implicitly grappling with in 'The Purveyor of Truth' and elsewhere (for example, what is called Russell's Paradox, a subset of which is sometimes called the Barber's Paradox, after the example that Russell gave of the barber who shaves all those, and only those, who do not shave themselves, or simply the paradox of self-inclusion). I will try to deal with some of these paradoxes in the next chapter, or at least try to show that Derrida often deals with them. But here I want to remain in a more literary space, or to stay focused on the question of literature.

For Derrida, then, the narrator of 'The Purloined Letter' is both inside and outside of the narration at once. He (and we have been assuming that it is a he) is both all-seeing and universal, able to control the narration from above, and located at a specific place, viewing the world from a particular perspective. To use a slightly different idiom, we might say that he is an example or an exception. He is taken out of the story to represent the story. But in so far as he is no longer inside the story, can he really be said to be representative? Moreover, this doubling of the narrator, this splitting of his function and all of the paradoxes it generates, is itself reflective of, or an example of, a whole range of further doublings in the story. We are getting a little clever here, but we might even say that the narrator is an example, and what he exemplifies is the logic of exemplification. Of all the other doubles that the narrator of the story doubles, undoubtedly the most important is the double of Dupin, on the one side, and the Minister, on the other. For the story (that is to say, the narrator) reminds us repeatedly of how similar these two are. And that would be one way of understanding that cryptic final message that Dupin leaves for his double or *doppelgänger* – the one that suggests that he and the Minister are akin to two warring brothers, bound together by their conflict, related by precisely that which separates them, caught up in an endless game of tit-for-tat through which they each get defined.[13]

Along with the other two stories that form Poe's Dupin trilogy or tales of 'ratiocination' as he called them ('The Murders in the Rue Morgue' and 'The Mystery of Marie Rogêt'), 'The Purloined Letter' is typically understood to be among the very first works of detective fiction – a genre that, one has to admit, if we include police drama and its various offshoots, has become all but ubiquitous today. But one also has to admit that 'The Purloined Letter' bears almost none of the traits that have come to define the genre it helped set in motion. There is, in fact, no mystery, and very nearly no action. The theme is secrecy, to be sure. But, in terms of the plot, not many secrets are concealed. A crime of sorts has occurred. But from the very beginning, we know who committed it (the Minister); we know why he committed it (to blackmail the Queen); we know where he has hidden his prize (somewhere in his apartment). In fact, we know everything that, in more typical examples of detective fiction, we would slowly be led to discover. In a sense, nothing is discovered in 'The Purloined Letter'. There is no plot, as such. No concealed information gets progressively exposed, no chain of events draws us towards an inevitable climax. In a sense, and without us really noticing, the author Edgar Allan Poe has himself performed a conjuring trick, or purloined something from us right under our noses – namely, a story, or the easy teleological, Aristotelian pleasure of a beginning, a middle and an end. So we know everything. But we also do not know what is written on the letter, which would seem to be the crucial bit of information. So we know nothing. We know everything and nothing at once. And that, it seems to me, would be the beginning of a pretty good definition of literature.

Oblique Rituals

I am trying, now, to build up to my discussion of '*Demeure*', Derrida's crucial essay on Blanchot, and on the relationships between literature and witnessing, secrecy and truth. But I am also doing a bit of plotting myself – holding that moment off, as it were, or waiting for the right time to reveal it. No doubt this gesture is somewhat manipulative, and hardly in the spirit of 'The Purloined Letter' which I just discussed – the work of literary fiction that, in essence, has no plot, but that, in its plotlessness, also seems to expose or reveal something essential about what Derrida liked to refer to as 'this strange institution called literature' ('P' 23). At any rate, those justifications (or alibis) having been proffered, in this section I would like to turn my attention to another of Derrida's articles – namely a relatively short piece called 'Passions: An Oblique Offering'. The context of Derrida's 'Passions' is crucial to understanding its movements, so I will explain. It is a piece that was solicited from him by the Derrida scholar David Wood for inclusion in a collection of essays, published in 1992, called *Derrida: A Critical Reader*, of which Wood is the editor. Wood apparently asked Derrida to respond in some 'oblique' fashion to the essays he had collected. And Derrida, in a move that we have to call characteristic, began by focusing his attention on the act of being asked to contribute in this manner, and the entire ritual of academic protocol and exchange.

At stake, then, in the opening sequences of 'Passions' is something very similar to what we have just been discussing with respect to the narrator of 'The Purloined Letter'. On the one hand, Derrida is the object of the essays collected in *Derrida: A Critical Reader*. So he is in some sense outside of the text. But on the other hand, he is being asked to contribute, or to inscribe himself within it. Thus, like Poe's narrator, he is something of a singular universal, simultaneously retreating from and advancing into the text. So Derrida begins with a discussion of ritual, and of the paradoxical, or perhaps abyssal, manner in which we are always involved in some ritual, and in trying to explain or make sense of that ritual as a whole from the perspective of our limited spot, role or function within it. In the case of being the object of a ritual called the academic 'critical reader', Derrida implies, the role one plays is that of sacrificial victim. So how, then, does the sacrificial victim perceive the ritual as a whole? How does she attain the necessary 'critical' distance to make sense of it, when she is clearly the one at the centre of it, staring into the abyss around which it circulates or revolves? Derrida's solution, it would seem, is to emphasise the concept of the secret, or to insist, in some manner, that he retains a certain secrecy, that no critical reader will ever be able to exhaust his thought or render him transparent, and that this secrecy is not specific to him, nor reducible to his mind or inner world, but almost part of the ontological makeup of everything.

After having made these gestures, and before moving into his consideration of the secret, Derrida develops an excursus, of sorts, on the theme of friendship. Here Derrida is presumably (if also silently) invoking his personal friendship with Wood and

with many of the other contributors to Wood's volume. And
here again, as in the consideration of ritual, Derrida raises the
question of the inside and the outside, or the paradoxical experience of being inside and outside of a system of rules, norms
or expectations at one and the same time. Thus he reflects on
what we might call the *aporia* or double bind of friendship: that
it is a rule that we cannot simply be following the rules; that
it is impolite to be polite merely out of politeness; or that the
expectation is that you will do what is expected, but not simply
because it is expected. In Derrida's own words: 'It is a rule that
one knows the rule but is never bound by it. It is impolite to
be merely polite' ('P' 9). Derrida then links this line of thought
(which, I have to say, seems exceptionally clear and level headed
to me, almost the exact opposite of the familiar caricature of
Derrida as an insanely hermetic or deliberately obscure Parisian
intellectual) to Kant's discussion of the moral law, and especially
his notion that respect for the moral law cannot be derived
from the law itself, but must ultimately be founded on 'an affect
(*Gefühl*)' (16).

Following the introductory remarks and the digression on
friendship, then, Derrida is finally lead to the question of the
secret. And, for the purposes of this book, it is important to note
that Derrida worked on 'Passions' around the same time that he
was preparing his 1991–2 seminars on *Questions de Responsabilité
I: Le Secret* – the seminar series that, in my Introduction, I speculated must be crucial to his later work. So there is little doubt that,
in this instance, he is drawing on the seminar material. Derrida
organises this part of the essay around a watchword, of sorts,
or a single sentence: 'There is something secret [*il y a du secret*]'
('P' 24). Like a ritual incantation, he repeats this sentence (or a
slightly altered version of it) seven times, providing it each time

with a different interpretation or inflection. Or, more accurately, and again as in a ritual, Derrida purifies the sentence, explaining each time either what he does not mean by it, or something that, while invoked by the phrase, cannot be said to exhaust it. And at the end of this seven-fold process of ritual purification, we arrive at, but of course are not told, the secret itself.

Here, rather than working through this part of the text systematically, or repeating Derrida's ritual step by step, I simply want to pinpoint or emphasise some of what I take to be the more important movements. But I also want to take issue with Derrida on one point. Specifically, I want to challenge his effort to link secrecy (and along with it, literature) to a political form that he insists on calling 'democracy'. And I will say openly that Derrida's almost uncritical insistence on this word, his almost rote repetition of the privilege it tends to get granted among a certain class of political thinkers or theorists, is the one thing about his later work that I find the most contentious and least convincing. But more on that topic later. For now, I will focus on Derrida's incantation.

'There is something secret' then. *Il y a du secret*. Derrida begins by admitting that this sentence or statement has 'apophanic' qualities, or that it articulates a desire to say the unsayable, or mark somehow what remains impossible to remark; but he also insists that it cannot be understood in the terms of negative theology (an issue I will take up again later, in the next chapter, when discussing Derrida's 'How to Avoid Speaking'). 'We testify [*témoignons*]', Derrida claims, 'to a secret that is without content' or 'without content separable from its performative tracing.' So something about this secret cannot be shown or revealed, it can only be enacted or performed. However, Derrida goes on, this secret is not 'an artistic or technical secret'. It is not 'the signature of talent or the mark of genius', nor is it 'the art hidden in the depths of the human soul' ('P' 24). It is neither 'private' nor 'public', Derrida continues, in a manner that is obviously very important for the argument I am making in this book. Nor can it be understood in terms of 'deprived interiority' (25) (which is, perhaps, how Simmel understood or misunderstood it). 'There is something secret', but it is not a 'learned ignorance'. It is not the stuff of a secret society, or a gnostic or monastic order. It is not 'the content of an esoteric doctrine', nor is it anything 'mystical'. It is not simply 'the hidden', 'the obscure', 'the nocturnal' or 'the invisible'. It 'exceeds', Derrida says, 'the play of veiling / unveiling, dissimulation / revelation, night / day, forgetting / anamnesis, earth / heaven, etc.' (26). It is, Derrida finishes, 'foreign to speech' – outside of responsibility, a kind of 'absolute nonresponse' (27).

Having purified his sentence 'there is something secret' in this fashion, Derrida then rushes, a little, to his conclusion, which he presents as a kind of confession or, in his words, a 'confidence'. He thus admits that, behind his discussion of the secret, he has also been seeking to 'confirm or confide' his 'taste', as he says, 'for literature' ('P', 27). That is to say, at this point in 'Passions', Derrida admits that, for him, the concept of the secret is closely connected to literature. And here is the paradox. For Derrida, the institution we call literature is a specifically modern and even very recent one. While it tries to ground itself in a much longer history, stretching all the way back to the classics, it really only takes shape in the nineteenth century. And, on Derrida's account, it is associated with a specifically modern right, namely what Derrida calls the 'right to say everything' (28), or the right for anyone to publish what, on another order, would be called a lie.

In this sense, Derrida proposes, there is an intimate connection between democracy and literature. 'No democracy without literature', Derrida asserts. But also, 'no literature without democracy'. And finally, this ostensibly democratic 'right to say everything' ('P' 28), or this right to create fictions and allow them to circulate in public, is also connected to what Derrida calls a 'right to absolute nonresponse', one that is both 'more original and more secret' than any 'power or duty', and in fact remains 'heterogeneous to them' (29). Put crudely, for Derrida, literature and democracy mean that people have a right to say anything, in private but also in public, and a right not to be compelled to give an account of what they say – simply to let their words circulate without having to be traced back to some intention, origin or inward truth. We all have a right, then, to repeat the words of Iago, cited in the previous chapter of this book: 'Demand of me nothing, what you know, you know.'

'Passions', therefore, is one of the places where Derrida clearly associates his treatment of the secret with both politics and literature. In this chapter, I am attempting to pursue these connections. But, as suggested, I must point out that I am not entirely in agreement with Derrida here. Or rather, while I agree, I think, with the spirit of these claims, I have reservations about the letter, and more precisely, about Derrida's use of two words, and his apparently axiomatic assumption that they belong together – namely, the word 'right' and the word 'democracy'. In simple terms, I wonder why we assume that the concept of right belongs with that of democracy?

Why should this juridical concept, which has a history that extends far into the past, and which has by no means always been bound to a specific political form, be associated with the institutions or the ideologies that go by the name 'democracy' today?

It seems to me that, at this point in his text, Derrida is partaking of a discourse that was very common at the time he was writing (that is, 1991), but that has no claim whatsoever on universality. In particular, it seems that, at this moment, Derrida is influenced by a discourse on political forms, one exemplified, perhaps, by Claude Lefort's work at the time – a discourse the purpose of which was less to define or enact democracy (whatever that might mean) than to mitigate against another ostensible political form, specifically what was called totalitarianism.[14] Here Derrida's 'right' to the secret risks having little performative status of its own. It risks having little positive content, and operating instead as a bulwark against a perceived evil. Thus the word democracy runs the risk of becoming little more than an effort to prevent something else – a chimera, really, that everyone fears, but that, in point of fact, does not exist.

As for the concept of right, or at least that of human rights, I think we need to pay some attention to the work of more recent thinkers like Samuel Moyn and Jessica Whyte.[15] From Moyn's perspective the contemporary discourse of human rights cannot be traced back to the French Revolution, as one line of thought would have it. Rather, it is more or less an invention of the twentieth century. It has its roots in the Christian personalism of the early part of that century. And it emerged in full force only in the 1970s, as one element of an ideological struggle against communism, or what we used to call 'really existing socialism'. This is not the place to attempt to provide a full account of this line of thought. But I will conclude this section by laying down some markers for a future investigation.

To continue reading Derrida's comments on rights and democracy in the wake of this more recent research into rights discourse, and especially the genesis of human rights, we would need to ask three questions, or three clusters of questions: First, is Moyn right? Does his brief history (of the very brief history) of rights correspond to the archive or the facts? Second, if Moyn is right, does Derrida form part of this history? Are his references to the concept of right bound up with an ideological drift of which he was more or less unaware? And finally, if they are, is that connection to an historical and political ideology something we can locate in his work, or separate from other elements of his work, or does it proceed from his general project, inflecting, in some sense, everything he has to say?

Recalling Derrida's invocation in 'Passions' of academic rituals, I will now repeat the phrase that we are supposed to use every time our argument comes up against a problem that it cannot easily resolve: This is not the place to try to deal with all of these issues and concerns. But I will also break with protocol a little, and confess that I am not adequate to these problems anyway. Here I mention them only to mark a distance between what I take to be Derrida's position on the question of rights and democracy, or at least the one that he presents here in 'Passions', and my own. In short, I am far more sceptical of this kind of language, and more or less convinced that it is inevitably bound up with liberalism, and even with the liberal distinctions or tensions between private and public, or privacy and security, that I am trying to challenge and evade. In the conclusion of this chapter, however, I will brush up against some of this material again when I consider most intently Derrida's notion that literature in particular is a recent phenomenon, and that it is connected to a particular juridical (or quasi- or para-juridical) set of rights. But for now I will bracket that issue, turn my attention to Derrida's '*Demeure*', and try to associate its major themes with what I have been saying in this chapter and this book thus far.

Singular Universal

At the end of my discussion of 'The Purloined Letter' above, I pointed to the strange or paradoxical manner in which Poe's text seems to have no secrets and yet to be fundamentally secretive as well – the sense in which, when reading it, we know everything and nothing at once, or need nothing to be revealed, but still remain completely ignorant. And I said that this paradox might be a good place to begin to develop a definition of literature. In the very final part of 'Passions', while confessing his taste for literature, Derrida hints at something similar. 'There is', he writes, 'in literature, in the exemplary secret of literature, a chance of saying everything without touching upon the secret' ('P' 29). In other words, and to repeat myself, there is a chance of saying everything and nothing – a chance of speaking in a manner that also withholds, of revealing while also concealing, or of telling the truth whilst keeping something essential essentially in the dark. This, I think, is the central paradox or, as he calls it, *aporia*, at stake in Derrida's essay '*Demeure*' – a reflection, among many other things, on the relationship, and the inseparability, of testimony, or individual truth, on the one side, and fiction, literature and deception, on the other.

'*Demeure*', we must say at the outset, is a very complex piece. It is repetitive. It seems to say the same thing over and over again, from a slightly different direction each time. But it is also relentlessly surprising. Each repetition of the basic claim concerning testimony and fiction, or truth and deception, gathers meaning together in a different manner. It is hard to break this kind of text down into digestible bits. But I will try to do so by provisionally separating out two basic themes or lines of thought, the first of which has to do with what we have been calling the singular universal, or a strange combination of absolute particularity and absolute generality, and the second of which has to do with what we have been calling the problem of time, which here Derrida addresses by reflecting on the ambiguous relationship between the instant, or the discrete moment in time, and the instance, or the example that is extracted from but also stands in for a larger collection or set. For the rest of this section I will try to explain the first of these. Then, in the next section, I will turn my attention to the second, keeping in mind all along that we cannot really separate the two out in this fashion, and that, for Derrida, they are related to one another far more fundamentally than they are separated from one another.

In most of Derrida's later works, the occasion or event of publication is integral to the argument. That is to say, Derrida refers us always to the performative dimension of his utterances, or to the act of saying or writing what he is saying or writing when and where he is saying or writing it. As we saw in 'Passions', for instance, Derrida begins by reflecting on having been asked to contribute to a volume dedicated to him and his work. In this sense, it is important to note that 'Demeure' is published in the same volume as Maurice Blanchot's 1994 short story 'L'Instant de ma mort' or 'The Instant of My Death', and takes shape as a kind of long afterword or commentary upon it. 'The Instant of My Death' tells the story of a young man, one who closely resembles Blanchot himself, and who, in the final days of the Second World War, narrowly escapes his own execution, and thus in some sense survives his own death. Blanchot, then, or Blanchot's narrator (and the ambiguity here is important), thus testifies to the only experience that is singularly his own – the only experience, as Heidegger might say, that any of us can genuinely call our own, namely death.

Derrida begins his consideration of Blanchot's apparently autobiographical story by reflecting on the meaning of autobiography, or, more generally, testimony – the act of telling my truth, or a truth that only I can know, to another. Testimony, Derrida explains, is unlike 'sharing a knowledge' or 'making known'. It is not simply an exchange of information about some external, objective phenomenon or fact, or something that might be verified by another. Rather, referring to Augustine, Derrida says that testimony involves 'a promise to *make truth*' ('D' 27). In testimony, some individual person claims to be speaking the truth about something only they can know. And that is the basic structure of all testimony. To put it formulaically, and in a phrase that I will probably repeat a number of times: I can only testify to what only I can know. No one else can testify in my place. And, when I testify, no one else can possibly verify the truth or falsehood of what I say. So testimony emerges from an absolutely singular place, or from the dark solitude of my thoughts, which no other person can intuit or ascertain. But at the same time, because testimony claims to be true, it makes an (implicit or explicit) demand on the universal. It demands that everyone who hears it agrees: 'yes, that is true; that is your truth'. Thus, testimony is both absolutely singular and absolutely universal. It retreats into the darkness of the soul even as it goes out into the illumination of the world.[16]

Derrida does not make this connection in '*Demeure*', but I think there is an important link here between what he calls testimony, in its singular universality, and Kant's analytic of the beautiful in his *Critique of Judgment*.[17] And this is interesting because, in my estimation, Kant's treatment of beauty is more compelling than his more widely discussed notion of the sublime. You will recall that, for Kant, aesthetics involves not 'determinate' but 'reflective judgement'. If, in the former, we come to understand our intuition or experience by aligning it with a pre-established concept (one with which we are already familiar or equipped), in the latter, the experience is new, and therefore requires the creation of a new concept. Art is the paradigmatic example here. If we read a novel, for instance, we can certainly make any number of determinate judgements about it (it is so many pages long, it was written on this or that date, it refers to these or those events, and so forth). But to treat it aesthetically, or to understand what is artistic about it, we must invent a new way of understanding in general. We must invent the concept adequate to making sense of it. However (and this is the key), when I make a reflective judgement, when I encounter something new and invent a new concept to make sense of it, part of the process of making that judgement is to assume that anyone else in my position, indeed everyone everywhere, would also agree with me. Thus, the judgement of beauty is an utterly singular judgement that operates by making a demand on the universal. And in this sense, it is very much like what Derrida calls testimony. It is a singular universal.

Returning now to Derrida, this line of thought means that testimony, or some crucial aspect of testimony, is bound up with secrecy. As Derrida puts it, in a paradoxical manner, 'I must be able to keep secret precisely what I testify to' ('D' 30). Or, to put the matter differently, even though testimony is by definition public or a public act (something I address to some audience or some other), it also relies on something that cannot be communicated or shared. It is, as Derrida says, 'the sharable and unsharable secret of what happened to me', 'both infinitely secret and infinitely public' (43). Moreover, and for the same reason, inasmuch as it is (and must be) conditioned by secrecy, or what no other person can ever intuit or know, testimony is also conditioned by the possibility of perjury and deception, fiction and literature. That is to say, on Derrida's account, such things are not accidental or secondary with respect to testimony. They are not things that only appear when testimony goes badly or when it is appropriated by a bad or less than scrupulous individual. On the contrary, perjury and fiction are absolutely necessary conditions for the possibility of testimonial truth. There is no testimony except in the shadow of deception.

We can reinforce this point by quoting some of Derrida's own language. 'Testimony always goes hand in hand with at least the possibility of fiction, perjury, and lie', Derrida maintains. 'Were this possibility to be eliminated, no testimony would be possible any longer; it could no longer have the meaning of testimony' ('D' 27). Or, as Derrida puts it a little later: 'In order to remain testimony, it must therefore allow itself to remain haunted. It must allow itself to be parasitised by precisely what it excludes from its inner depths, the possibility, at least, of literature' (30). Or again, one more time, as Derrida puts it towards the end of his piece: 'Without the possibility of this fiction, without the spectral virtuality of this simulacrum and as a result of this lie, or this fragmentation of the true, no truthful testimony would be possible.' As a result, 'the possibility of literary fiction haunts so-called truthful, responsible, serious, real testimony as its proper possibility' (72). No fiction, then, or no literature, no testimony. Or, to put the matter a bit more aggressively: No lies, no truth. No dark and hidden inner world of the singular, no bright and illuminated outer world of the universal.

Before we move any further here, it is important, I think, to get a sense of the exact scope of what Derrida is attempting to address. Early on in '*Demeure*', Derrida notes that his subtitle – 'Fiction and Testimony' – is intended to mimic or reflect the subtitle of Goethe's autobiographical *Aus meinem Leben: Dichtung und Wahrheit* – a phrase which is usually, and inadequately, translated into English as 'Poetry and Truth'. One of Derrida's topics, then, is autobiography, or of the way we speak about our own lives. To this he adds what we have just been considering, namely testimony, or the more formal, and often juridically framed act of telling one's own truth. But in a far more profound and expansive sense, throughout '*Demeure*', Derrida implies that he is concerned, not simply with the literary genre of autobiography or the juridical phenomenon of testimony, but with truth, language, communication or inter-action in the widest possible senses of those words.

As we saw in the previous chapter, for Derrida, all language relies on an act of faith, or a sworn oath to be truthful and to believe that the other is being truthful as well. And in this same sense, Derrida suggests, all language is testimony. In fact (and I am going to emphasise this point), 'language' here is not the best word for capturing what Derrida has in mind. Particularly when talking about Derrida, who is still far too frequently associated with all kinds of misunderstandings of that infamous phrase 'there is nothing outside of the text' (*OG* 163), it confuses too many people. So Derrida is not just saying that all language is testimony. He is saying that all engagement with others (and not only human others) consists, on some level, of testimony – both sharing and not sharing, both offering and retracting, both revealing and concealing, my singular, unique truth.

That point having been established, we now need to return to and complicate what Derrida says about the strange proximity or what he calls 'disturbing complicity' ('D' 67) between fiction and testimony, deception and truth. To be very clear, and to forestall another whole range of desiccated but still somehow circulating criticisms of a caricature of Derrida's position (zombie critiques, as I like to call them), Derrida is not saying that there is no difference between testimonial truth and fiction or deception. He is not saying that we cannot separate the two sides from one another, or that, because they are essentially the same, we live in a world without either. Rather, and far more complexly, Derrida's point is that the border between testimony and fiction (or truth and deception) also runs through both testimony and fiction, such that each is internally divided by the division between the two. That is to say, for Derrida, even before we begin to distinguish between testimony and fiction or truth and deception (which, if we want to have any politics, ethics, law or knowledge whatsoever, we must assuredly attempt to do), neither one can make sense or operate without the other. As Derrida puts it, 'the limits between fiction and testimony . . . are also interior each to the other' (56). Or, to put the matter differently, and invert the image, the line that divides them is itself divided by them.

But to come back to the basic point about the singular universal, or Derrida's treatment of that paradox, another way to get at the issue would be to focus on the event of testimony, or the kind of performative speech act that constitutes testimony (keeping in mind, once again, that all language and all engagement involves something like testimony). When someone testifies, they must be exemplary. That is, and as mentioned, they must be irreplaceable. The one who testifies tells their truth, one that no one else can appropriate or know. They speak of what, at that very moment, they believe to be true. However, they also speak about something that happened in the past. They speak of an example from their experience. Thus they must be exemplary, or irreplaceable. But they must also say something that constitutes an example. They must repeat something from the past that will also be repeatable in the future. As Derrida puts it, 'the example is not substitutable: but at the same time, the same *aporia* always remains: this irreplaceability must be exemplary, that is, replaceable. The irreplaceability must always allow itself to be replaced on the spot' ('D' 41). In other words, along with being a singular universal in the manner we described above, testimony is singular universal in the manner in which it is temporalised: at this singular instant, I speak my unique truth, by repeating something from the past, that can, in principle at least, be universalised, or repeated indefinitely into the future. Testimony splits the instant, as it were. It divides the indivisible element of time. And it is to this question of time that I will now turn.

Instant and Instance

I would like to begin this section with a digression, of sorts, on a thinker whose understanding of testimony contrasts in helpful ways with that of Derrida, and might particularly help us introduce the very complicated the problem of time. I am thinking of Levinas, who Derrida does not really discuss in '*Demeure*', but who seems to be negatively invoked. In particular, when reading Derrida's text, it is difficult not to be reminded of Levinas's 'Truth of Disclosure and Truth of Testimony' – an essay much of which Levinas later integrated into *Otherwise than Being*, and one that Derrida unquestionably knew well.[18] In this work, Levinas develops a theory of testimony that points in some of the same directions as Derrida's, but that ultimately takes an almost diametrically opposed line, especially with respect to the questions of secrecy and time. Indeed, if, for Derrida, testimony is inextricably bound to secrecy, if Derrida believes we cannot testify without, at the same moment, concealing or hiding, for Levinas, on the contrary, testimony constitutes the opposite – a sudden and completely transparent illumination of the one who testifies. Moreover, and more importantly for the problem that we are addressing here, or the problem of time, if, for Derrida, testimony involves secrecy in part because it is temporalised (in that it is an instant that is also an instance, as we have already suggested, and will explain in more detail below), for Levinas testimony is purely present – the pure presence of a non-dialectical and non-representational performance or, in his words, a Saying of the Infinite.

We can set the context for Levinas's essay on testimony by emphasising his frequent use of a figure with whom we are already familiar – the figure of Gyges. Levinas references the Myth of Gyges at regular intervals throughout all of his work, including in his two most important books, *Totality and Infinity* and *Otherwise than Being*. For Levinas, Gyges is the model of the metaphysical subject *par excellence* – the subject who does not relate to the other, much less have the ethical experience of becoming their 'hostage', but who desires to see without being seen. As Levinas puts it in *Totality and Infinity*, the one who attempts 'seeing without being seen, like Gyges' configures 'the myth of the "I"', or 'a determination of the Other by the same, without the same being determined by the other'.[19] Thus, for Levinas, the Myth of Gyges is not simply a bit of counterfactual moral philosophy. Rather, it captures the 'ontological structure' of metaphysics in general, or the way that, by beginning with the disclosure of being rather than the ethical relation, metaphysics from Plato to Heidegger reduces the other to the same, or to simple cognition, thus missing any relation to the genuine alterity, difference, or otherness of the other.

'Truth of Disclosure and Truth of Testimony' begins by rehearsing Levinas's general critique of metaphysics and ontology (a critique that always has phenomenology, and especially Heidegger, in the background). Inasmuch as we think of truth as the un-veiling or dis-covering of being, Levinas maintains, we are bound to understand it exclusively in terms of a correlation between subjects and objects, or consciousness and being.[20] Indeed, this is the case whether we think of truth in terms of adequation, or consciousness adequately representing something that exists outside of it, or in terms of revelation and disclosure, where being exposes itself to our being in the world. For Levinas, on the contrary, truth is not primarily about a correlation between consciousness and being, however that correlation gets defined. Rather, it concerns my relationship with the non-representable – something that is 'Infinite', as he says, or 'beyond being'. On Levinas's account, then, testimony is not an effort to express my knowledge of being, or what exists. Instead, it articulates (or, more accurately, performs, enacts, or makes manifest) this relation to the infinite, the unrepresentable, or the absolute other.

Thus, and to put the matter simply, for Levinas truth does not concern a representation of being; rather, it is something that emanates directly out of the subject, with no prior source or ground other than that which is infinite and beyond being. Levinas calls this Saying as opposed to the Said.[21] And it is very important for him to specify that this Saying has nothing to do with an individual person's opinion or judgement, and nothing to do with revealing a previously existing inwardness, privacy, secret, or concealed thought. For Levinas, there is nothing invisible or hidden about the subject who testifies to the infinite. On the contrary, they are shot through with light, as it were, and rendered entirely transparent. Thus, for Levinas, testimony operates by 'breaking open the secret of Gyges, the invisible-seeing-subject [*suject-voyant-invisible*]'.[22] It constitutes, in Levinas's very striking and powerful words, 'a blazing sun that eradicates every residue of mystery, every ulterior motive, every loosening of the thread that would allow for evasion'. Or, as he puts it a little later, 'in Saying, by which the subject, driven out, leaves its clandestinaity, the Infinite comes to pass'.[23]

This general challenge to secrecy and invisibility, and privileging of beatific transparency, is reinforced in many of Levinas's other writings. Indeed, it would not be too much to say that, along with being the great recent thinker of ethics, the infinite and the other, Levinas is the great critic of the secret. Thus, in *God, Death, and Time*, for example, he speaks of the subject 'bearing witness', and maintains that 'there is no refuge for this subject in the secrecy that would protect him from the neighbour'. Rather, he says, 'it is a question of exposure without shelter, as under a leaden sun without protective shade' and 'exposure without reserve'.[24] But, despite its somewhat sinister overtones, this line of thinking cannot really be associated with a political conception of transparency – either the transparency of the people to the state, or of the state to the people. Rather, what Levinas has in mind here is something that, on his account, precedes all politics. He is attempting to describe the sense in which the act of testimony or Saying is purely non-representational, and absolutely present. When someone says, for example, 'I believe in God', it is not as though they are expressing a belief that existed before the expression in an object or thing that also existed before the expression. No, the testimony itself, in its pure performance or Saying, is the belief of which it speaks. In other words, on Levinas's account, testimony is without secrecy because it is purely performative (it is its expression, as it were), purely non-representational (it speaks of nothing but itself), and therefore purely in the present.

Now, let us turn our attention back to Derrida's text on testimony. As I noted at the outset, '*Demeure*' is both repetitive and surprising, making the same argument over and over again, but with completely different consequences or associations each time. This is, perhaps, something of a performance of the logic of the singular universal we have been discussing, as well as the temporality we are trying to explain here. That issue set aside, one of the more surprising moments in '*Demeure*' appears towards the end of the text, where Derrida addresses the question of the miracle. Here Derrida seems to be invoking something very similar to what Levinas says. For Derrida's point is that, while there is a long history of people testifying to miracles, or seeking to establish the truth of a miracle through testimony, what is miraculous in testimony is not the particular experience or event of which it speaks, but the event, the moment, or the instant of the testimony itself. That is to say, in a manner that would appear to resonate with Levinas's approach, Derrida proposes that the miracle of testimony is found, not in the constative mode, or that which it ostensibly represents or refers to, but in the performative – in the speech act that we call testimony or, better, testifying or avowal. The miracle is not something I experienced back there in the past, that is to say; it is right here and now, in the fact that I can, to recall Augustine's words, cited by Derrida, 'make truth' when I speak.

But, I want to contend, the apparent proximity between what Levinas and Derrida say about the miraculous performance of testimony is entirely superficial. In fact, when Derrida treats testimony in this fashion, he is, as I have already suggested, saying almost the exact opposite. For Levinas sees testimony as a manifestation of my relation with the Infinite – a kind of sublime experience of having the Infinite speak through me, and illuminate me with its all-penetrating light. But Derrida sees it as something fundamentally mundane and average. In speaking of testimony, he is not at all invoking something transcendental, but describing, in clear and phenomenological terms, the most everyday experience imaginable – namely, the experience of believing another and being believed by them despite the fact that they might be lying, or what, in the last chapter, I called the act of faith required for every exchange, and even the most minimal interaction with another. As Derrida puts it, 'any testimony testifies in essence to the miraculous and the extraordinary from the moment it must, by definition, appeal to an act of faith beyond any proof. When one testifies, even on the subject of the most ordinary and most "normal" event, one asks the other to believe one and one's word as if it were a matter of a miracle' ('D' 75). The miracle of testimony, then, is the miracle of every exchange imaginable. It is our miraculous ability to trust one another in a manner that proceeds, not only without evidence, but without even the possibility of evidence, verification or proof.

Having established what I take to be the basic difference between Levinas's and Derrida's conception of the miracle of testimony, we can now pursue the more complicated differ-ence – the one that has to do with time. For Levinas, we recall, testimony consists of the absolute presence of the Saying. The truth of testimony is found in the act itself. To say 'I believe in God', for instance, is to manifest or even constitute that belief in the here and now. For Derrida, on the contrary, testimony has a far more sophisticated temporality. Yes, as in Levinas, the truth of testimony is manifest in the act of testifying, or what, borrowing from the title of Blanchot's story, Derrida calls the instant. And this is another sense in which testimony is, for Derrida, miraculous. It is a completely new and discrete event. It breaks, in some sense, with the determined chain of causes and effects. But at the same time, on Derrida's account, testimony always testifies as well to some past experience or event – one that, more importantly, once testified to, must be repeatable or iterable by the one who testifies and by others into the future indefinitely. That is to say, testimony must be an instant (something singular and unique); but it must also be an instance (something exemplary and iterable).

This relationship between the instant and the instance is, if we can put it this way, the nuts and bolts of a very complicated conception of time that Derrida worked on throughout his life. I will return to this problem in the next chapter, and try to explain it from a number of different directions. For now, I will simply provide a sketch or outline. For Derrida, it is not simply that the instant (or the now) is temporalised, or receives its determination only from other past and / or future instants or nows, and thus is never fully present, but ecstatic, as Heidegger might say.[25] While I am associating it with Heidegger here, this kind of argument has been around for a very long time, and arguably goes back to the ancient Greeks (and it is not quite what Heidegger says either, but that is a topic for another time). Rather, Derrida's point is that every instant is utterly singular but also, and at the exact same instant, utterly split. The instant is a point, and thus indivisible. But, impossibly, it is also divided.

Here it is helpful to recall Derrida's point of departure in 'Demeure', namely Blanchot's 'The Instant of My Death'. For even just the title of Blanchot's story points to the paradox. From Heidegger we can take the notion that there is no more singular event than death. This, of course, is one of the key claims of *Being and Time*. Only death is individual, and only death individuates, or gives us our unique existence, at the precise moment it robs us of that existence, or takes it away. But, as 'The Instant of My Death' recounts or testifies to, owing to a strange course of events, there is at least some sense in which Blanchot (or, rather, the narrator of his story) survived his own death, and thus became able to testify to (or repeat) it in the future. In other words, in 'The Instant of My Death', the absolute instant, the instant of all instants, or the instant *par excellence*, namely death, becomes an instance, an example, something that can be repeated or recounted. Impossibly, miraculously, what is absolutely indivisible, namely death, is divided.

Derrida's suggestion in '*Demeure*' is that this curious *aporia* of the instant and the instance is true, not only of Blanchot's experience of surviving and later testifying to his own death, but of testimony (and, by extension, language, experience, relation and interaction) in general. Each instant is instantaneous or unique and an instance or an example. This is a logic, I think, that Derrida reflected on throughout his life. It is closely related to his many treatments of death. It is already being opened up in his early deconstructions of the metaphysics of presence. It is almost always at stake in what we have called his more experimental middle period. But it becomes completely urgent in his later writings. And this is something we can see very clearly in his late seminars on *The Death Penalty* and *The Beast and the Sovereign*. I will explore these texts a little more in the next chapter. But here, I want to focus on two consequences of (or two lines of thought that get disclosed in) Derrida's discussion of the instant and the instance in '*Demeure*'. Specifically, I want to consider his treatment of what we might call the truth-status of literary language or fiction, on the one side, and what, in the previous chapter, when discussing Derrida's reading of Thomas's *La Parjure*, I called the substitutability of the 'I', or simply the nature of the self, on the other.

Derrida's attitude towards literature is a little confusing, and I will expand on this confusion in the next and concluding section of this chapter. But basically, and as I mentioned already, sometimes Derrida characterises literature as a recent historical phenomenon, bound to the nineteenth century, and to a certain parcel of juridical rights and political institutions (especially one he insists on calling democracy). At other times, however, he treats literary language, and especially fiction, as a kind of paradigm of all language. More accurately, he treats the *aporia* of the fact that we can read and understand fiction as a general *aporia* of experience.

In '*Demeure*', Derrida explains this second notion with reference to Blanchot's 'The Instant of My Death'. Put simply, he says that, even though fiction does not refer to something real in the world or in the past, we as readers can still understand it. How is that possible, since it is language with no referent? Moreover, Derrida continues, this strange capacity to understand what we cannot possibly know is central to testimony as well. As I mentioned above, on Derrida's account, I can only testify to what only I can know. I testify to a secret – my truth, a truth that no one else can appropriate or own. Blanchot's 'The Instant of My Death' exemplifies this testimonial secret, or rather amplifies it, because in that text, Blanchot testifies to that which is absolutely his and only his, namely his death. But, once again, we need to remember that, for Derrida, what goes for Blanchot's testimony to his own death also goes for all communication, every interaction, and even experience in the broadest sense. So, for Derrida, literary language, and especially fiction, puts on display, as it were, a paradox that surrounds us all the time. Every day and everywhere, we are always understanding something that we cannot possibly see, verify, or comprehend – something that is, in Derrida's words, 'singular in general' ('D' 91).

Now, to turn to the second point, concerning the substitutability of the 'I', I want to propose that, if this paradox is in play during every act of communicating, exchanging or relating to another, or simply to otherness as such, it is also, and by definition, in play whenever I relate to myself as well. When I engage in testimony, or speak of a past experience, how does the I who exists today, in this instant, understand the I who existed back then? How do I turn that instant, which also revolved around a fundamental and impenetrable secret, into an instance? The larger question here is probably something like 'what is memory?' or 'how do we account for the consistency of the self through time?' These are, of course, colossal issues, and I have no intention of addressing them here. But I think we can at least hint at, or begin to intuit, Derrida's response, if we say that the self or the I is structured by the logic of the singular universal as well. Every I is, at one and the same time, both absolutely singular, indivisible or unique, and utterly general, replaceable or substitutable with any other I. This would be another meaning of that untranslatable phrase we have been repeating in this book – *tout autre est tout autre*, one apparently simple, but actually very complex and profound, rendering of which would be 'every other is every other'. On this account, and to recall the text that we discussed at the beginning of the first chapter, we are all like Othello, or singular universals. Which is to say, exactly none of us is anything like Othello. At every instant, we are all instances and instants, divided and undivided, or split at an absolutely unsplitable point.

The Experience of Literature

To conclude this chapter, I will return to the point I made above about Derrida's recourse to a discourse of rights and democracy, and his claim that literature is bound to a 'right to say everything' and a 'right to absolute nonresponse' ('P' 28–9), both of which can only make sense in the context of a juridical and political order that has taken shape approximately since the nineteenth century. As you will recall, this is the part of Derrida's later work that I find the least convincing, and most vulnerable to attack. The recent research of Samuel Moyn in particular would seem to present a significant challenge to anyone who wants to defend this element of Derrida's thought today. I myself will basically avoid the question, and not seek to defend it. Rather, and as I suggested already, I want to come at the issue a little obliquely or peripherally. Instead of either challenging or reinforcing the explicitly political stakes of Derrida's use of this kind of language, in sum, I want to explore whether or not what Derrida claims about the 'right to say everything' and the 'right to absolute nonresponse' really provides us with an accurate or helpful definition of literature.

But I am going to play a bit of a trick here; or rather, I am going to try to show how Derrida (perhaps deliberately, but we will never know) effectively played a trick on himself. Because, instead of simply rejecting Derrida's argument that this 'strange institution' called literature is inextricably bound to the institutions of democracy, and thus dismissing Derrida's conception of literature altogether, I am going to point to another, alternative genealogy of literature in Derrida's own work (and especially in an essay called 'Literature in Secret: An Impossible Filiation'), and suggest that it is more fecund than the one just sketched. That is to say, I am going to try to prove that someone has a better argument about literature than Derrida: namely, Derrida.

To the best of my knowledge, in his later work, Derrida develops three quite different lines of thought on the origins of literature. The first is the one we have just been discussing, or the notion that literature is a product of the nineteenth century, and especially democracy. To repeat the crucial phrases from 'Passions' cited above: 'no democracy without literature' and 'no literature without democracy'. Alongside these assertions, Derrida also develops a slightly more elaborate, and far more historically protracted, consideration of the connection between literature and rights, or literature and a community of rights. In '*Demeure*', for example, but elsewhere as well, he refers us to the work of the great German literary scholar and philologist Ernst Robert Curtius, and especially to Curtius's argument for a continuous literary tradition that runs from the Greeks to the French Revolution, or Homer to Goethe – a tradition that is called to a close at the end of the eighteenth century with the advent of nationalism.[26] This might sound like the opposite of Derrida's claim that literature takes shape alongside democracy in the nineteenth century; and, historically speaking, no doubt it is. But what Derrida emphasises about Curtius's argument is less its historical periodisation (or rather, lack of periodisation), than his notion that literature must be understood, not in terms of nations, but in terms of a 'juridical institution' and a system of 'acquired rights', at the centre of which sits 'the Roman figure of citizenship' or '*civitas*'. Here, and again as Derrida emphasises in '*Demeure*', literature would be bound up, not only with rights, but with Roman law, and even with the Latin language ('D' 24).

Derrida presents, then, at least two conceptions of literature as something essentially tied to law. In '*Demeure*', he explains why he takes this approach. 'There is', he writes, 'no essence or substance of literature' ('D' 29). What we call literature has no naturally existing unifying features. And this claim is self-evidently true. Go to any literature department at any university in the world. Look at the texts assigned on their syllabi. What do they all have in common? Phillip K. Dick. Emily Dickinson. The Oxford English Dictionary. The answer is nothing. They have nothing in common. Except, perhaps, for words (but then, why call it literature? Why not call it philology, as they did in the nineteenth century?). What is more, you will find on those syllabi books with pictures too. And films. Not to mention countless other objects. Therefore, and as Derrida puts it, 'even where it seems to reside [*demeure*], literature remains an unstable function, and it depends on a precarious juridical status' (29). It has no natural unity. Therefore, it requires an artificial one. Literature, in other words, is a legal fiction. Or, if we wanted to be crafty, we might say that fiction is a legal fiction. And this is part of the reason why Derrida talks about literature in terms of 'passion' or passivity. As he explains in '*Demeure*', literature's 'passion comes from this – that it receives its determination from something other than itself' (29). And in this instance, that 'something other than itself' is law, or a system of rights, either positively set out in some legislation, or more loosely implied. What rights? Well, presumably, rights like 'the right to say everything' and 'the right to absolute nonresponse' ('P' 28).

But to say that literature is a legal fiction does not at all justify the existence of literature departments at universities, nor does it do much to justify their continuation. It is, as far as I can tell, an essentially defensive posture. 'We must retain and defend the legal status of literature, and all the juridical and political institutions that make this status possible, because if we did not do so, literature would simply vanish. For nothing other than this fragile artificial legal frame holds literature together.' To which one could obviously respond: Who cares? Why are we defending and supporting this product of the nineteenth century anyway? From the right, we could hear someone say: 'It is expensive and pointless.' From the left, they might say: 'Exactly, it is a colonialist, classist, racist, sexist, homophobic, transphobic, heteronormative, micro- and macro-aggressive nineteenth-century institution. Get rid of it.' And this is more or less what has been going on. Literature gets Balkanised. Its former adherents find themselves elsewhere: Comparative Literature; Continental Philosophy; Languages and Linguistics; Film Studies; Cultural Studies; Women's Studies; Art History; Digital Humanities; and so on, very nearly *ad infinitum*. As we saw with society in the previous chapter of this book, this thing called literature cannot really stand up to persistent scrutiny (to use a word that will surely resonate with those familiar with the history of English Literature studies and departments). It is as if we have laser vision that we cannot turn off. When we look at it closely, it liquefies, and drops through our fingers.

So, to put the matter bluntly, I do not think we are going to get very far if we are simply attempting to defend the institution called literature. Or, more accurately, I do not think we will get very far if our planned defence of that institution is simply to point out that it is an institution, and that it is built, not on something natural or given, but on an artificial juridical and political foundation. Moreover, I am not entirely sure we should be attempting to defend the institution called literature. In fact, I am probably in agreement with much of the leftist critique that I gently lampooned a moment ago. But, the defence or nondefense of the institution called literature notwithstanding, I would be committed to defending what we might call the *experience* of literature, or the experience that many of those objects we call literary both exemplify and provide or enact. We might call the experience I have in mind something like 'the experience of the secret'. And there is no doubt that many objects that we do not call literature offer this experience as well. In fact, and as I will argue now, this experience is something we have every moment of every day. It is, perhaps, experience itself. And it is related to the third genealogy of literature in Derrida's later work that I mentioned at the outset.

So far, then, we have seen Derrida root literature in the nineteenth century, and in the mode of democracy that comes out of that century; and we have seen him more or less affirm Curtius's notion that literature is not founded on nations (not, therefore, German, French, English, Australian literature, and so forth) but on a system of rights, at the core of which are the rights first developed by the citizens or Rome. And as we explained, while obviously very different in terms of their historical investments and claims, both of these genealogies conceive of literature in juridical terms, or link it to the question of rights. The third genealogy of literature found in the later Derrida, however, appears very different. As we will see, it certainly deals with the law, or some kind of order or command delivered by some kind of authority, but it does not necessarily deal with the modern institution or institutions called law. In terms of Derrida's texts, the principal source of what I am referring to here as Derrida's third genealogy of literature is a short essay called 'Literature in Secret'. And it is to this essay that I will turn my attention now.

'Literature in Secret' is organised around a reading of three texts: first, as in *The Gift of Death*, which we analysed above, there is the Biblical story of Abraham, from Genesis; second, and again as in *The Gift of Death*, there is Kierkegaard, and especially *Fear and Trembling*, or Kierkegaard's reading of the story of Abraham; and finally, there is Franz Kafka's *Letter to His Father*. It is important to note that all three of these texts skirt the boundaries of what we usually mean when we say 'literature'. Even today, the Bible is not really literature. It is a great sacred text, or, depending on the state of one's soul, the word of God. Kierkegaard's *Fear and Trembling* is something like a work of philosophy, although it is also profoundly ironic, which is something we often do associate with literature. And finally, Kafka's *Letter to His Father* is a posthumously published bit of archival material. It was written by someone who is typically considered a literary author, to be sure. But it was not written for publication (unless, and this is a serious question, we consider sending a letter to another individual a kind of publication). So, in other words, Derrida writes about 'literature in secret' without writing about anything we would typically call literature. And that, perhaps, is part of what he means by his title. Literature itself or literature as such remains a little hidden here – in secret.

The major themes of Derrida's essay (the principal one of which, as we will see below, is forgiveness) are also not fundamentally or essentially literary. That is to say, while one could certainly write a piece of literature about forgiveness, quite clearly, not everything we call literature is. But what Derrida does want to propose is that both the experience of forgiveness and the experience of literature revolve around something like a secret. Thus, about half way through the text, Derrida sets out a kind of provisional definition of literature. 'Every text', he maintains, 'that is consigned to public space, that is relatively legible or intelligible, but whose content, sense, referent, signatory, and addressee are not fully determinable realities – realities that are at the same time non-fictive or immune from all fiction, realities that are delivered as such by some intuition, to a determinate judgement – can become a literary object' ('LS' 131). That is to say, every text that is not a strict description of some external and verifiable fact can be treated as literature. Or, put differently, every text that is founded in some sense on something that cannot be known (that is, something secret) is potentially literary. It can be approached, we might say, from a literary perspective.

Now on this definition, not only would the Bible, *Fear and Trembling*, and *Letter to His Father* be potentially literary. No, and far, far more expansively (with the possible exception of the most technical manual for the operation of some machine, where there might be an exact one-to-one correspondence between what the words tell one to do and what one then must go about doing), every text, and arguably every sign (or, as Derrida would likely prefer, and as we saw in our discussion of Derrida and Lacan above, every trace), and perhaps even more so, every experience of everything everywhere, is potentially literary. Fascinatingly, it seems to me, in 'Literature in Secret', the particular image that Derrida invokes to describe this experience of literature as the experience of the secret (and perhaps even the experience of experience full stop), is that of the meteorite (from the Greek *meta*, or over and above, and *aoros*, or lifted and hovering in the air). And, as Derrida explains, he likes this image because what appears to characterise the meteor is its unknown and unknowable origins. It lights up only once it hits earth's atmosphere. And that it was there beforehand, or where it was beforehand, we do not and cannot know. Inasmuch as it does not have a determinate or discoverable origin, referent or source, literary language, Derrida implies, is the same. And so too, in some profound sense, is all experience.

At the very beginning of this chapter, I mentioned the possibility of a secret or secrecy that exceeds the order of the sovereign. But I also declined to address it straight away, and suggested that we circle around the issue for a while first, or come at it indirectly. In some sense, that is what we have been doing throughout this chapter. Here, however, I think it is fair to say that we are passing very close to that issue. For we have set up this conception of the secret at the root of literature (and, arguably, at the root of language and experience in general) in opposition to Derrida's other efforts to define literature in more juridical and institutional terms. If we have a concept of literature as an institution founded on certain rights, and associated, ultimately, with a Roman conception of citizenship and law, then we are undoubtedly placing it under the auspices or the protection of some sovereign. But if we have a concept of literature as something more akin to an experience, and especially an experience of the secret, or a paradoxical experience of that which we cannot comprehend, master, or know, it is not entirely certain that we need a sovereign power to define it. In fact, on this second model, literature might become the very thing (or one of the things) that dismantles the sovereign, and does so repeatedly, each time it is set in motion, or each time its operation is performed.

You will recall that, a moment ago, we suggested that the connection that Derrida announces in 'Literature in Secret' between the theme of literature and that of forgiveness initially seemed a little tenuous. Now, however, under the rubric of the problem of sovereignty, and of the experience of literature as that of a secret that somehow exceeds and even dismantles the sovereign order, the pieces of Derrida's text begin to come together. For when Derrida discusses forgiveness here, he does so primarily in terms of relationships between fathers and sons, or filial bonds (hence his subtitle as well: 'An Impossible Filiation'). The texts Derrida reads offer any number of examples of fathers and sons: Abraham and Isaac, of course, but also in some sense God and Abraham, as well as, perhaps, Abraham or God and Kierkegaard, and, finally but most importantly, Kafka's father and Kafka. There is sovereignty in each one of these relationships, no doubt. But, through his reading, Derrida shows how, owing to a certain secrecy inscribed in it as well, the problem or what he calls the *aporia* of forgiveness evades and destabilises this sovereignty.

By way of conclusion, I will try to explain: 'Literature in Secret' begins by making the same point we have seen Derrida make a number of times so far, the point that is in many ways at the centre of this book as a whole, namely that society is organised around, not just communication, but also secrecy. Paradoxically, the secret is integral to the social bond. As Derrida writes 'the secret of secrecy about which we shall speak does not consist in hiding something, in not revealing the truth, but in respecting the absolute singularity, the infinite separation of what binds me or exposes me to the unique, to one as to the other, to the One as to the Other' ('LS' 152). In other words, and as I have said a dozen or more times, we share what divides us, and are held together by what holds us apart. Here Derrida explores this strange paradox by looking closely at Abraham's relationship with God. As you will recall, Abraham is told to take his son Isaac to Mount Moriah, and to sacrifice him. This is a test, Derrida suggests. And Abraham passes. But Abraham is also not told why he must perform this sacrifice. And, in a sense, the secret that God does not share with Abraham binds the two together just as powerfully as does the one that God does share. Or, to put the point differently, Abraham's ignorance as to God's purpose or intention is precisely what renders his obedience to God's command so powerful.

The story of Abraham is, then, a kind of allegory for society in general, or for our relation, not only with God as infinite other, but with the otherness of everyone and, arguably, everything as well. Here, however, and in order to explore the paradox or *aporia* of forgiveness, Derrida seems to intervene in the original text, and to add a scene that we do not in fact find in Genesis. He proposes that, immediately after God stops Abraham from sacrificing his son, Abraham might seek to apologise to God, or to ask God to forgive him for doing what he has been told, or for his willingness to kill his son. In this instance, Derrida proposes, Abraham would be saying something like 'forgive me for being too faithful to you, or for following you too closely, and agreeing with you too readily'. 'Forgive me', in short, 'for being true to you.' Or, as Derrida puts it, 'forgive me for preferring the secret that binds me to you rather than the secret that binds me to the other other, to each and every other' ('LS' 154). This is the issue we discussed in the first chapter, under the headings of 'The Contaminated Third' and 'Perjury Squared'. Every act of fidelity, every promise to be faithful includes (and not merely as some future possibility, but in the act of swearing an oath or promising fidelity itself), an infidelity, a perjury, or a breaking of the promise or the oath. We live with what Desdemona calls a 'divided duty', and I can only keep my bond with one in so far as I break it with another.

As Derrida explains it in 'Literature in Secret', something similar is at stake in the act of forgiveness (which, we should point out, in French is '*pardon*', which carries a far more obvious juridical meaning than the English). Forgiveness necessitates the unforgivable. Or, as Derrida puts it, a 'law inscribes the unforgivable, and fault itself, within the heart of forgiveness'. For Derrida, this notion appears to have at least two separate meanings, which I will sketch here. First, and perhaps a little obviously, 'one never asks for forgiveness except for the unforgivable, one never has to forgive the forgivable' ('LS' 127). So the unforgivable is inescapably part of forgiveness. But also, and in a more complicated sense, both the act of forgiving another and the act of asking for forgiveness include, as part of their very structure, something that is unforgivable. Both forgiving and being forgiven entail what, elsewhere, Derrida calls a 'double bind'. For I can only forgive someone, and I can only ask to be forgiven, if I in some sense presume their position, or presume that I know that they feel guilty, and thus need to be forgiven, or, in the other case, presume that I know they feel generous, and are thus capable of forgiving. In Derrida's words, all forgiving and all asking to be forgiven involve a 'specular identification' (137) with the other, and thus a reduction of their otherness, or an unforgivable violation or invasion of the secret that constitutes them as other.

Kafka's *Letter to His Father*, or rather the posthumous publication of Kafka's *Letter to His Father*, provides a kind of performance or enactment of this unforgivable violation of the other that is built into the act of forgiveness. Before we ask the question 'how are we to read it?' we would have to ask 'are we to read it at all?'

Is this intended to be seen by anyone other than its addressee? Even after his death, and in a strange way especially after his death (because now he can no longer explain himself, or explain what he meant when he wrote it), are we not violating Kafka's singular secret? What is a letter, after all? We know that, today at least, Kafka's letter has been 'consigned to public space' and that, given the fact that its author and its intended recipient are both long dead, its origin or referent are not 'fully determinable realities'. Thus, on Derrida's definition, it has the potential to be literature, or to be treated like literature. But so too does nearly every text, every sign or trace, and probably every experience. If every utterance involves something like secrecy and something like literature (if every utterance is something like a letter to one's father), then how do we distinguish between reading as generous interpretation and reading as personal violation? How do we distinguish between endeavouring, in good faith, to understand the other, and reducing, in bad faith, the other to the same?

With respect to Kafka's *Letter to His Father*, and to be clear, I am not saying we should not read it. On the contrary, I think we have to read it. But we also have to ask to be forgiven, in some sense, for having read it. And, what is more, in asking to be forgiven, we will also have committed the unforgivable on another level. And this is something that probably extends to all readings, all interactions, all engagements, perhaps all relations and experiences in general. We are always breaking our oath. We are always violating the secret that holds us together while holding us apart. We are always assuming that we know what we can never possibly know. Thus we always need to be forgiven, and we always need to forgive others. And in asking and in granting forgiveness, we are always, and constantly, perpetrating the unforgivable.

Notes

1 See Jodi Dean's *Publicity's Secret: How Technoculture Capitalizes on Democracy*.
2 Birchall, 'Aesthetics', 26.
3 Birchall, 'Aesthetics', 26.
4 Davide Panagia, 'On Datapolitk', http://www.academia.edu6875336/On_Dataolitik.
5 Liliana Bounegru, 'GetHub as Transparency Device in Data Journalism, Open Date and Data Activism', http://lilianabounegru.org/category/data-visualization.
6 See David Wills's *Prosthesis*.
7 For a careful discussion of this issue, see Jacques De Ville, 'Derrida's *Purveyor of Truth* and Constitutional Reading'.
8 Poe, 'The Purloined Letter', in *Poe's Tales of Mystery and Terror*, 289.
9 Poe, 'Purloined', 289.
10 Poe, 'Purloined', 289.
11 Poe, 'Purloined', 319.
12 Lacan, 'Seminar of "The Purloined Letter"', 44.
13 For a discussion of this phenomenon, see Dimitris Vardoulakis's *The Doppelgänger: Literature's Philosophy*.
14 See Claude Lefort's *The Political Forms of Modern Society: Bureaucracy, Democracy, Totalitarianism* and *Democracy and Political Theory*. Here I would like to mention a number of Derrida's texts that I am decidedly not dealing with in detail in this book – books like *The Politics of Friendship*, *Specters of Marx*, *Rogues*, as well as essays such as 'The Force of Law: The "Mystical Foundation" of Authority'. The question of Derrida's treatment of democracy in terms of 'democracy-to-come', as well as his concern with constitutional and public law, especially around the question of sovereignty, has received an enormous amount of attention in the secondary literature. For particularly good examples, see Fritsch, 'Derrida's Democracy to Come' and De Ville, *Jacques Derrida: Law as Absolute Hospitality*. In this book, I take it for granted that this particular aspect of Derrida's later work has been explored in some detail, by scholars who are more qualified than I.
15 See Moyn's *The Last Utopia: Human Rights in History* and *Christian Human Rights*; and Whyte, 'The Fortunes of Natural Man: Robinson Crusoe, Political Economy, and the Universal Declaration of Human Rights'.
16 For a more politically engaged discussion of the structure of testimony, and the manner in which it appears to require a certain loneliness, even as a

condition of its possibility, see Jill Stauffer's *Ethical Loneliness: The Injustice of Not Being Heard*. What I argue here with respect to Derrida and testimony certainly resonates with Stauffer's position, although her approach is rooted more in Levinas than in Derrida.

17 Kant, *Critique of the Power of Judgment*, 89–127.
18 Levinas, 'Truth of Disclosure and Truth of Testimony', in *Basic Philosophical Writings*.
19 Levinas, *Totality*, 61, 170.
20 As an aside, there may be a fruitful connection here between the way that Levinas critiques a conception of knowledge as 'correlation' and the Speculative Realist critique of 'correlationism', discussed in my Introduction above.
21 Levinas, 'Essence and Disinterestedness', in *Basic Philosophical Writings*, 112–25.
22 Levinas, 'Truth of Disclosure', 104.
23 Levinas, 'Truth of Disclosure', 104.
24 Levinas, *God, Death, and Time*, 196.
25 Heidegger, *Being and Time*, 314.
26 Curtius, *European Literature and the Latin Middle Ages*.

3

Between Two Solitudes: Self-Deception, Consciousness and the Other Mind

State Secrets

In the previous chapter, I attempted to draw together Derrida's discussion, particularly in his later work, of politics, literature and the secret. I focused my attention on the theory of testimony or avowal developed in most detail in the essay '*Demeure*', in which, by way of an extended discussion of Blanchot's 'The Instant of My Death', Derrida suggests that testimony is, at one and the same time, utterly singular, or having to do with a secret knowledge that only the one who testifies can genuinely possess (I can only testify to what only I can know, as I put it), and something like universal, or at any rate a repetition of a past experience or event that itself becomes infinitely repeatable or iterable. I tried to show that this paradox or *aporia* of the singular universal also has a bearing on Derrida's approach to literature, on the one hand, and time or temporality, on the other. According to Derrida, I claimed, literature is a paradigmatic example of the singular universal, and thus a paradigmatic or exemplary example of the logic of the example as such. That is to say, literature is always an instant that is also an instance. Indeed, I even went so far as to propose that, on Derrida's account, this logic of the example (or of the open secret, as it were, or the thing that cannot possibly be known but that must also be entirely knowable) configures experience or our relations with others and with the world in the broadest possible sense. Finally, if only briefly, I began to sketch what all of this might have to do with Derrida's lifelong concern (indeed, near obsession) with the problem of time, and especially death.

In this chapter, I want to continue with this line of thought. But I also want to place more emphasis on its discretely or predominantly philosophical stakes. In fact, initially at least, I want to try to show how Derrida's treatment of the secret might be seen to inform a number of debates among philosophers who do not typically pay much attention to his work, and often repudiate it – namely, Analytic or Anglo-American ones. I am thinking in particular of two sets of debates within what is called the philosophy of mind: first, the problem or paradox of self-deception (a subset, really, of the Liar's Paradox, which explores whether or not it is possible to lie to oneself, and which has an affinity with Russell's Paradox as well, which I mentioned above in relation to the problem of the example and the exception); and second, the problem of consciousness (or what, approximately twenty years ago now, the Australian philosopher David Chalmers first dubbed 'the hard problem', or roughly the fact that there can be no purely physical or functional explanation of our mental experience, or the feeling that accompanies our awareness of things).[1] As we will see, both of these problems open onto a third problem – what is sometimes referred to as the problem of other minds, or how and whether I can know anything determinate about the mind of another.

One way (but, to be clear, not the only or even most significant way) to understand the title of this chapter – 'Between Two Solitudes' – would be to hear it as a comment on the notorious division between Continental and Analytic philosophers. In bringing Derrida into conversation with Analytic philosophy of mind, I hope it is understood that I am attempting to be less polemical than ecumenical. I simply want to suggest, in a gentle and unobtrusive manner, that Derrida's thought, and especially his approach to the secret, could conceivably contribute to conversations from which he and his followers are all too often excluded out of hand, or turned away at the door. Along the way, if only in passing, I am also trying to address a number of the criticisms that have been levelled at Derrida by the Speculative Realists – a group of thinkers who, in their own fashion, have also sought a rapprochement of sorts between Continental and Analytic philosophy. As with the Analytic philosophers, my gesture in the case of the Speculative Realists is not polemical but ecumenical. I merely want to propose, gently here as well, that Derrida might not be dead just yet, or that, if he is, he might also be among the living dead, or those philosophers from the past still worth giving a second glance.

But while those will be, as it were, the surface concerns of this chapter, I also want to make it clear that, just underneath the surface, political questions will continue to be churning away. Indeed, I am interested in the problem of self-deception primarily in so far as it is related to the question of politics, secrecy and the lie. And I am touching on 'the hard problem' of consciousness largely because I think it helps expose what we might call a new political ontology, or a new way of thinking the relationship between what is typically called the human and its other, or the non-human. Thus, in order to emphasise at the outset the political concerns that will be silently present, or just under the surface, throughout, I will begin with two very concrete, practical, local (for me, at least) and explicitly political or juridical events. Specifically, I will analyse two laws that have recently been passed by the Australian parliament, and that might operate as flares, of sorts, or ways of briefly lighting up the larger political terrain that, I would contend, is taking shape in our age – a terrain that sometimes, and probably too often, goes by the name neo-liberalism, but for which, in my estimation, we still have not developed an adequate critical vocabulary. The laws in question are called the Border Force Act, which was passed in the Australian parliament with bi-partisan support on 15 May 2015, and the Mandatory Data Retention Regime, which was passed, again with bi-partisan support, on 21 March 2015. As we will see, along with illuminating a little that thing we have inadequately named neo-liberalism, both of these laws also involve the question of secrecy and the secret.

First, then, the Border Force Act. The thrust of this law is to make it a criminal offence, punishable by a sentence of up to two years in prison, for anyone working at the Naru or Manus Island detention centres (the reputation of which I hope I do not need to rehearse here) to provide information about these centres to the media, or to any other individual of group. Government employees or (and this point is crucial) government contractees must only communicate about their work with Department of Immigration officials, and no one else. The law is clearly designed to intercept whistle-blowers, and its chief target is not really civil servants, but people who work for Non-Governmental Organis-ations or NGOs. Here we need to understand that a great deal of the work performed in the detention centres gets contracted out, as it were, to NGOs. This follows the neo-liberal logic of deregulation. Every effort is made to diminish the state. So rather than having civil servants performing the roles, in a bizarre pantomime of a market economy, organisations like the Red

Cross or the Salvation Army or Save the Children compete for the opportunity to do the work. However, the problem emerges when people who work for the NGOs cannot be controlled as directly or as effectively as traditional civil servants. Rather than simply following orders, they have intentions to do things like, for example, attempting to save the children. So, in the form of ordinances like the Border Force Act, the law steps in to contain their actions.

This, it seems to me, is a pretty good example of the way what we are provisionally calling neo-liberalism works. It involves what I will dub a deregulating regulation (a clumsy phrase, I know, but the best one I can come up with at this moment). At the same time that the state retreats, at the same time that it contracts out its traditional activities and allows for the development of 'the market', regulation or the law expands. The two phenomena, which seem to be contradictory at first glance (less state, more law), in fact go hand in hand. And it would be hard to understand this deregulating regulation from the perspective of traditional political theory. We will not get at it, for example, if we think in terms of the specificity or autonomy or concept of the political. It is not exclusively about friends and enemies, or the sovereign exception, or any of the ideas typically associated with the thought of Carl Schmitt.[2] There is clearly an economic element to all of this. But at the same time, we will also miss the mark if we think in classically Marxist or economic reductionist terms. There is definitely an economic logic of decentralisation, efficiency, austerity and so forth. But there is not really any economic production going on in the detention centres – at least not yet, or not in any obvious sense.

To be clear, with respect to my claim that nothing is being produced at the detention centres, I should note that I am aware of one good challenge to my position, namely Antonio Negri's proposal that we are living in a state of what Marx called 'real subsumption' – one in which capitalism has absorbed all relations and all activities, such that surplus value can be created, not only in recognisably productive industrial contexts, but literally everywhere and all the time.[3] On this account, for which I have considerable sympathy (and which seems to be in many ways borne out by the kind of evidence I am presenting right now), profit can be sucked out of anything, even, for instance, horrifying and terrifically expensive acts of state-sanctioned racist hate. Here we must note in passing that the portion of the Australian budget that goes to protecting borders and locking up asylum seekers (at least in comparison to the amount spent on refugees) is astronomical. And, naturally, much of that money finds its way into the hands of private individuals and corporations – for example, security companies, but also building, equipment, shipping, manufacture and a complex web of related enterprises. All of that granted and said, however, the problem with the theory of real subsumption is that, under it, terms like economics and production begin to do what we saw happen to the concepts of society and literature in the previous two chapters. That is to say, they appear to liquefy, or fall through our fingers and get absorbed into the sand beneath our feet.

Rather than a specifically political or economic reductionist approach, then, to understand things like the Border Force Act we would do well, I think, to refer to Giorgio Agamben's work, and especially his book *The Kingdom and the Glory*. I am invoking Agamben here only in passing. But I should note that an entire, and entirely different, book could be written on his thought and the question of the secret – one that would emphasise the way that he himself puts the secret to work in his writings, or uses it, in deft and fascinating ways, to seduce his readers into a protracted study of exceptionally hermetic and arcane material that he then reveals to be illuminative of the most pressing issues of our time. I will come back to Agamben, and to some of what I am hinting at here, in my Conclusion. For now, I simply want to recall his concept, which he develops in *The Kingdom and the Glory*, of the 'bi-polar machine'[4] of politics and economics, sovereignty and governance, or state and society, and his notion, in particular, that such things are related in their very separation, or held together by being held apart. And, as you may know, in an example of the seductive hermeticism I have just mentioned, Agamben traces this logic of the bi-polar machine all the way back to early Christian debates about the doctrine of the Trinity. Thus, just as God the Father can withdraw into transcendent and sovereign isolation, while God the Spirit providentially governs or administers every aspect of our worldly existence, so too can the state retreat while law and regulation expand.

Let us now turn our attention to the second law mentioned above – the Mandatory Data Retention Regime. What does this regime mandate, you might ask? Well, it mandates that two years' worth of the phone and internet records of Australian citizens and residents must be retained. But this retention will not be the work of, for example, the state, the police, or ASIO (the Australian secret service). No, according to the Mandatory Data Retention Regime, two years of communications meta-data must be retained by the service provider. That is to say, the records must be retained by the communications corporations themselves. And those corporations are then required to make that data available to the state when it requests it. So, in essence, what this law does is take the most scandalous revelation of the Snowden Affair – namely that a so-called democratic government was collecting meta-data, or simply spying, on its citizens – and make that legally mandatory. And, for good measure and along the way, it also privatises or deregulates it.

The law, in other words, or rather the law in conjunction with capital or the market (again, the bi-polar machine), absorbs the scandal. What was once its shadowy grey area or, as Agamben might say, 'zone of indistinction'[5] (in what sense did FISA, or the American secret courts, legitimate spying on innocent civilians – was it operating within, or above, or before the law?), and it renders that grey area internal to the law's operation. But again, and crucially, the Mandatory Data Retention Regime is an example of deregulating regulation or the bi-polar machine of sovereignty and governance, politics and economics, state and society. The state withdraws or retracts, in other words, while, through a twisted alliance with something like the market, law and regulation expand.

Not surprisingly, the Mandatory Data Retention Regime stipulates that corporations must bear the cost of collecting and storing this meta-data, which is currently estimated to be about $400 million. And that translates into roughly $3.98 per year per customer (who is obviously the one who will wind up paying for it). So, in essence, as a result of this law, Australian citizens and residents will be paying communications corporations about $4 a year to spy on them for the state. $4 then: it is a bargain! And, not to be facetious, but that is exactly how I imagine a neo-liberal economist would think. Setting down their Ayn Rand for just a moment, peering at us over the brim of their designer glasses, and probably stabbing at their desk with their index finger to emphasise each word, they would say: 'Look at this incredible law. It somehow manages to decrease the operation of the state while at the same time performing and improving upon the only legitimate function of the state, namely security.' And this would be another way of expressing what we are calling deregulating regulation, or again, drawing on Agamben, the bi-polar machine of sovereignty and governance. At every turn, whenever possible, it seeks to decrease the operation of the state (or, crudely put, state spending, and thus taxation) whilst almost magically increasing the function of the state (crudely again, security, and the protection in particular of private property). This is the point at which the most arcane and speculative aspect of Agamben's approach seems most valid. It is a mystery, how this came about – nothing less than the mystery of the Trinity.

I mention all of this because I think that, when we approach the political question of secrecy (and surveillance) today, we have to keep in mind what is unique about what we are consenting now to calling neo-liberalism. We will not really understand this phenomenon if we rely on a political vocabulary that predates this period, or if we simply repeat that vocabulary without submitting it to a transformative critique. Hannah Arendt, for example, in her famous essay 'Truth and Politics' (which Derrida also deals with in his 'History of the Lie', and which I will come back to below), posits a distinction between what she calls the 'traditional' and the 'modern' or totalitarian lie.[6] On Arendt's account, the first has always been part of politics, for as long as there has been politics. Basically, it involves trying to conceal some particular fact or position from an enemy. The second, however, only takes shape in modern conditions, and especially with the emergence of what Arendt avers to be the completely new political form called totalitarianism (and, as an aside, I have already indicated my mistrust of this concept, a mistrust that I will return to later as well). It involves, not simply concealing a fact, but rather attempting to reinvent the context or fabric of reality in which all facts first appear. Thus, for example, we do not merely tell the people that Trotsky was a traitor to the revolution. No, we completely and effectively rewrite history, such that Trotsky never even existed in the first place.

But that concept of the modern or totalitarian lie does not really get at what is going on in things like the Border Force Act or the Mandatory Data Retention Regime or countless other laws like them in countless other jurisdictions or political spaces. Here it would probably be more fruitful to refer back to what I said in the first section of my second chapter about the work of people like Clare Birchall, Davide Panagia and Lilliana Bounegru. In that emerging field, an attempt is being made to compose a vocabulary for politics in the digital age. When I mentioned it above, I expressed my interest in, but also mild suspicion of, this politicisation of data, if it can be put that way. In either case, my strategy here is simply different. I want to come at the issue on a lower level, as it were, or closer to the ground, and thus perhaps under the radar. For me, and as I suggested in the Introduction, alongside the effort to think what is entirely unique and new about our age, and the technologies that define or determine it, we should also be revisiting fundamental philosophical or ontological questions. Along with wondering how modern politics and technology manipulate and control the secret, or use and abuse it, we should also be trying to explain what, exactly, a secret is, and what a self (or, for that matter, a state) is, such that it might be able to keep or divulge such a thing. That, at any rate, is the task I would like to try to approach now.

This chapter begins, then, with a consideration of the two more overtly philosophical questions or debates mentioned above – the question of self-deception, on the one hand, and that of consciousness, on the other. To address the first, I will begin by returning to Derrida's 'History of the Lie: Prolegomena', a piece in which he makes a number of interesting and provocative statements about what he calls 'the self-lie', or self-deception, particularly with reference to the paper by Arendt already mentioned, 'Truth and Politics'. In my estimation, these comments clearly refer to the same paradox of self-deception that has vexed Analytic philosophers for some time. And, as I will try to show, Derrida's own consideration of what, throughout his later writings, he calls 'autoimmunity' offers a neat way of addressing, if not exactly resolving, the paradox. To help explain what I mean, I will also insert a digression on a short and still relatively unknown text by Simmel called 'The Maker of Lies' – one of a series of brief pieces on art, literature and theatre that Simmel called '*Momentbilder*' or 'Snapshots: *sub specie aeternitatus*'. This will lead into my consideration of the second question or debate mentioned above, or the 'hard problem' of consciousness. Here, and a little unexpectedly no doubt, I will refer primarily to Derrida's 'How to Avoid Speaking: Denials' – a text that, on face value, appears to be about the mysteries of negative theology, but that, in my opinion, is really, or just as much, about the far more mundane experience of consciousness.

If, for the bulk of this chapter, I will attempt to bring Derrida, and especially Derrida's treatment of the secret, into conversation with Analytic philosophy, or to show how his ideas might inform debates among Analytic philosophers, in the final section, I will return to the Continental side of the equation, and show how what Derrida has to say about things like the paradox of self-deception and the 'hard problem' of consciousness have a bearing on his reading of someone as resolutely Continental as Hans-Georg Gadamer. In particular, I will explore an essay (or a tribute, really) that Derrida wrote about Gadamer shortly after his death (and shortly before Derrida's own) called 'Rams: Uninterrupted Dialogue – Between Two Solitudes, the Poem'. Here the central issue is not merely whether or not it is possible for me to lie to myself, or how I might account for my experience of consciousness. Rather, it is how, and in what sense, I might claim to know the mind of another – how and in what sense, that is to say, I might be able to communicate or understand anything at all. And this, as I indicated above, is also an issue that has a great deal of traction among philosophers of the Analytic bent.

Deceiving Myself

The notion that one has lied to oneself or deceived oneself is something like idiomatic in more than one European language, and perhaps in others as well. In French, for example, one could speak of '*l'aveuglement*' or '*auto-tromperie*'; in German, '*Selbsttäuschung*'. This same idea is also deeply ensconced in our literary and cultural traditions. The great figure of King Lear, who we watch deceive himself in so many ways, from the moment he arrives on stage to the moment he dies on it, immediately comes to mind. So too do nearly all of the main characters in Jane Austen's novels, not to mention a whole array of film creations. Perhaps the most familiar philosophical expression of self-deception is Jean-Paul Sartre's notion of 'bad faith', where, under the pressure of external forces and expectations, the subject refuses to exercise her existential freedom, to which she is properly condemned.[7] But even in more colloquial terms, the notion that 'I was fooling myself' or that someone else was 'tricking themselves', and as a result behaved in a manner that was objectively at odds with their own interests or desires, is common enough to be called ubiquitous. We speak this way with a great deal of frequency. And it performs any number of functions in our day to day lives.

Nevertheless, at the same time, a very long philosophical lineage has sought to point out, and then somehow resolve, the paradox inscribed within the notion of self-deception. In simple terms, and as I have already explained a number of times, a lie is an intentional act – one in which the liar conceals, not an objective fact, but the content of her own thoughts. And this intentional act is directed at another. To recall the formal definition set out in my first chapter, to lie I must deliberately endeavour to make you believe that I believe something other than what I genuinely believe. But, if that is the case, then how could one intentionally conceal one's own thoughts from, precisely, one's own thoughts? In other words, how could I intentionally attempt to trick my own intentionality? How could I deliberately deceive the seat of my own deliberation, or wilfully confuse my will? To say that I lied to myself or fooled myself is a little like saying that I hid an object from myself by holding it behind my own back. The agent of deception is also the target of deception. The liar is also the lied to. And, so long as we assume that the self is unified, or that it is one agent rather than many, that scenario makes no sense.

Derrida addresses this issue directly in his reading of Arendt in 'History of the Lie'. As I mentioned a moment ago, in 'Truth and Politics', Arendt distinguishes between the traditional and the modern or totalitarian lie. The first, she says, conceals a fact from an enemy; the second seeks to destroy and then completely reinvent the context in which all facts appear. For Arendt, the ultimate conclusion of the second form of deception is what she calls the 'absolute lie', or the one in which the liar comes to believe her own lie.[8] And, Arendt maintains, this act of self-deception would be one of the many irrational horrors of what she calls totalitarianism. Like Eichmann, perhaps, the criminals come genuinely to believe that they have done no wrong, and that their own lies are the truth. And when this form of deception becomes a form of politics, or even a form of life, the world risks falling out from under our feet. We are left treading water on a shifting ocean of perpetual invention and illusion, process and change.

In 'History of the Lie', Derrida takes exception to this notion. First, he suggests that Arendt needs to think more profoundly about what it means to lie – that she is taking it for granted that she knows the lie, and is thus unwittingly getting lost in what, above, we saw Augustine call its 'cavern-like windings [*cavernosis anfractibus*]', or its eternal labyrinth or maze. Then, Derrida invokes the philosophical lineage I have just described, or the tradition of pointing to the paradox of 'self-deception' or the 'self-lie'. 'Is "self-deception" possible?', Derrida wonders. 'Is it a rigorous and pertinent concept?' 'In strictest terms', he continues, 'does one ever lie to oneself' (*WA* 40). And then again, a little later on in the text, he proclaims: 'To lie will always mean to deceive the other intentionally and consciously, while knowing what it is that one is deliberately hiding, therefore while not lying to oneself.' Thus, for Derrida, 'the self, if this word has a sense, excludes the self-lie' (60).

To be clear, at this point, Derrida is not merely challenging Arendt's understanding of truth, lies and politics. Rather, he is going after her unreflective presuppositions, especially as they concern the concept of the lie and that of the self. To put this another way, Derrida is not simply saying that we cannot lie to ourselves, or that self-deception is an impossible act. No, he is saying that, if we are going to understand the very common notion (and, probably, the very common experience) that one has tricked or fooled oneself, we are going to have to rethink what we mean by deception and what we mean by a self. In the case of the first, or what we mean by deception, in 'History of the Lie' Derrida insists that we must do away with a certain, as he puts it, 'optimism' – the optimism which says that, ultimately, the truth is more powerful than the lie, and that the lie is a secondary and transitory phenomenon (*WA* 60). That is to say, to think the lie, we must try to think the abyssal notion of a lie that is never revealed, and the effects of which last indefinitely, or even infinitely – what Derrida calls 'the indefinite survival of mystification' as opposed to a 'truth that must always win out and end up being revealed', and that does so because it 'indefinitely outlives lies, fictions, and images' (65). Here, and as Derrida explains, the consequences of his investigation begin to undermine its premise or project. For how could we have a 'history' of a lie that is never revealed? How can we have a history of that which never appeared, neither in the present, nor in the past, nor in the present that once was in the past? But this is a topic that we could easily get lost in (a cavern-like winding, as it were), so I will set it aside, and address the other issue, namely what would a self have to be if it were capable of deceiving itself.

I will come back to Derrida and to his 'History of the Lie' in a moment. But first I would like to recall that this question is at the root of a considerable debate among Analytic philosophers, the basic parameters of which I will try to sketch here. The history of this debate undoubtedly extends back further than we could possibly explain. But for our purposes, we can point out that it is already in play in Kant, who, in his *Metaphysics of Morals*, notes: 'It is easy to show that man is actually guilty of many inner lies, but it seems more difficult to explain how they are possible; for a lie requires a second person whom one intends to deceive, whereas to deceive oneself on purpose seems to contain a contradiction.'[9] Sartre formalises the same paradox in *Being and Nothingness*, when addressing the concept of 'bad faith', which we have already glimpsed above: 'It follows that the one to whom the lie is told and the one who lies are one and the same person', Sartre explains, 'which means that I must know in my capacity as deceiver the truth which is hidden from me in my capacity as the one deceived.'[10]

Kant and Sartre notwithstanding, the more recent literature has broken the paradox of self-deception down into two separate but related issues: first, what is called the 'doxastic' or 'static' paradox (simultaneously, in one static moment, both believing and not believing in some state of affairs); and second, the 'strategic' or 'dynamic' paradox (the notion that one cannot successfully employ a deceptive strategy against someone who is aware of this strategy).[11] The first, then, has to do with belief, or what the deceiver does or does not hold to be true. The second, which is weaker, perhaps, but still difficult to resolve, has to do with function – not whether or not I can believe my own lie, but simply whether or not such a lie could work.

The most common solution to both the doxastic and the strategic aspects of the paradox of self-deception is not really a solution at all. On this approach, philosophers simply partition the mind or the self, and propose that one part is capable of deceiving the other. Here, for example, they might take a sort of psychoanalytic line, and suggest that the unconscious mind can deceive the conscious one. Or, alternatively, philosophers will work with concepts like awareness or disposition, and propose that we can be partially but not fully aware of something, or aware at one moment but not at the next, or that we can be disposed to one thought here but not so disposed there. But, as many working in the field today would agree, such lines of investigation do not really resolve anything, they merely displace the problem. The paradox of self-deception concerns the presupposition of a unified self. And that is really what it is attempting to address. Simply to set that aside is to skirt the issue. Instead, we must face it head on: a self must be unified, otherwise it is not a self. But at the same time, our simple moral experience tells us that we often do trick, deceive or lie to ourselves. And those two things cannot both be possible. So we must either get rid of the concept of the unified self (which is to say, get rid of the self altogether). Or we must come up with a model of the practice of deception that escapes the contradiction.

Aside from the partitioning of the self, and thus merely avoiding the problem, the other important solution (and probably the most interesting one I have come across in my admittedly far from exhaustive research) is presented by the American philosopher Herbert Fingarette, in his short, eminently sensible, and eminently fascinating little book *Self-Deception*. Fingarette is kind of an anomaly in the field, because, even when he was working on this problem in the 1960s (the book was first published in 1969), he was already moving across the border that divides what we now call Continental and Analytic philosophy. Thus his approach is heavily influenced by Sartre, and by the theory of 'bad faith' sketched above, as well as by Freud. But the most important influence is undoubtedly Wittgenstein, and it is probably fair to call Fingarette's treatment of the paradox of self-deception a specifically Wittgensteinian one.

Basically, Fingarette suggests that we try to escape the presupposition of an inner world where thought takes place (that, in other words, we accept Wittgenstein's critique of private languages). Instead of thinking in terms of what he calls 'cognitive-perception', or the realm of belief in general, he proposes that we think in terms of 'volition-action', or the realm of engaging and performing. That is to say, Fingarette sees consciousness primarily in terms of actively and practically doing things in the world. So, on his account, we can experience something passively, to be sure. But we can only become aware of it by actively and deliberately 'spelling it out' to ourselves.[12] More accurately, for Fingarette, we can and do actively engage with the world in all kinds of ways. But we only become aware of our own engagement when we, again, spell it out to ourselves, or as Fingarette also says, 'avow'.[13] Self-deception, then, stems from an engagement with the world that one does not or cannot avow, or actively and deliberately make one's own. Self-deception occurs, in other words, not so much when we lie to ourselves, as when we fail to give ourselves an account of ourselves.

Fingarette's work invokes a whole array of very complicated questions and problems in the philosophy of mind that I have neither the space nor the talent to explore. But I will say - with respect to this roughly Wittgensteinian account, where consciousness is understood primarily in terms of practical activity, and language in terms of its function or use - that it seems to me to slip too easily into a behaviourist programme, where the inner world becomes little more than a reflex of an outer one. Or, to put the point differently, it does not really explore the division between the inner and the outer, it merely evaporates it. Thus, in the case of Fingarette, he might be able to explain how, when

I am unaware of some aspect of my engagement with the world, or do not spell it out to myself, I can live in a contradiction, and perhaps even in some sense deceive myself; but this does exactly nothing to explain why I become aware of this part of my life, but remain essentially unaware of that one. What is the motivation behind the motivation, as it were? If it is merely accidental, then we are basically eliminating mental life altogether. On such an account, sometimes I am aware, sometimes I am not, and there is no reason to pursue the matter any further. But this goes against, not only a long tradition (in fact, more or less the whole tradition) of philosophy, but also our (or, at any rate, my) most average and everyday experience.

It is certainly possible to be unaware of part of our engagement with the world, or to fail to 'spell it out' to ourselves. But when we are unaware in this fashion, and then later become aware, we can also look back, and trace out unconscious motivations for our lack of awareness. And, not to be crudely psychoanalytic, these motivations are frequently associated with traumatic experiences that we wish to avoid. It is not enough, then, to speak of what it means to be aware. We must also consider what it means to be unaware, and explore all the ways in which our lack of awareness informs and even overdetermines what we take to be our awareness. To put the same point from another direction, even if we spell things out to ourselves, as Fingarette proposes, we are also, and in that very act, compelled and driven by countless other things that we have not spelled out, as it were, or that remain silent. Or, to employ yet another idiom, there will always be an unconscious motivation – one that, while not reducible to the (essentially Cartesian) 'cognitive-perception' model, also cannot be understood in terms of the (essentially Wittgensteinian) 'volition-action' one. There is always an excess, a supplement, or an extra to the distinction between the cognitive and the active, or thought and performance. And this, I want to propose, is the space in which what we experience as self-deception takes shape.

The Maker of Lies

Here I would like to return to Derrida. For while I am not sure it would be acknowledged by those engaged in these debates today, I do think he has something interesting to contribute. You will recall that we left him challenging Arendt on the problem of self-deception, or rather the question of what kind of self could conceivably deceive itself. At this point in his argument, Derrida refers us to three thinkers or lines of thought that, somehow, Arendt overlooks when she is considering the issue: Freud, Heidegger and Marx. He places particular emphasis on the Marxist concept of ideology, which, as he explains, offers a way of speaking about political deception or illusion without requiring intentional consciousness, which is a presupposition for the concept of the lie. In other words, the concept of ideology allows us to speak of deception on a structural and systemic level, rather than on the level of the self. It thus does not get bogged down in the paradox of self-deception. But at the same time, it also does not resolve that paradox. And Derrida's point here is not to resolve it, but only to suggest that Arendt could have had recourse to the concept of ideology rather than using that of the lie, and made many of the same political points she was trying to make using it. Or, perhaps, and a little more critically, Derrida is expressing suspicion as to why Arendt avoids this concept, and why she insists on using the concept of the lie instead.

Is Arendt ultimately committed to a picture of political life and political action that can always be brought back, at some point, to intentional individuals? Is this part of her larger effort to exclude from public life issues that she thinks of as being bound up with what, in *On Revolution*, she calls 'the social question'? In Arendt, is politics finally about heroic individuals speaking great words and performing great deeds? And if so, is that not a very limited picture of our public existence? Freud and Heidegger too offer Arendt approaches that she seems unwilling or unable to accept. In the case of Freud, there is the psycho-analytic insight that everything that even partly resembles the lie ('all those betrayed truths', as Derrida puts it, 'that are the lapses, the disavowal, the dream, all of the rhetorical resources of the unconscious, and so forth') also operates as a symptom, and thus 'the avowal of another truth' (*WA* 69). Heidegger as well, with his treatment of *aletheia*, and the existential analytic of *Dasein* as the being to which beings are dis-closed or re-vealed, would seem to offer a more sophisticated conception of the lie, and particularly of the possibility of an indestructible lie, as it were, or a lie that was not inevitably or even just regulatively destined to be eliminated, or rendered transparent, thus exposing once and for all the full illumination of the truth.[14]

But if we want to remain focused on the paradox of self-deception, I think that, while he does not mention it 'The History of the Lie' (in fact, he may not have begun developing it yet), Derrida himself has a concept that might allow us to negotiate the problem – namely what, in his later work, he came to call autoimmunity. This is a term Derrida borrowed from medical biology (or rather, reappropriated from medical biology, and returned to its philosophical significance), but he also deployed it in a wide array of fashions. Indeed, because it features prominently in his last writings on politics (particularly in his very late and very political text *Rogues: Two Essays on Reason*), its political inflection and its relationship to what he often called 'democracy to come' is where most commentators have placed their emphasis. But at the same time, in *Rogues* and elsewhere, Derrida explicitly says, 'I have granted to this autoimmune scheme a range without limits' (R 34). That is, he affirms its application, not just to politics, but to any field or arena whatsoever.

The term first begins to appear in Derrida's work in his extended essay on religion 'Faith and Knowledge: Two Sources of "Religion" at the Limits of Reason Alone'. There Derrida uses it to configure the manner in which contemporary religions both thrive on and rail against technological modernity, and especially communications technologies. This process is auto-immune in so far as, through it, religion seeks to protect itself from the very thing that protects it, and keeps it alive. Beyond that particular application, Derrida also notes 'we feel authorised to speak of a sort of general logic of auto-immunization', or of a system that operates by 'protecting itself against its self-protection by destroying its own immune system' (*AR* 85n31).

What Derrida appears to like about this 'general logic' is the way it allows him to speak of a structure or a process that is constituently open to its own destruction, and that can only be distinguished or separated from what lays outside of it in so far as it contains the fundamental possibility of self-destruction. What surrounds the self, as it were, what secures its borders, what establishes its limits, or marks a line between the inside and the outside, is what, at every single moment could destroy, not only the self, but the thing that surrounds, secures or establishes it. With the concept of autoimmunity, it is almost as if Derrida takes Heidegger's Being-towards-death, or his notion that the only event that individuates us is also the event that eliminates us (namely death), pulverises it, and spreads it throughout every moment and every part of every life everywhere. We are always dying. And that is part of how we live.

It is my proposal here that self-deception could be understood in terms of the double bind of autoimmunity as well. That is to say, it is precisely in the act of protecting ourselves from the potential bad faith of others that we wind up deceiving ourselves. We have spoken a great deal about the act of faith required for even the most minimal engagement or relation – the trust, belief or affirmation that we must have already extended, even before we open our mouths or exchange a glance. But we have not emphasised the shadow that looms over this faith, or the manner in which it generates and necessitates suspicion. We must trust, but precisely in so far as we are aware of this, we must also doubt and wonder. This experience can overtake a person, as in the state we call paranoia. But we are all paranoid, and we must be, as a correlative to the faith required to interact with anyone anywhere. Self-deception would occur when this protective doubt, or this capacity that immunises us against external threats, real or perceived, explicit or concealed, gets turned towards ourselves, or even attacks itself, as it were, such that we become suspicious of our own capacity for suspicion, and thus lose our ability to operate in the ambiguous, undecidable zone between trust and doubt, or, if you prefer, faith and knowledge, that we must occupy, if we are going to negotiate the essential secrecy or opacity of our relations, perhaps our experience as such.

What I am saying now, I understand, is not especially clear. But if I could be permitted a brief digression, I will try to use it to explain. In the first chapter, we quite extensively considered

Simmel's work on the secret, and especially his essay or chapter 'The Sociology of Secrecy and of the Secret Society'. But Simmel also wrote a number of other, lesser known, pieces on the topic, one of which is, in my estimation, an entirely compelling short story, or vignette really, called 'Der Lügenmacher' or 'The Maker of Lies'. This story, which has received exactly no critical attention, save a short article that I myself wrote a few years ago,[15] is one of eight pieces that Simmel published pseudonymously, between 1899 and 1903 (again, I would say his most fertile period intellectually) in the cultural journal (and organ of the artistic movement of the same name) *Der Jugend* under the general heading '*Momentbilder*' or 'Snapshots: *sub specie aeternitatus*'. These pieces are very rich, sometimes playful, and often gnomic. The subtitle – under the species of eternity – is actually a quotation from Spinoza. We could, and someone (else) should, write a book on all of their connotations and implications. But here it is enough to say that, in the 'Snapshots', Simmel finds another way to exercise his methodological principle, or what, in the first chapter above, we explained in terms of his 'sociological aesthetics'. That is to say, and as you will recall, for Simmel, every point, when looked at properly, contains the infinite, every particular the universal. So each of these 'snapshots' points out into a plenitude of possible meanings and interpretations. Each one is, in Spinoza's words, a species of eternity.

The particular snapshot we are interested in – 'The Maker of Lies' – is but a few paragraphs long. It tells the story of a man to whom a magician grants the power to make others lie – not, that is to say, the power to make them believe what he says, but the power to make them say something other than what they believe. The man uses this strange ability with what the story calls 'the wantonness of a torturer [*der Wolluste Folterknechts*]', forcing people to say things they know are not true, even when they genuinely desire to be honest, thus leaving them racked with guilt, or 'the scars of shame [*den Narben der Schmach*]', over having lied.[16] Eventually this man falls in love with a woman who neither loves nor hates him. He uses his power on her, forces her to lie, and the two become lovers (here we might recall our confusion, way back in the Introduction, when Plato presented us with the image of a shepherd who could seduce a Queen simply because he was invisible). But the man soon realises that, in compelling the woman to deceive him, he had also 'deceived himself [*sich doch getäuscht*]', or fooled himself into thinking he might be happy with someone who does not genuinely love him. And so, he turns this 'lie-making power [*Kraft des Lügenmachens*]' back on himself, and thus deceives himself again, this time into believing (or at least saying) that they are both happy. This plan, the story concludes, 'worked admirably', and 'everything was as good as it could be, or at least almost so'. Only then did the man 'realise what good intentions the magician had towards him'.[17]

As you can already see from this brief synopsis, the relationships that Simmel sets up in the story (between the magician and the man, between the man and those on whom he uses his power, and, of course, between the man and the woman) are all extremely complex, as though Simmel were deliberately subverting or inverting our expectations. Thus, and crucially, the man is not given the power to lie successfully (a mythological power that has often been explored in literature), but the power to make others lie (unsuccessfully, because he would know they were doing so). And this means, among many other things, that the referent of the title – 'The Maker of Lies' – remains somewhat ambiguous. It could be the man, it could be those he compels to lie, it could be the woman, and it could even be the magician. But what is most important here for our purposes is that Simmel explores the question of self-deception by locating it, not only in the head of one individual, but in a network of relationships between an individual and others. Moreover, the story opens up another, related paradox of deception, specifically that of the forced lie, or the lie that one is compelled to tell. Can one really be compelled to lie? The reference to a torturer (*Folterknechts*) certainly creates space for thinking about this issue. If I am forced to lie, is it my intention that is at stake, and ultimately at fault? Or is it that of the one who forced or tortured me? And yet, on the other hand, is not every lie at least in some measure a forced lie, or at least in some measure compelled or drawn out of the liar by external circumstances that they themselves cannot control?

What Simmel's little story is doing, then, is showing us how intentionality and will are always in the world, or part of an inter-subjective set of relations and exchanges, and never the simple, original volition of an isolated and inwardly defined individual or subject. The will is not simply at the origin of action. It is not something that exists prior to its expression in an act. Rather, it exists first and exclusively in some action, or in its performative articulation. If this is the case, then at least some of the confusion around the notion of self-deception begins to evaporate. I am not deceiving myself exclusively in my mind first, and then acting on the false convictions that result. Rather, and as Fingarette's work helps us understand as well, self-deception involves the whole network or arc of volition and action, or desire and its expression. In so far as we have a will, it is bound up with our bodily existence, or our physical and material life. And, while more or less everyone interested in the topic, myself included, has tended to remain concerned with mental acts, as though they could be separated from the body and held in isolation, the analysis of self-deception should include some effort to make sense of the more or less undeniable fact of the body, and of the embodied nature of the will. Or, at any rate, if we wanted to understand the paradox in more depth, I would wager that that would be one extremely fruitful line of inquiry.

But what we want to foreground here is the relational character of self-deception – the fact that it takes shape in the context of an exchange of lies with others, or an exchange of betrayals. It is the ability of the man in the story to compel others to deceive him that ultimately compels him, in a manner that I would say follows the logic of what Derrida calls auto-immunity, to deceive himself. I deceive myself when my own absolutely necessary sense of suspicion is turned back on me, such that I can no longer trust my own expressions, or lose track of where my thoughts would connect to my words, or my desires to my convictions and beliefs. And again, as in what Derrida says about autoimmunity, this process is both damaging and required. It is like the *pharmakon* that Derrida explored in his early work on Plato – both a medicine and a poison, both the cure and the disease (*DIS* 12). It is the part of the uncertainty about ourselves that we must possess in order to negotiate an uncertain world, and especially an uncertain relation with others. Indeed, in Simmel's story, the man ultimately comes to realise that the power of self-deception is part of what it makes him capable of living in his world, rendering 'everything . . . as good as it could be'.[18] Unless of course that statement is ironic, or Simmel intended irony. Which, like so many other things we have encountered in this book, is also something we will never know, at least not for certain, as we will never know whether anyone is being genuine or ironic. And that would be a good place to begin a line of thought on the very thorny problem of irony, which is clearly related to the questions of secrecy and deception. But that is a consideration that will have to be set aside for another time.

The Hidden Share

A. How to Avoid

In an article called 'Public Secrets: "Being-With" in an Era of Perpetual Disclosure' the cultural theorist Jeremy Gilbert takes issue with the later Derrida's fascination with the problem of the secret. For Gilbert, no matter how sophisticated Derrida might try to make it, the basic concept of the secret is inescapably bound up with the individual and individualism. Even what Derrida sometimes calls the 'unconditional secret' can ultimately entail nothing more and nothing other than a retreat from public life – a kind of Stoic turn inward, an isolationism or even solipsism. Indeed, for Gilbert, the 'unconditional secret' is something of an absurd term. An unconditional secret (or a secret that does not get revealed, an example of which we saw in our consideration of Derrida's reading of the story of Abraham above), would not really be a secret at all, Gilbert claims. It would simply be the unknown. Thus, as an alternative to Derrida, Gilbert proposes we turn to the work of Jean-Luc Nancy, and especially Nancy's notion of 'being-with', which consists of a critical reformulation of what Heidegger calls *Mitsein*. If we start with a fundamental secrecy, this argument contends, we are invariably in the realm of the individual, and thus of the private; if we start with a fundamental being-with, plurality, or being-together (what Nancy also likes to refer to as 'the share' or *partage*),[19] we find a new way of addressing our public existence, and potentially a new way of composing democracy.

My hope is that, by this point, it is clear that and why I would disagree with Gilbert. For Derrida's understanding of the secret has exactly nothing to do with privacy, the individual or the inner world. Rather, on Derrida's account, and as I have stressed over and over, it is precisely the secret that allows for our relations with others. We share what divides us. The fact that we can hide our thoughts from one another is constituent of the social bond. And here I want to be clear as to why I am using the phrase 'social bond' rather than 'public'. If we want to adopt Nancy's language, we can affirm that Derrida's treatment of the secret is entirely concerned with the problem of 'being-with'. But, the level on which Derrida is locating being-with is much deeper than the one implied by the term 'public'. It is, as we have said many times, an act of faith that must precede any interaction whatsoever. The concept of the public, on the other hand, has at least two crucial limitations: first, it seems to imply a distinction between private and public, one that I am not convinced we can disentangle from liberalism, and thus from the individualism Gilbert wants to challenge; and second, and in a related sense, it is very closely associated with a conception of reason or rationality, or the notion of democracy as the public use of reason. And this is also something we would have a hard time disentangling from liberalism. Indeed, and at the risk of sounding a little glib, I would be inclined to suggest that, if we want to challenge liberal individualism at its root, the concept that should ignite our suspicion is not that of the secret, but that of the public.

I will come back to these issues later, when I discuss Arendt again in my Conclusion. Here I mention them as a way of introducing, as it were, the opposite misreading of Derrida's discussion of the secret – the misreading that seeks, not to chastise him for using an inescapably individualistic term and thus shirking some kind of duty to public reason, but rather to draw him and his comments on the secret closer to hermeticism, mysticism and theology, especially of the negative sort. The suggestion that Derrida's work has an affinity with negative theology has been circulating for many decades. As Toby Foshay pointed out some time ago, in his Introduction to the 1992 collection *Derrida and Negative Theology*, Derrida had already acknowledged the apparent relationship between his thought and this tradition in his early manifesto '*Différance*'.[20] There Derrida admits that the 'detours, locutions, and syntax' of his argument 'resemble those of negative theology, occasionally even to the point of being indistinguishable from negative theology' (*MP* 5). That is to say, Derrida recognised that his notion that *différance* is neither a concept nor a thing, but rather something like the prior and withdrawing condition for all concepts and things, appears to sit quite well alongside the *deus absconditus* of negative theology, or the God who, as the creator of all beings, cannot be represented in or by any specific being, and whose absence, infinite distance, or absolute alterity generates an impassioned and unquenchable longing or desire. And this apparent opening has led and continues to lead to a whole array of speculations about deconstruction and theology.[21]

In 1989, however, or about two years before he delivered his seminars on *Questions de Responsabilité I: Le Secret*, and thus presumably while the ideas were beginning to germinate, Derrida addressed this issue directly, or applied himself to the tradition of negative theology, in his essay 'How to Avoid Speaking: Denials'. In that essay, Derrida essentially tries to deny any robust connection between his work and negative theology. But, from psychoanalysis and other discourses, he takes the principle that every denial includes an affirmation, or is symptomatic of a repressed or disavowed agreement. And, as in other works we have explored in this book, Derrida begins by interrogating the performative act of his own text – he begins, that is to say, not with the denial itself, but with a long reflection on what it might mean to deny something like negative theology, which is itself a kind of negation or denial, namely a denial of our ability to know or directly represent the divine. So, put briefly, Derrida's conundrum is how to deny without, to employ the idiom of popular psychology, being in denial. Or, to get at the point from another direction, Derrida begins by exploring the question of how one might negate (or deny) something that is itself negative (namely, negative theology) without becoming affirmative, or opening himself up to the flippant riposte, 'well, if you are not a negative theologian, then you must be an affirmative or positive one, which is to say, a metaphysician or an onto-theologian, which is something that, in numerous other places or at other moments, you also claim to negate or deny'.

As Derrida suggests, even in his title alone, one easy way to answer or avoid these conundrums would be to avoid speaking about the matter altogether (which is basically what he did between the time of his comments on negative theology in '*Différance*' and that of 'How to Avoid Speaking'). But this answer or avoidance merely reinscribes the problem on another level. For in doing so, he would be trying to avoid speaking about a tradition that is more or less all about the avoidance of speech, or the avoidance of any attempt to represent an unrepresentable

God. In 'How to Avoid Speaking', then, Derrida's solution is a bit of a dodge. Instead of either speaking to or avoiding the topic of the relationship between his work and the tradition of negative theology, he defers or delays, and offers a long digression – a digression on a question that is central to both his work and negative theology, namely the question of the secret. So, basically, in 'How to Avoid Speaking', Derrida does not directly tackle the issue of his relationship with negative theology or theology in general. Rather, he shifts the terrain, as it were. He performs something like what Gilbert Ryle calls a 'knight's move', or, as I mentioned in my Introduction, moving sideways in order to move forward.[22] And, to put the matter directly, in 'How to Avoid Speaking', what this 'knight's move' entails is a kind of bracketing or diminishing of the problem of the nature of God or our relationship with God (the problem at the heart of negative theology) in favour of a consideration of the far more mundane and worldly question of the nature of consciousness. The secret that interests Derrida, then, is not the absolute alterity of God, but the absolute alterity of the other, or the sense in which, to repeat, 'every other is every bit other' (*GD* 84).

At this point a more detailed analysis of 'How to Avoid Speaking' would seem to be in order. The text develops many of the themes we have already discussed in this book. Indeed, one might even speculate that this is where Derrida first sets out some of the themes that would come to characterise his later work. Thus, and as we have attempted to explain many times, Derrida suggests that the secret is paradoxically the condition of the social bond, and that, because we have the capacity to hide our thoughts from one another, every interaction and exchange involves a kind of silent and a priori promise, oath or affirmation – a 'yes, yes'. As Derrida puts it here, 'a promise has committed me even before I begin the briefest speech . . . From the moment I open my mouth, I have already promised' ('HAS' 84). He then goes on to discuss the secret, and to negotiate its, as it were, negative aspects in light of this a priori affirmation. And he basically maintains that, even though the secret does involve a kind of negation or 'separation', it remains under the law of affirmation. 'The secret as such, as secret, separates and already institutes a negativity', Derrida writes. However, he continues, this 'is a negation that denies itself' or 'de-negates itself'. And this 'denegation does not happen to it by accident: it is essential and originary' (95). The secret, then, is a negation or a separation. But it is one that, in the very act of negating and separating, also fails to negate or separate. It already implies a relation with the other – one that is conditioned by the promise, oath or affirmation just described.

What does Derrida mean when he says that a secret negates and de-negates, and that it therefore ultimately involves a more fundamental affirmation? It seems a bit opaque, no doubt, but actually, I think it is rather straightforward. He is saying that there is no real secret as such – nothing that is fully hidden from view, and completely unshared. Every secret, as a condition of its being a secret, has always already been shared, and is thus not a secret at all. With reference to David Fincher's well-known film, we might call this the *Fight Club* problem. The first rule of fight club, as you will recall, is never to speak about fight club. But in articulating this rule, in inviting another person into the secret society of the fight club, you have already broken it. And that breaking of the rule or divulging of the secret is not something that happens to the secret, as Derrida says, 'by accident'. On the contrary, it is an 'essential and originary' aspect of any secret. Moreover, according to Derrida, this principle holds even for a secret that one individual keeps to herself. That is to say, it holds 'not only [for] the sharing of the secret with the other' or with another person, but also for 'the shared secret within oneself', or within the hidden dialogue or endless conversation with ourselves that makes up our inner world (recall the narrator in the opening scene of 'The Purloined Letter', sitting in silence with Dupin, thinking to himself, but also, in his own head, having a conversation with a kind of prosthetic or double Dupin). Thus, on Derrida's account, the secret 'cannot [even] appear to one alone except in starting to be lost'. And in this sense, Derrida concludes: 'There is no secret as such: I deny it' ('HAS' 95).

However, while the inner world of the individual may always involve some kind of dialogue, or entail some kind of relationship with a (perhaps fantastic or imaginary, but nevertheless operative) other, thus negating the negation that is the secret, the individual does have a capacity to keep this entire process to herself. And that, I think, is the capacity that really interests Derrida in 'How to Avoid Speaking'. Or, at any rate, in my interpretation of not only this essay but all of Derrida's later work, I am inclined to take the emphasis off the many (but I believe often misleading) references to theology and religion, and place it here, on Derrida's consideration of an everyday experience – in this case, the experience of consciousness itself. So, at a crucial moment in 'How to Avoid Speaking', Derrida introduces the question of the animal (another question, as we have already seen, that would come to fascinate him more and more throughout the later part of his life). He wonders about the very traditional notion that animals cannot keep secrets (recall his disagreement with Lacan, discussed above, over whether or not animals can lie). Ostensibly, this argument goes, animals cannot keep secrets 'because they cannot represent as such, as an object before consciousness, something that they would then forbid themselves from sharing'. This is a colossal issue, Derrida implies. And in order to even begin to consider it, 'it would be necessary to reelaborate the problem of consciousness'. At this point in the text, it is as though Derrida distracts himself. He starts to muse: 'is any problem more novel today than that of consciousness?' ('HAS' 87). He then devotes a handful of what I take to be very provocative and important paragraphs to the issue.

In essence, and as I implied earlier when considering his text on Lacan, Derrida argues that consciousness is – or at least may be – nothing other than the capacity to keep secrets, or to keep things to oneself. 'Here we would be tempted to designate, if not to define, consciousness as that place in which is retained the singular power not to say what one knows, to keep a secret in the form of a representation', Derrida writes. 'A conscious being is a being capable of lying, of not presenting in speech that of which it yet has an articulated representation' ('HAS' 87). Put differently, Derrida continues (here giving us a fairly good clue as to the meaning of his title), a conscious being is 'a being that can avoid speaking'. Derrida reinforces and elaborates on this point a short time later. The ability to lie, he says, while indicative of consciousness, is also 'a second and already mediated possibility'. In order to commit a lie, 'it is first and more essentially necessary to be able to keep for (and say to) oneself what one already knows'. In other words, the lie is always directed at some other, even if it is the other within myself. It is thus 'second' and 'mediated', as Derrida puts it. The more fundamental capacity, the one on which the lie relies, is simply the capacity not to speak, or to hold a representation and not divulge or reveal it. 'To keep something to oneself', Derrida continues to muse, 'is the most incredible and thought provoking power' (87). It is, in fact, the power we call consciousness. However, and crucially, Derrida insists that this power, while deeply secretive, is nevertheless still governed by the law of affirmation discussed above. As Derrida puts it, 'this keeping-for-oneself' or 'dissimulation' also requires that the self be 'multiple', or that I 'differ from' myself. And thus, and as we have repeatedly said of all relations and interactions, it 'presupposes the space of a promised speech' (87). It presupposes, that is, the oath and the social bond.

B. Speculative Fiction

To complete this section, I want to make three points about Derrida's claims concerning the nature of consciousness, or the relationship between the secret and consciousness. The first one is critical. I simply want to suggest that my interpretation of 'How to Avoid Speaking' is superior to a couple of the readings we find among the theologians. I will particularly refer to Mark C. Taylor and John Caputo. But I think I could make the same point in relation to others as well. Second, I want to lay out a few markers for how Derrida's conception of consciousness might help us address, or perhaps reorient our relationship with, what David Chalmers calls 'the hard problem'. Basically, I merely want to note that, if we are going to discuss the experience of consciousness, we must include some consideration of the secret. And, taken to its obvious conclusion, this means that everything we say about consciousness is and always will be marked by a fundamental uncertainty – an uncertainty that cannot be overcome, and that, as a result, renders our discussion ineluctably speculative, even fictive, fantastic, or (why not risk it) literary. Finally, I want to reiterate a speculation of my own, one that I introduced earlier. In particular, I want to emphasise that Derrida's conception of consciousness as a capacity to keep secrets has the potential to open onto an extraordinarily expansive ontology (or, as Derrida might have put it, hauntology). For if consciousness is the capacity to keep secrets, then there is, by definition, no way of knowing whether or not we are encountering it. In principle, everything, or everything we might define as an object (monkeys, microorganisms, machines, meteorites, music, mathematics) could possess what we call consciousness.

First, then, let us consider the theological interpretation of 'How to Avoid Speaking', and of Derrida's treatment of the secret in general. Let us start with Taylor. On his account, Derrida's approach to the secret has to do with something like anti-foundationalism, or a challenge to the concept of origins. 'Since "the genesis of secrecy" is always missing, there is nothing to tell. The secret is that there is no secret.'[23] But, as I have tried to explain, this is not what Derrida means when he says that there is no secret. He does not mean that the genesis of the secret is missing (a missing origin that the negative theologian can then align with a missing or withdrawing deity). No, Derrida means that every secret is always already shared, and thus compromised in its secrecy.

Caputo makes a similar error. 'The secret', he says, 'has no semantic content. The secret has nothing to hide.' It is thus 'an odd sort of secret, something of a non-secret, the secret that there is no secret in the sense of some sort of secret knowledge, some secret knowing, some positive content'.[24] Of course, this is not what Derrida is saying either. It is not even, I would venture to say, in the spirit of Derrida's comments on the secret. For it does something that Derrida does not and never would do – namely, nominalise or hypostatise this concept of 'the secret' (a nominalisation and hypostatisation that, as we saw with Taylor, renders the concept amenable to theological meaning). Derrida is not taking about *the* secret. Derrida is talking about secrets, and the entirely mundane human capacity to hide things from one another. Of course, all secrets are going to have 'semantic content'. Some particular representation is going to be concealed. But, and again, even when it is concealed in the mind of one individual, it will have already been shared, and thus not a secret as such. That is what Derrida means when he says 'there is no secret as such: I deny it' ('HAS' 87).

Let me turn now to the problem of consciousness. This is, of course, a huge field, and I am by no means an expert. In fact, I probably cannot even claim the position of interested amateur. But it does seem to me intriguing that, about six years before David Chalmers published his path-breaking paper 'Facing Up to the Problem of Consciousness', Derrida was already indicating his fascination with the same problem – a problem that had been out of fashion for quite some time, not only in Analytic philosophical circles, but also, and probably more so, in Continental ones (where it was generally associated with phenomenology, a school of thought that had ostensibly been eclipsed by structuralism, which itself sought to attend to, not only consciousness and individual intentional acts, but much larger social and political formations, or language and signification in general, or simply structures). Questions of priority aside, what does Chalmers claim? What is 'the hard problem' up to which we must face? In a nutshell, it goes something like this: It is easy enough to explain in physical and materialist terms the functions of consciousness, or the way that perception and thought work; it is much more difficult, and perhaps ultimately impossible within a physicalist and materialist framework, to explain the experience of consciousness, or the way that I experience all of these individual and discrete functions as unified and as mine. The easy problems have to do with function. The hard one has to do with experience, and especially my inward experience of things.

Now, in my opinion, Derrida would agree with all of this. He would have no problem with any of it. But he would also insist that the problem at stake is actually much harder than Chalmers pretends. For, in order genuinely to address it, not only would we have to account for our experience of consciousness; we would also have to account for our experience of trying to solve the problem of consciousness, and the way that our investigation of the problem relies in some measure on its already having been solved. We could not ask the question unless we had already presupposed some kind of answer. That is to say, Derrida would insist on inscribing the performative act of studying consciousness within the object or field being studied. And, as we have seen, Derrida would also insist that a defining feature of consciousness is its capacity to keep secrets. And so, genuinely to address 'the hard problem', I would, as it were, have to inscribe my secret (my particular experience of consciousness) within a field of secrets (the experience of consciousness for others or in general). To put the point differently, and to recall our earlier discussions, we would have to think the paradox of the singular universal. And one consequence of this would be that everything we say about consciousness or the hard problem, indeed everything we say about everything, would be framed, as it were, by speculation, fiction, fantasy or literature.

To be clear, and to forestall an expected criticism, none of this is intended to stop anyone from trying to solve the hard problem of consciousness, or to explain how it might be possible to move from a description of the physical phenomenon we call mind (or, if you would rather, the brain) to an explanation of thought or experience. Nor is it intended to stop science in general, or any effort to understand the world or our relationship with it. On the contrary, and to invoke the philosopher of science Karl Popper for a moment, inasmuch as the speculative frame renders every statement 'falsifiable', or open to contestation, it is in fact a condition of science. That is to say, there would be no science unless it presupposed a fictive frame. Or, to put the point more robustly, and no doubt (or at least among some) controversially, there could be no science without literature.[25]

I want to reiterate once again my own speculative interpretation of Derrida's notion that consciousness consists of the capacity to keep secrets. Ultimately, it seems to me, this means that we can never recognise, or even just intuit, the consciousness of the other. 'Every other is every bit other.' And if we can put it this way, that is the extremely hard problem of consciousness – much harder, I would propose, than the difference between the function and the experience of the mind. The nature of consciousness is to conceal itself. It exists precisely in so far as it eludes our perception and fails to appear. Thus we cannot know when, where, or whether we are encountering it. We might propose that there are certain outward signs that give us clues. In our intellectual tradition, language is the one that has been proposed most often. But any pattern or order could be interpreted as a kind of language (and this, in my estimation, is all that Derrida meant when, in *Of Grammatology*, he wrote those so frequently maligned and misunderstood words 'there is nothing outside of the text'). And, depending on where you sit with Kant, you will either say that the world is full of order, or that it is given full order by, precisely, consciousness (whatever that is).

This is probably a good place to insert another brief comment on the Speculative Realist challenge to Derrida. There is certainly something like a 'correlationist' moment here. Derrida is proposing that we cannot know the other – but less because of the limitations of our linguistic or discursive framing of our experience than because of the fundamentally secretive nature of the other mind, or the other's capacity to keep secrets. But in fact I think the issue is slightly different still. It goes to what the Speculative Realists, on the one side, and Derrida, on the other, are attempting to analyse or achieve. If the former are concerned with our ability to know the world, the latter is concerned with our performative engagement or encounter with the world – not constative representations of things, but performative acts and events. Meillassoux uses the metaphor of 'the great outdoors' – this being what, since Berkeley, the correlationists barred from consideration.[26] But the metaphor is precise. It concerns, not being as such in its pure exteriority, but that which is outside of a door. It is, in other words, a precisely correlationist metaphor. It concerns what comes in-between the inside and the outside, allowing each one access to the other. Derrida's point would be that this door can certainly be opened. But it can also be closed. It is a metaphor, not of direct knowledge, but of revelation and concealment – that is, of the secret.

Once we have this definition of consciousness as secrecy, there is no way of limiting its scope. We humans must submit to sharing it with everything. It slips into every imaginable corner of being, and becomes part of everything we encounter. It opens up a universal ontology of thought – what, again, particularly in his later work, Derrida tries to capture with an idiom of spectres, ghosts and haunting – or, as he puts it in more than one place, a 'hauntology'. And that is not a wild speculation. It is not a reinvention of philosophical idealism, or an effort to trap anyone in the prison-house of language (do not worry, those who still want to worry, there is and always has been something outside of the text). Nor, moreover, is it in any way intended to promote some theological notion of a universal consciousness or something like a god. On the contrary, it is an entirely logical consequence of a fairly convincing phenomenological account of our completely average experience – namely, the one Derrida provides, and thankfully speaks about quite extensively, in 'How to Avoid Speaking'.

A Missed Encounter

Our speculative itch having been scratched, perhaps now is a good time to return to the earth, or rather the world, and to consider something more obvious and less contrived. For while I think it is possible, and even logically consistent, to expand Derrida's notion that 'every other is every bit other' into a universal ontology or hauntology, I also think that it can and should be applied in its more transparent meaning – that is to say, as a way of configuring relationships between two or more human beings. In this section, and as indicated above, I will explore Derrida's late essay on Gadamer, 'Rams: Uninterrupted Dialogue – Between Two Solitudes, the Poem'. The main point of this essay (or homage) is, I think, carried in the title. If it is the case that 'every other is every bit other', then every encounter or dialogue must be 'between two solitudes', or two minds that cannot possibly know anything certain or determinate about one another. Among Analytic philosophers, the issue Derrida takes up here is often called 'the problem of other minds', or the fact that we have access only to the behaviour, and not the intentions or thoughts, of the other.[27] And, as we saw with respect to the paradox of self-deception and the hard problem of consciousness above, I believe Derrida also has something to contribute to this field. But, to get at what Derrida might have to say about the problem of other minds, we must pass through his consideration of death – an issue that Analytic philosophers do not often explore. The consideration of death in this section will then segue into the next chapter, which will focus on Derrida's treatment of that topic.

'Rams', then, is framed by a reflection on an infamous 'encounter' that took place between Derrida and Gadamer at the Goethe Institute in Paris in 1981. This encounter (which was subsequently translated and published, along with a series of secondary commentaries, as *Dialogue and Deconstruction: The Gadamer-Derrida Encounter*) is typically understood to have been something of a failure, or missed opportunity.[28] This, I think, is one of the ways we should hear Derrida's title: 'Rams'. Derrida and Gadamer did not really encounter one another at all. Rather, like rams in rutting season, they butted heads. My own impression of this episode has always been that Derrida comes off as impish at best, and juvenile at worst. He was the younger ram, trying to prove something, or competing for dominance. Gadamer, on the other hand, seems measured, sensible and direct. In short, his age notwithstanding (and given that his opponent's only real strategy is strategically to back down), Gadamer wins the fight. That judgement aside, what Derrida appeared to be doing in his encounter with Gadamer in 1981 was attempting to avoid a dialogue, or to avoid the reciprocal and balanced exchange that

Gadamer ostensibly wanted. And Derrida did so, it seems to me, in order performatively to assert that all dialogue is constituently fractured or interrupted.

In 'Rams', however, which was written roughly two decades later, Derrida essentially turns this argument inside out. That is to say, he attempts to characterise the failure of his encounter with Gadamer as its greatest success, and suggests (as if scripting a Hollywood romance like *When Harry Met Sally*) that he and Gadamer had a lasting relationship afterwards precisely because it went so badly in the beginning. Thus, as Derrida puts it, the event in question was 'all the more fortunate, if not successful, precisely for having been a missed encounter'. Moreover, he continues, 'it succeeded so well at being missed that it left an active and provocative trace, a promising trace, with more of a future ahead than if it had been a harmonious and consensual dialogue' (*SQ* 136–7). In other words, the fact that it failed in Gadamer's hermeneutic terms is correlative to the fact that it succeeded in Derrida's deconstructive ones. Precisely there where it failed to produce consensual communication, it opened onto an unknown and unknowable future – what Derrida so often refers to as a future yet 'to come'.[29]

On face value, Derrida's point here borders on the prosaic. If he and Gadamer had understood one another perfectly, he appears to be saying, there would have been nothing left to say. So, in a perverse sense, the less two people in a dialogue actually understand one another, or the less they harmoniously and consensually agree, the more of a future they open up, or the more they leave for future discussion. Friendship would thus require enmity. But, while Derrida clearly means something like that, that cannot be all that he means. Rather, in 'Rams', he uses his 'missed encounter' with Gadamer in Paris in 1981 as a passageway or point of departure into a larger set of arguments concerning the manner in which every encounter is a missed encounter, or the way that missing the other (and here I mean 'missing' both in the sense of missing a target or misunderstanding the words of another, and in the sense of a melancholically longing or desire for someone who is no longer present or with us, often someone who is dead) is internal to encountering them.

At the centre of 'Rams' is a consideration of Gadamer's reading of a poem by Celan called 'Vast, Glowing Vault'. The poem is something of an elegy. The speaker is staring at the stars at night, and noticing in particular the constellation we call Aries, or the Ram (this being another, and perhaps the primary, referent of Derrida's title). She is overwhelmed by this sight, and experiences something like the sublime. Then, in the concluding lines, on which Gadamer focuses his reading, she says: 'The world is gone, I must carry you [*Die welt ist fort, ich muß dich tragen*]'. The question at stake here is, how do we characterise the relationship between the speaker and the one she must carry? Gadamer's proposal is that it involves something like what he calls a 'fusion of horizons'.[30] Derrida's proposal, on the other hand, is that it cannot be such a hermeneutic fusion. Or rather, it cannot be about dialogue, reciprocity and consensus. Rather, the relationship between the speaker and the one she must carry is the same as the relationship between us, or the readers of Celan's poem, and the poem itself. That is to say, it is a relationship between two solitudes. And, as we have already begun to explain, for Derrida, this relationship between two solitudes is mirrored in his relationship with Gadamer (and indeed, in any relationship between any two people anywhere at any time).

We can put this another way. On Derrida's account, Celan's 'Vast, Glowing Vault' is a performative, or an example of what it states. Or, in Derrida's own words, 'what this poem gives to be read might also be the scene of reading' (*SQ* 144). In other words, this poem, and indeed every poem (in fact, and as we discussed earlier, all testimony, and thus all language, and perhaps all experience) has no fixed or identifiable meaning. Rather, it 'retains an apparently sovereign, unpredictable, untranslatable, almost unreadable initiative'. It is not the expression of a subject who, through dialogue, we might come to know and understand. Rather, 'it remains an abandoned trace, suddenly independent of the intentional and conscious meaning of the signatory' (146). As Celan himself puts it in 'The Meridian' (something we will come back to in the next chapter): 'The poem is alone. It is alone and under way.' And to read it is to participate in what Celan calls 'the secret of an encounter [*Geheimnis der Begegnung*]'.[31] Or, returning to Derrida, the poem 'wanders, but in a secretly regulated fashion, from one referent to another – destined to outlive, in an "infinite process", the decipherments of any reader to come'. It is, in other words, 'destinally abandoned, cut off from its origin and from its end' (*SQ* 146). Moreover, Derrida continues, it is precisely this sovereign secret or destinal abandonment of origins and ends that renders the poem readable, or open to an interpretation. I can read and interpret a poem (and by extension any language, any experience), not because its meaning can be revealed to me through dialogue, but precisely because its meaning is absolutely and irreversibly concealed – in short, a secret.

So, for Derrida, what is true of the relationship between us and this poem is true of the relationship between us and any poem, indeed any utterance whatsoever. But, and more to the point, and as suggested above, it is also true of two more relationships: the relationship within the poem between the speaker and the one she must carry; and the relationship between Derrida and Gadamer. Let us explore these two separately. For Derrida, the relationship between the speaker and the one she must carry is also a relationship between two solitudes. Using rather poetic language himself now, Derrida gets at this point by focusing on the stanza break that separates the final line in the poem from the rest. 'The sentence is all alone', he writes. 'It stands, it supports itself, it carries itself all alone, on the line between two abysses, isolated, islanded, separated like an aphorism, the sentence no doubt says something essential about solitude' (*SQ* 158). So, this isolated sentence is about isolation. Very clever. 'When the world is no more', Derrida continues, now starting to reference the German text specifically, and surreptitiously throwing in a reference to Freud for good measure, 'when it is on the way to being no longer here but over there, when the world is no longer near, when it is no longer right here (*da*), but over there (*fort*), when it is no longer even present there (*da*) but gone far away (*fort*), perhaps infinitely inaccessible', well, 'that is when I must carry you, you alone, you alone in me or on me alone' (158).

What all of this means is a little confusing. It enacts the principle it appears to be trying to express, namely that poetic language is fundamentally secretive, and has no fixed meaning. But Derrida does us the favour of punctuating this line of thought with at least one or two relatively clear statements concerning the experience of two solitudes that he is trying to capture. 'I am alone with, alone to you alone, we are alone: this declaration is also an engagement', he writes (158). Here we might recall the formula I developed above with respect to testimony: I can only testify to what only I can know. Part of what it means to testify (or write a poem, or use any sign or leave any trace whatsoever) is to avow a truth that only one person can properly possess. So solitude or loneliness is built into any exchange or relationship. We are always alone, even when we are together. We can only be alone together. But this is also the condition for being together (or for being-with, if you prefer, or *Mitsein*). It is 'also an engagement'. And all of this stems from what, at this moment in 'Rams', Derrida calls 'the absolute singularity of the other' (158) – which is to say, our capacity to keep secrets.

Now let us turn to the other relationship invoked a moment ago, the relationship between Derrida and Gadamer. On Derrida's account, it too is characterised by a double solitude, if you will, or 'the absolute singularity' of each to the other. We have seen Derrida make this point many times. But here, and importantly, he amplifies it by connecting it to the death of the other. What makes the other singular, what interrupts every dialogue between us, what fundamentally prevents us from understanding one another, is the fact that we will die, and even more profoundly, the fact that one of us will die before the other. As Derrida puts it, all relationships are conditioned by 'a sad and invasive certainty: one day death will necessarily separate us' and 'one of two friends will always see the other die' (*SQ* 139) (as an aside, there is also the possibility that both will see the other die, as in the case of *Romeo and Juliet* or *Thelma and Louise*). But more importantly, for Derrida, this death that separates one from the other, or that interrupts their dialogue, is not something that remains off in the future, as a kind of emerging possibility, destiny or teleological goal. No, for Derrida, inasmuch as it is a possibility (or the ever-present possibility of the impossible), death is immanent to every aspect of life. It is always there, haunting every relationship we have with one another, and indeed with anything other. In fact, on Derrida's account, we cannot really speak about either life or death independently; we can only speak of life-death, or an inescapable co-mingling of our infinite and our finite being – or, once again, something like a singular universal.

At this point we arrive at what I take to be the crucial passage in 'Rams', and in Derrida's homage to Gadamer – one that, inasmuch as it was written shortly after his death, also has some of the characteristics of an elegy, or a work of mourning. 'The melancholic certainty of which I am speaking . . . begins', Derrida writes, 'in the friend's lifetime' (*SQ* 140). Death interrupts our dialogue from the very first encounter. Thus, and to refer again to the final line of Celan's 'Vast, Glowing Vault', from the moment we meet, we must already start carrying one another's memory. And from the moment we meet, the world that is the other has already come to an end. We are thus always already living in what Derrida calls 'the world after the end of the world' (140). And here Derrida ups the stakes, not just considerably or exponentially, but infinitely, offering us one more understanding of what we have been calling the singular universal, and of that enigmatic phrase '*tout autre est tout autre*', which, as mentioned before, could also be translated 'every other is everything other', or just 'every other is everything': 'For each time, and each time singularly, each time irreplaceably, each time infinitely, death is nothing less than the end of the world', Derrida asserts. 'Not only one end among others, the end of someone or of something in the world, the end of a life or of a living being.' No, on Derrida's account, 'death marks each time, each time in defiance of arithmetic, the absolute end of the one and only world, the end of the unique world, the end of the totality of what can be presented as the origin of the world for any unique living being, be it human or not' (140).

How are we to make sense of this outrageous hyperbole? Every single death of any unique living thing constitutes the end of everything, the end of the entire and only world, Derrida says. But he cannot possibly mean that. It is in defiance, not only of arithmetic, but of the most basic principles of reason and common sense. In fact, it is in defiance of what I would consider many of the most basic principles of affect, emotion or feeling as well. When someone dies, we can certainly feel melancholic, often profoundly so. When it is someone close to us, or someone we love, we can even feel that it constitutes the end of the world. But I cannot imagine a person who would actually experience, in their emotional being, every single death of a unique and living creature as if it were the end of the entire and only world. And even if we could imagine such a deity of emotional capacity (this person would have to possess some kind of vast, glowing vault within them), where would we draw the line between a unique living being and a non-unique one? Somewhere within that impossibly gigantic class of creatures we unthinkingly refer to as animals? But if so, where? And more importantly, why? Why stop there? What is not unique about a mosquito, a maggot, a mushroom, an amoeba, a bit of mitochondria? What would a world and what would an end have to be for Derrida's sentiment here to have any meaning whatsoever? What does it mean to proclaim that every single death is the end of the entire and only world?

I am not sure I have answers to all of these questions. In fact, I am sure that I do not. But in the next chapter, I want to continue to hone in on Derrida's conception of time, and its relationship to death. Initially, this will involve taking a closer look at Derrida's readings of Celan, and especially his interpretation of Celan's 'The Meridian' in the 'Eighth Session' and the 'Tenth

Session' of *The Beast and the Sovereign, Volume 1*. At the far end of this engagement with Celan, or at the point of the greatest abstraction, if you will, Derrida has Celan describing time as a series of absolutely isolated punctual points, each one fully distinct from the other. And on this account, perhaps we could say that, not only death, but the simple passage of time constitutes something like an infinite number of ends to an infinite number of discrete and independent worlds. That, at any rate, might begin to give us one way of approaching the outrageous hyperbole just discussed. After exploring that highly speculative and mildly bizarre notion, I will shift my focus to *The Beast and the Sovereign, Volume 2*. There, I will emphasise what Derrida has to say about what he calls 'living death' or '*survivance*', on the one hand, and his extended reflection on prayer, solitude and death that concludes this, his very last seminar, on the other.

Notes

1 Chalmers, 'Facing Up to the Problem of Consciousness'.
2 Schmitt, *The Concept of the Political* and *Political Theology: Four Chapters of the Concept of Sovereignty.*
3 Negri, *The Politics of Subversion. A Manifesto for the Twenty-First Century.*
4 Agamben, *The Kingdom and the Glory*, 114.
5 Agamben, *State of Exception*, 26.
6 Arendt, 'Truth and Politics', in *Between Past and Future.*
7 Sartre, *Being and Nothingness*, 86–118.
8 Arendt, 'Truth and Politics', 167.
9 Kant, *The Metaphysics of Morals*, 183.
10 Sartre, *Being and Nothingness*, 49.
11 See Mele, 'Recent Work in Self-Deception' and 'Real Self-Deception'; Talbot, 'Intentional Self-Deception in a Single Coherent Self'; Foss, 'Rethinking Self-Deception'; Davidson, 'Who is Fooled?'.
12 Fingarette, *Self-Deception*, 47.

13 Fingarette, *Self-Deception*, 68–9.

14 I will note here that Heidegger explicitly explores the concept of the secret in his 1942–3 lecture course on *Parmenides*. He connects it quite clearly with the treatment of truth as *aletheia*. See Bernet, 'The Secret According to Heidegger and "The Purloined Letter" by Poe'.

15 Barbour, 'The Maker of Lies: Simmel, Mendacity and the Economy of Faith'.

16 Simmel, 'The Maker of Lies', 273–5.

17 Simmel, 'Maker of Lies', 273.

18 Simmel, 'Maker of Lies', 275.

19 Nancy, *Being Singular Plural*.

20 Coward and Foshay (eds), *Derrida and Negative Theology*, 2.

21 I have already referenced some of this literature above – notably John D. Caputo and Martin Hägglund. Other important contributions include: Hart, *The Trespass of the Sign: Deconstruction, Theology and Philosophy*; Sherwood and Hart (eds), *Derrida and Religion: Other Testaments*; de Vries, *Religion and Violence: Philosophical Perspectives from Kant to Derrida*; Taylor, *Erring: A Postmodern A/theology*.

22 Ryle, 'Thinking and Self-Teaching', 217.

23 Taylor, *Nots*, 17.

24 Caputo, *Prayers and Tears*, 107.

25 For a fascinating discussion of this topic, one that also addresses the Speculative Realists in important ways, see Steven Shaviro's *Discognition*.

26 Meillassoux, *After Finitude*, 26.

27 There is a huge literature on this topic, much of it from a phenomenological perspective, and just as much from a, roughly, Wittgensteinian one. Here I will quickly note John Wisdom's *Other Minds* and Anita Avaramides's *Other Minds*. My point here is not genuinely to contribute to this discussion, but merely to gesture towards the kind of contribution one might make from a broadly Derridian perspective. As far as I can tell, the closest anyone has come to taking up this task is Henry Staten, in his study *Wittgenstein and Derrida*. But even there the specific issue is not explored in any depth.

28 Michelfelder and Palmer (eds), *Dialogue and Deconstruction: The Gadamer-Derrida Encounter*.

29 Derrida's most extensive discussions of this notion are to be found in his more political writings, especially around the notion of 'democracy to come' (see *Specters of Marx* and *Rogues* in particular). Here I will only point out that, along with having this specifically political application (one that

has attracted an enormous amount of attention among Derrida's readers and followers), the notion of the 'to come' is also rooted in a more general theory of time – one that I am attempting to explore here.

30 Gadamer, *Truth and Method*.
31 Celan, *The Meridian*, 5.

<h1 style="text-align:center">4</h1>

Being Alone: Death, Solitude and the End of the World

The Measure of Grief

At the end of the last chapter, we left Derrida saying, in effect, that every single death or end is the death or the end of everything – not the end of one particular world, but the end of the entire and only world. Playing on his aphorism '*tout autre est tout autre*', which I have repeated numerous times in this book, we might invent a phrase that, to the best of my knowledge, Derrida never used, but that would, I think, have suited him well, at least in this context: '*toute fin est la fin de tout*', or every end is the end of everything. As I said above, this is a very poetic and affected notion. It is also shockingly hyperbolic – an exaggeration beyond exaggeration. How could anyone think, indeed how could anyone feel, such a sentiment? What would it really mean to believe, or even simply to intuit or sense, that every single death of every unique living creature constitutes the end of the entire and the only world, or that '*toute fin est la fin de tout*'? Without submitting to Derrida's hyperbole outright (and here it is worth pointing out that, in his autobiographical work *Monolingualism of the Other*, Derrida amenably confesses that he is

201

'an incorrigible hyperbolite. A generalized hyperbolite. In short, I always exaggerate' [*MO* 48]), or without either accepting or rejecting it, this chapter constitutes a reflection on this problem of death and the end, especially as it is developed in Derrida's later seminars. In it, I will try to gather together some of the points I made in the previous three chapters about sociology or the social bond, literature and philosophy. And I will try to come to some conclusions about Derrida's lifelong meditation on (indeed, near obsession with) the problem of the conclusion, or the conclusion of life that we like to call death.

Particularly since his death, a great deal of work has been done by Derrida scholars and critics on Derrida's theories of mourning, or mourning and melancholy.[1] As others have noted before me, among the many things that Derrida will be remembered for, he will undoubtedly be remembered as a master of the genre of remembrance – that is, the work of mourning, or the eulogy. Some of his most profound statements can be found in his remarks on the deaths of his many friends. In this chapter, however, I am going to take it for granted that Derrida's explicit eulogies have received a sufficient amount of critical attention from others. Instead of focusing there (and while acknowledging that that would be one fruitful way of pursuing the themes I am introducing here), I want to place the emphasis on Derrida's seminars – or, at least, on the ones that have been made available so far in print and translation. In particular, I want to provide a number of close readings of what I take to be key sections of *The Beast and the Sovereign, Volume 1* and *The Beast and the Sovereign, Volume 2*. My central claim will be the same as it has been throughout this book – namely that the concept of the secret is not incidental, but crucial for, or integral to, Derrida's overall project. The secret secretly conditions more or less everything in the later Derrida, including these, his final seminars, and in many ways, his final work.

Following these introductory comments, then, this chapter is broken down into four further sections. The first one deals primarily with a reading of Paul Celan that Derrida develops in the 'Eighth Session' and the 'Tenth Session' of *The Beast and the Sovereign, Volume 1*. Some of what Derrida says here covers terrain that we have already seen him traverse elsewhere, or re-iterates claims that we have already established, especially when we were considering Derrida's engagement with Gadamer in the last chapter – an engagement that, as you will recall, was organised around a reading of one of Celan's poems. So we will see once again how, for Derrida, Celan's work emphasises or explains the principle of 'two solitudes', or the notion that we remain absolutely other with respect to one another (and ourselves, or the other that each of us carries within us), and that the death of the other already haunts my relationship with her as soon as I meet her, even for the first time. But, and as I want to explain, in the 'Eighth Session' and the 'Tenth Session' of *The Beast and the Sovereign, Volume 1*, Derrida links this insight about the relationship with the other more explicitly, and more elaborately, to a general theory of time – one that I am calling here 'the divided instant', and one that is related to the singular universal. So that is what the next section of this chapter is intended to illuminate.

After discussing Derrida's interpretation of Celan in *The Beast and the Sovereign, Volume 1*, I will turn my attention in the subsequent three sections to *Volume 2*. Here I want to pick out and analyse in detail two of what I take to be Derrida's most important themes in these seminars – namely, the theme of what he calls 'living death' and *'survivance'*, which he discusses most extensively in the 'Fifth Session', and that of prayer and solitude, which occupy a central position in the 'Eighth Session', the 'Ninth Session' and the concluding 'Tenth Session'. This part of the chapter will, I have to admit at the outset, get rather complex, and I may not be able to maintain my commitment to writing clearly or lucidly about this philosopher who is so often accused of being obscure or obtuse. It will also, I have to admit as well, get rather affected. For in these final seminars, although no one knows it yet, Derrida is dying, and he is reflecting on death itself. In a sense, in *The Beast and the Sovereign, Volume 2*, we encounter Derrida in a state of 'living death' - not only because we are reading him now, after his death, but also because, at the moment he was writing and speaking back then, his death was close at hand. In other words, in these final seminars, Derrida was speaking about the 'living death' and *'survivance'* while he was approaching a living death and *survivance*.

The mood of this chapter, therefore, and arguably the predominant mood in all of Derrida's work, is melancholy. And this permits me, I hope, a brief and parenthetical reflection on Lars von Trier's 2011 film *Melancholia* — a film that sits quite neatly alongside Derrida's considerations of the same theme.[2] As you may remember, the film (significantly, in the context of Derrida's concern with division or doubles) is divided into two parts, each of which is named after one of the two sisters at the centre of the plot — first, 'Justine', and second, 'Claire'. Justine is the melancholic. The part of the film named after her focuses on her wedding to the unbearably bland and ineffectual Michael, and her relationships with her narcissistic father Dexter, her impossibly cruel mother Gaby, her apparently together and somewhat self-righteous sister Claire, her insufferable boss Jack and his extraordinarily lucky assistant Tim, and her arrogant and manipulative brother-in-law John. The wedding takes place in a castle, isolated from the rest of the world. The events, and especially the departure of each of the guests at the end of a disastrous evening, are overlain with a tone of foreboding, the reason for which only becomes clear in the second section of the film, or 'Claire'.

In this second section, it quickly comes into focus that a giant, previously hidden, rogue planet named Melancholia is about to smash into the earth, destroying everything and everyone on it. We remain at the isolated castle. But now the only inhabitants are Justine, Claire and John, and their son Leo. In his arrogance, John remains convinced, and relentlessly seeks to convince others, that Melancholia will pass safely by the earth – until, at almost the very last moment, his calculations show that this is not the case, and, in an act of profound cowardice, he not only kills himself, but uses all of the available sedatives to do so. Leaving aside many things for the sake of concision, as their doom (that is, the end of the world, the one and only world) impends, Claire (the sensible sister) becomes completely unhinged (a terror she seems to project onto her confused but somehow also resolute son Leo), whilst Justine (the melancholic, or the sister with all of the problems) remains calm and composed.

The melancholic lives with disaster at every moment, von Trier seems to be proposing. Or, borrowing Derrida's language now, we might say that the melancholic experiences every death of every unique creature as the end of the only and entire world. For Justine, in other words, '*toute fin est la fin de tout*'. Every single end is the end of everything (this being yet another kind of singular universal). For her, that is to say, a planet called Melancholia smashes into the world, destroying everything and everyone, at every second of every day. To live with this is already and always to have lived with the end of the world (and to have survived it, impossibly and repeatedly, as we will see Derrida say a little later). It is thus to be prepared, or to remain calm, when this end comes about on the register of what we a little unthinkingly refer to as 'real life'.

Some of these same themes are taken up in another of Derrida's seminars – namely the seminar that has recently been published and translated as *The Death Penalty, Volume 1*. As its editors note in their prefatory material, the full measure of what is going on in *The Death Penalty, Volume 1* will likely have to wait until the publication of its second volume. But even a cursory glance makes one thing very clear – the death penalty is not only an issue that Derrida speculated on, or produced philosophical theories of, it is also an issue that he investigated empirically in great depth. In fact, it would seem that Derrida's study of the death penalty represents the most extensive empirical investigation of his entire career. Along with this empirical investigation, the death penalty seminars also betray an enormous sense of projection. Derrida speaks of being condemned to death; but he also seems to identify, in some sense, with those who are condemned to death. He imagines himself in their place. And, while fully aware of the difficulty of turning someone else's concrete (and singularly terrifying and horrendous) experience into a philosophical abstraction, it is nevertheless true that, in a sense, we are all living with a death sentence. In a sense, we are all on death row. Melancholia is illuminating the sky, preparing to smash into the world, destroying everything and everyone, for all of us, right now, tomorrow, the next day, and in fact all of the time.

Instead of trying to offer a full or synoptic consideration of *The Death Penalty, Volume 1*, I want to focus on two sections that are germane to what I have been discussing in this book, and what I will be discussing in this chapter. First, I will look closely at Derrida's consideration of Nietzsche's analysis of the relationship between cruelty and belief, trust or credit in the 'Sixth Session' (which, as we will see, complicates in important ways what I have been saying about the oath and the social bond, or the sense in which all of our interactions and relations rely on an a priori act of faith). Then, and less elaborately, I will note Derrida's effort to, as he puts it, 'deconstruct' the concept of death itself in the 'Ninth Session' (or his effort to show that the ostensible line that separates life from death cannot really be calculated, and that the fantasy or illusion that we can draw such a line is at the root of all notions of calculation, including recognisably economic ones). My consideration of these two sessions will endeavour to bring together what I have said so far about mourning and melancholy, and point towards what I will have to say about the two volumes of *The Beast and the Sovereign*.

Some context first: In the earlier parts of *The Death Penalty, Volume 1*, Derrida sets up a debate between the proponents and the critics of the death penalty, especially as they have existed since the Enlightenment or the eighteenth century. He mentions many names, but arguably the two most significant ones are Victor Hugo and Immanuel Kant. Hugo, of course, was a fierce opponent of the practice of state-sanctioned execution. And, put briefly, for Derrida, the rhetorical ploy of Hugo's challenge involved attempting to show the Christian state that it is un-Christian to kill as a means of punishment. Kant, on the other hand, argued in favour of the death penalty. His proposal (which might initially appear to be at odds with his own categorical imperative, or the imperative to treat others and ends in themselves, rather than means to an end) hovered around a theory of calculation. Or rather, Kant attempted to show that the death penalty is consistent with the categorical imperative that is beyond calculation. Put briefly, for Kant, if someone arbitrarily takes the life of another, in that very act, they have wilfully or autonomously consented to having their life arbitrarily taken. They have already said 'yes', as it were, to their own execution.

The spanner arrives in the 'Sixth Session', when Derrida begins to examine the theme of cruelty, and to consider what Nietzsche says about cruelty in *The Genealogy of Morals*. Here, Derrida suggests, and despite their diametrically opposed positions on the death penalty itself, both Hugo and Kant share a desire the avoid cruelty. That is to say, both Hugo's challenge to the death penalty, and Kant's advocacy of it, are premised on the same wish. They both want to exclude what the American constitution calls 'cruel and unusual punishment' – the first by claiming that the death penalty is always cruel, the second by claiming that it is not at all, or that it is merely a matter of moral reason. For Nietzsche, however, and as Derrida explains, cruelty is an 'originary' concept (*BS2* 159). In other words, it is a concept that has no opposite. All human activity entails cruelty, even and perhaps especially the effort to escape or expunge, precisely, cruelty. Thus, on Nietzsche's account, both Christianity and the Kantian categorical imperative are shot through with what they attempt to disavow or deny. They both set up what Derrida calls 'the theatre of cruelty'. Just barely beneath the surface, pulsating away behind their respective proclamations of love and reason, they both entail a dramaturgy of irrational hate.

Indeed, and what seems more important for the argument I am making here, on Derrida's reading of Nietzsche, not only the effort not to be cruel, but every manifestation of faith, trust or belief (faith in God, faith in reason, faith in one another) is ultimately or fundamentally bound up with cruelty, and with the cruel or sadistic pleasure of watching (or, and even more to the point, making) another suffer. In fact, Derrida explains, from Nietzsche's perspective, it is not just our capacity for belief that is bound up with a long and forgotten history of cruelty; it is also our capacity for memory, or our capacity to hold one thought in our mind over a period of time. For Nietzsche, Derrida says, we exchange trust, we exchange faith, we exchange belief, not (as I have proposed in this book) because 'every other is every bit other', or because we are compelled to by the fact that we cannot see into one another's heads. No, we do so because, over the course of countless generations, millennia in fact, those who incurred a debt and did not live up to their agreement were compelled to repay that debt by offering the creditor the cruel pleasure of inflicting pain on them and their body. For Nietzsche, this cruel pleasure (and not some rational calculus, or fantasy about deterrence) is the real source of the concept of law and punishment. And what we call belief, faith, credit, promising or trust (in fact, what we call memory, the inner world, the interiority of the self, or the citadel of the soul) is little more than an efflux, as it were, of a brutal and blood-drenched history of violence.

We can come at the same point from a slightly different direction. For Nietzsche, our credit or belief in one another, or our ability to exchange faith and trust (which is also the origin of society, of economy, and perhaps of calculation in general) is founded, ultimately, on the completely incredible or unbelievable notion that we can equate a crime with a punishment — that there might be some equivalence between what I am owed and what I take in return, or what is called '*jus talionis*'. Belief, then, is founded in something that we cannot possibly believe, or something entirely unbelievable; credit is founded in the incredible. Derrida calls this 'the caustic force of Nietzsche's genealogy', or the notion that, 'at bottom, we do not believe; we do not believe even in what we believe or say we believe', and that we (must) do this 'in order to make the market possible, to make commerce, contract, exchange, and finally language possible and thus a social contract, a law that is always first of all commercial law' (*BS2* 153). Nietzsche's point here resonates well with what I said above, in the first chapter of this book, about Simmel's treatment of money, which, as you will recall, Simmel characterises, not as one social phenomenon among many, but as a general 'form of sociation', or a paradigm of social relations and interaction as such.

There is no reason not to be forthright at this stage. The logic that Nietzsche pursues, and that Derrida outlines in *The Death Penalty, Volume 1*, puts to the test, and even threatens to collapse, many of the general claims I have been developing in this book. The trust, faith, or belief that we must have in one another, by virtue of the fact that 'every other is every bit other', here run the risk of becoming a by-product or epiphenomenon of a more originary cruelty and violence – not a mode of belief, but a pure chimera, a fantasy, and, moreover, a dangerous fantasy, one that secretly amplifies the cruelty that it pretends to extinguish, or that institutes a kind of cruelty to the second degree, or cruelty squared. I am not sure a robust defence is available to me here. Nietzsche is, in my opinion, the great destroyer, and I cannot think of a single philosophical argument that completely eludes the onslaught of his thought (he smashes into every world, we might say, like a colossal and previously hidden rogue planet). Nevertheless, in this context, one thing is worth noting. Whatever else this incredible and unbelievable equivalence or calculation that Nietzsche posits beneath all belief, credit and calculation might be, it cannot be a hidden truth, or some reality that might be exposed, once the illusion of belief has been properly stripped away. It cannot be a hidden essence or originary state to which we might seek to return. On the contrary, everything that Nietzsche says here (and elsewhere too) is already framed by, if not belief, at least fiction. And whatever we mean by truth, it is already the effect of a more fundamental matrix of illusions.

This brings us to the 'Ninth Session', where Derrida proposes to 'deconstruct' the concept of death. In fact, in doing so, he seems to offer an alternative to Nietzsche's notion that belief and calculation begin with the unbelievable effort to posit a calculable equivalence between crime and punishment. Derrida's central claim here is that any thinking or philosophy of death (and the notable if not exclusive case is obviously Heidegger) relies on an unjustifiable precomprehension of death. It must assume that it already knows what it goes on to characterise in terms of the absolutely unknowable, or, as I have said a few times here, the secret par excellence. But, Derrida maintains, nothing is less certain than what constitutes the instant of death, or the boundary or threshold between what we call life and what we call death. And this is where Derrida introduces what could be read as an implicit response to Nietzsche, and to Nietzsche's notion that all belief and calculation can ultimately be traced back to cruelty. For Derrida, on the contrary, what makes belief and calculation possible in the first place is not the unbelievable effort to equate crime with punishment, but an effort (an impossible and even insane effort) to master death by claiming to identify its very instant. In a certain sense everything else, from the crassest and basest economic calculation to the most mystical and sublime devotion to God, would fall out from this originary effort to situate, locate or rigidly identify something that, in fact, has no identity, and no single point or moment of occurrence.

The Divided Point

A. Marionettes and Majesties

In this section I would like to continue this consideration of time and death by turning my attention to *The Beast the Sovereign, Volume 1.* Unlike the last section, however, where I merely touched upon a few elements of *The Death Penalty, Volume 1,* here I would like to work a little more methodically and patiently through Derrida's text. Thus, and as mentioned above, I will consider in some detail Derrida's reading of Celan, primarily as it gets developed in the 'Eighth Session' and the 'Tenth Session of *The Beast and the Sovereign, Volume 1.* And I will begin with a fairly straightforward hermeneutic reconstruction of Derrida's claims. At the same time, things are going to get relatively complicated and abstract. For I will be pursuing what is, perhaps, the most complicated aspect of all of Derrida's work, and arguably the most complicated philosophical question that there is – namely, the question of time. Through our reconstruction of Derrida's reading of Celan, then, we are trying to hone in on what Derrida means by time, or how he characterises (if we can put it this way) the basic structure of time. In essence, and to telegraph my conclusion, I will try to show that, for Derrida, time consists of an infinite number of utterly discrete and singular instants or moments that are also (paradoxically, impossibly) divided or split in relation to other instants. Put differently, for Derrida, time is an infinite number of singular universals.

So, let us begin with the 'Eighth Session'. To provide just one point of context, we can say that the immediately previous 'Seventh Session' is organised around the question concerning technology. At its centre is one of Derrida's favourite images – the image of the marionette. Since the same image will return in the 'Eighth Session' and the 'Tenth Session', or the ones that interest us here, we do not need to elaborate on it right now. But it is worth noting that, just as the entirety of *The Beast and the Sovereign, Volume 1* and *Volume 2* challenge the distinction between the human and the animal, the 'Seventh Session' leaves us wondering whether it is really possible to distinguish between the human and the machine. For Derrida, and as we will see, the marionette configures the difficulty of making both of these distinctions (between human and animal, as well as between human and machine), not to mention many other distinctions as well.

This leads directly to the 'Eighth Session', in which Derrida begins to wonder, if we cannot easily distinguish man from either animal or machine, then is there anything essentially human? What, in other words, is 'proper to man'? At the same time, Derrida develops the theme of sexual difference. 'The phallus', he asks at the very beginning of the session: 'is it proper to man?' (*BS1* 206). This investigation quickly turns back to the central question in the seminar, namely that of sovereignty, and the sense in which legal right seems to require the protection of the very violence or force that it is designed to protect against. Here Derrida briefly engages with Aristotle's famous definition of man as a political animal or *zoon politikon*. Thus he supplements the questions 'what is proper to man?' and 'is the phallus proper to man?' with another question, one that will become integral to his reading of Celan – namely, 'what is sovereignty?', or even more specifically, 'what is majesty?' (214). On Derrida's reading, the traditional responses to the question of majesty all suggest that it is something superlative, grand, high, of great magnitude, above all others, and so forth. And, Derrida says, such imagery can also be associated with the phallus or the erection. Thus, according to the traditional (or at any rate most familiar) account, it could be said that what is proper to man (what is sovereign and unique about man, what affords man his majesty and his dignity) is, ultimately, the phallus and the erection. In short, the traditional conception of man, or what is proper to man, is phallocentric.

In an effort to dismantle this conception of man (as a dick), Derrida turns to Celan, and especially Celan's notoriously cryptographic text 'The Meridian' – a text that consists of the transcript of a speech that Celan gave on 22 October 1960, after having been awarded the prestigious Georg Büchner Prize for literature. It is worth pointing out here that nearly all of Celan's work is deliberately cryptographic, secretive and hermetic. It is invariably, and even singularly, overdetermined by what is missing but silently implied. And both Celan and his followers (and Derrida can be included here) clearly delight in this aspect of his work. I am not a member of the monastic order of Celan experts, so I will not pretend to unlock any of his so tightly locked secrets. I will simply note that anyone who is interested in just how secretive and hermetic 'The Meridian' can be should have a glance at the meticulously detailed character of contemporary Celan scholarship, especially as it relates to this one piece. For instance, the 1999 German edition *Der Meridian, Endfassung, Vorstufen, Materialien*, edited by Bernard Böschen-stein and Heino Schmull (an edition that was translated into English in 2011 by Pierre Joris under the title *The Meridian:*

Final Version–Drafts–Materials, and that includes, along with the text of the speech itself, an assemblage of drafts, sketches, documents and preparatory notes) provides a case in point.

Regardless, Derrida approaches 'The Meridian' by way of its discussion of the marionette, or those uncanny wooden puppets on strings already mentioned, and at the centre of the 'Seventh Session'. In Celan, Derrida points out, the image of the marionette is one of a handful intended to explain the meaning of art, and poetry in particular. For Derrida, Celan's reference to the marionette certainly has that meaning. But it is also much more. Specifically, Derrida maintains that, via Celan, we always encounter at least two marionettes, or two possible interpretations of the marionette. First, the marionette is stiff and hard like an erection. It is a little hard penis – and as a result, a little silly or ridiculous as well. Second, however, the marionette is also the 'little Mary', or the virginal little girl. It is the Virgin Mary, or the miracle of all miracles. Thus, for Derrida, the image of the marionette carries with it a suggestion of sexual difference – a difference that, on Derrida's account, necessarily sits alongside a whole array of other differences or doubles. For example, Derrida proposes, just as the marionette is both man and woman, or an erection and a little girl, it is also in a sense both human and machine, or a machine-like puppet that acts in uncannily human ways. Similarly, it is also both living and not-living; or rather, the marionette marks a border or meridian between life and its other. Moreover, it is, in some sense, both human and animal. For (and to recall what we said about Derrida's reading of Lacan in the first chapter), while witnessing its performance, we can never be sure whether the marionette is spontaneously responding, or merely reacting, to the motions of the puppeteer's hands, motions which appear incredibly miniscule and discrete in comparison to wild gesticulations of the puppet itself.

This discussion of the two marionettes prepares us for what I take to be Derrida's more profound consideration of two majesties, or the two ways of thinking majesty that Celan's 'The Meridian' offers up. To put the matter quickly, before going into more detail below, Derrida essentially claims that Celan's 'meridian' is the line that runs between these two majesties. And he further claims that this same meridian or line runs through what Celan calls 'the present', or the immediate instant of the now. That is to say, and to prepare for what I try to explain in the next section, Derrida ultimately reads 'The Meridian' as a reflection on majesty or sovereignty and time. He maintains that, from Celan's perspective, or from within the logic of his text, every present now or discrete, singular instant, every moment in time, must be constitutively divided or split in two, and that, somehow and paradoxically, this splitting of the instant, or this relating of the singular instant to another instant in time (what, and as I mentioned long ago in the Introduction, in his earlier work Derrida refers to as 'spacing', or 'the becoming-space of time' and 'the becoming-time of space' [*MP* 13]), must take place without depriving either of any of their singularity. Indeed, this relation or, as Derrida puts it, borrowing from Celan, 'encounter' between singular instants will become, for Derrida, something like the essential structure of time in general, or the basis of temporality in general. In other words, for Derrida, time is composed of singular instants that are also, and impossibly, split via their encounters with other instants, and thus not merely instants, but also instances. Or, to recall what I suggested at the beginning of this section, for Derrida, time is composed of singular universals.

But in the 'Eighth Session' Derrida warns us to be patient, or to move patiently through 'The Meridian' before we jump to too many conclusions. And that warning undoubtedly applies to our reading of his text as well. So let us back up a bit, and trace out how Derrida's argument unfolds. In the 'Eighth Session' and the 'Tenth Session' of *The Beast and the Sovereign, Volume 1*, Derrida's reading of Celan establishes two basic and related points, both of which hover around the question of time. The first basic point has to do with dates and dating. The second has to do with the nature of art, and poetry in particular. While, as we will see, these two points are intricately bound up with one another, here I will try to explain them separately and in succession.

First, there is the question of dates and dating. Celan was obsessed with dates, in part because they seem to speak to the paradox of time, or the paradox of what we have been calling the instant and the instance. A date is that which is absolutely discrete (it only occurs once and is then gone forever); but, it is also that which returns with regularity, and gets marked as the same, each and every year. The very title of Celan's text – 'The Meridian', one meaning of which is the imaginary line that stretches from the North to the South Pole, and thus spins around the globe once each day – seems to mark this marking of time. Derrida explores this issue a little in *The Beast and the Sovereign, Volume 1*. But as he notes there as well, he deals with it more extensively in his earlier text 'Shibboleth: For Paul Celan'. In that text, he puts the paradox as such: 'How can one date what does not repeat if dating also calls for some form of return?' (*SQ* 2).

Owing to the fact that he deals with it at some length elsewhere, Derrida's discussion of dates and dating in *The Beast and the Sovereign, Volume 1* is somewhat curtailed. But he does point to, or rather confess, an interesting error on his part with respect to dates – one that illuminates the issue, and that will help me transition to the second basic point in his reading of Celan. Derrida's confession has to do with the date January 20, which figures prominently in 'The Meridian', where Celan points out that it is the date that the character Lenz from Büchner's novella of the same name walks through the mountains, wishing he were able to walk on his head (and thus, on Celan's reading, imagining that he might have the abyss of the sky beneath his feet). At this moment, Celan suggests, inasmuch as Lenz imagines a kind of groundlessness, he discovers something essential about art, namely its singularity and solitude – an artistic discovery about art that, impossibly, Celan attempts to commemorate or repeat by writing a similar story on the same date.

Now in 'Shibboleth' (which is itself the transcript of a speech he gave at a conference on Celan's work in Seattle, Washington, on 14 October 1984, and which, as mentioned above, was first published in French in 1986), Derrida sets this passage from Celan's 'The Meridian' up as the principal example of the theory of dates and dating just discussed, or the notion that each date is both singular and repeated, or exists both in abject solitude and in an encounter with the other. In *The Beast and the Sovereign, Volume 1*, however, Derrida informs us of a crucial bit of information (a secret, as it were) that he did not know, or of which he was unaware, when composing 'Shibboleth' some two decades earlier. Specifically, Derrida reveals that January 20 was also the date of the Wannsee Conference in a Berlin suburb in 1942, the conference at which the Nazi regime first designed and decided to implement the 'final solution', or the mass murder of Europe's Jews (*BS1* 226).

It would be hard to imagine a bit of information (which Derrida explains he first came across in a footnote to a French edition of Celan's work edited by Jean Launay, which itself was first published in early 2002, or about a month before Derrida delivered the 'Eighth Session' of *The Beast and the Sovereign, Volume 1*) that would change the meaning of Celan's references to the date January 20, and cast new light, or a new pattern of light and shadow, across both Celan's text and Derrida's reading of it in 'Shibboleth' more dramatically or completely than this one. Now the date signifies, not only the discovery of a singular work of art, but also the implementation of the singular crime – although the word 'crime', and perhaps every word, is entirely insufficient, and necessarily diminishes the magnitude of what is at stake. But the point we are making here, or the point we are using Derrida's confession to make, is simple enough. It is not only the case that each date is singular and repeated, occurring only once, but destined also to return. It is also the case that the meaning of each date, from the past, is never fixed, but will always shift and get reoriented, depending on what information and context we bring to our effort to understand or make sense of it. Somehow, the singular date remains singular without remaining the same.

We can come at this point from another, possibly a little less obtuse, direction. The question I want to ask here is not whether or how Derrida's discovery and confession about the meaning of the date January 20 should alter our reading of either 'The Meridian' or Derrida's interpretation of it in 'Shibboleth' (which, again, he wrote whilst unaware of this apparently crucial bit of information). Rather, I want to ask whether the revelation of this secret information (or, indeed, any secret information, or even, if one could possibly imagine it, *all* secrets of this sort, or all of the information encrypted within 'The Meridian', whether intentionally, unconsciously, or simply by accident), could exhaust the meaning of what Celan calls a poem, or a poetic utterance, or even something as miniscule as a single date. And I want to reply by saying that, for both Derrida and Celan, the answer to that question is emphatically 'no'. And this impossibility of exhausting meaning with information is integral to what Celan wants to say about art (poetry in particular), as well as what Derrida wants to say about sovereignty and time.

B. *The Time of the Poem*

This brings me to the second main point that Derrida draws out of Celan's text – the one about the nature of art and poetry. As we mentioned, Celan's work is decidedly cryptographic. It is overdetermined by secret information, or what Celan leaves out but also hints at or implies. Celan's discourse is, we might say, an assemblage of clues. At the same time, for Celan, beyond all such hidden information, or secrets that might be concealed and revealed, there is also a kind of absolute secrecy or absolute singularity conditioning every poem or poetic utterance. Or, to put the point differently, for Celan, there is an absolute solitude operative in any poem; and, paradoxically, this singularity or solitude is precisely what makes it possible for us to read, engage with, or, in Celan's terms, 'encounter' it (and, conversely, for it to encounter us).

As we will see, whilst deceptively simple on first glance, this idea is actually a passageway into a labyrinth. But if we had to express it directly, we might say that, for Celan, the instant a poem is finished, or the instant a poetic word is uttered, it becomes detached from the intention of the author, and from all fixed referents or meaning. As Celan puts it, in a well-known passage that we have already mentioned and that Derrida also cites: 'The poem is alone. It is alone and under way.' And yet, for the same reason, Celan continues, or precisely because it is alone, the poem can 'participate in an encounter'. Even more to the point, for Celan, because it is alone, the poem can participate in what, in a phrase that Derrida takes to be crucial, Celan calls 'the secret of an encounter [*Geheimnis der Begegnung*]' (*BS1* 262–3). Put directly, the solitude of the poem, the absolute secrecy inscribed in its heart (the fact that it begins without fixed meaning, and walks on its head, as it were, with the sky beneath its feet), is also what makes possible its encounter with a reader – indeed, in principle, its encounter with an infinite number of readers, each one different from the last.

Now, to be clear, while this may be a useful way into what Celan means here, and what Derrida wants to take away from him, this image of a poem that is 'alone' or 'alone and under way', and thus capable of participating in 'the secret of an encounter', cannot be reduced to a particular occluded version of what used to be called 'reader response criticism', in which the text is said to acquire whatever meaning it might have, not at the moment of its creation, but at that of its interpretation. Indeed, we could probably say that, for Celan and Derrida alike, this consideration of the singularity and solitude of the poem is not merely about poetry per se, but something akin to an allegory for language and experience in general, and that what is really at stake in this line of thought is less how we read or make sense of poetry and literature, than how we experience all of our relations with subjects and objects, or with one another and with the world. Thus the point here is that, as with the poem, every relation or interaction involves 'the secret of an encounter', or an encounter between two or more absolute singularities – what, as I mentioned in the previous section of this chapter, the subtitle of 'Rams' refers to as 'two solitudes'.

No doubt this conception of our relationship or engagement with others and the world in terms of an encounter between singularities or solitudes is complicated enough. But, as I have already implied, in the 'Eighth Session' and the 'Tenth Session' of *The Beast and the Sovereign, Volume 1*, Derrida insists on connecting Celan's notion of 'the secret of an encounter' to the problem of time and temporality. In other words, from Derrida's perspective, what is important in Celan's approach here is not merely the encounter between, for example, myself and another, or an I and a thou. No, for Derrida, what is most important is the encounter between my time and the time of another, or what Derrida refers to as 'the time of the other' (*BS1* 231). Derrida gets at this notion by focusing our attention on another moment in Celan's text – one in which Celan describes art and poetry in terms of 'presence', and more specifically, in terms of what he calls the 'one, unique, punctual present [*eine, einmalige, punktuelle Gegenwart*]' (231).

To understand this point, it is helpful to recall what we said above about the two marionettes, and how they configure, on Derrida's reading of Celan, two majesties, or two understandings of majesty. Here Derrida draws our attention to a point in 'The Meridian' where Celan refers to a moment in Büchner's play *Danton's Death* when the character Lucile suddenly shouts 'Long live the King!' Setting aside the context for the purposes of concision, Derrida proposes that, for Celan, these words have two different meanings, or gesture towards two different conceptions of majesty, which are separated by a meridian or a line. On the one side, there is the majesty associated with what is said, in the constative mode – namely, the projected eternal life of the sovereign, or the utterance, as is discussed most famously in Ernst Kantorowicz's *The King's Two Bodies*, that 'the King is dead, long live the King'. But on the other side, there is what we might call the majesty of the saying of these words, in the performative mode – a saying and a performance that Celan refers to as a 'counterstatement [*Gegenwort*]' (229).

Now, on Derrida's account, this second, performative meaning of the phrase 'Long live the King!' is integral to what Celan means by poetry. And it implies a completely different temporality – not the eternal life of the sovereign, but the truth that can only be manifest in, once again, 'one, unique, punctual present'. This Derrida calls 'the majesty of the present' (*BS1* 229). And it is very close, if not identical, to what we were discussing in the previous chapter under the rubric of testimony, avowal or witnessing. It is the articulation of a truth that only the one who articulates can possibly know – and only at the precise moment that they articulate it. To repeat our formula, I can only testify to what only I can know.

But at the same time, and most importantly, this performance or this testimony, this expression that can only ever be absolutely singular and punctual in its presence, is also always, and from the very beginning, destined to be encountered by another, or by the other. Precisely as indivisible presence, it paradoxically bears within it the presence or the time of the other. And, for Derrida, this is what Celan means by 'the secret of the encounter'. In Derrida's terms, it is singular, but it is also already given to the other, or to the time of the other. And this giving must take place before it is possessed. It is thus a giving that is not a gift, or a giving that operates outside of any restricted economy of reciprocal exchange, or any expectation of a return. The other, the foreigner, or what Celan calls the *unheimliche* (a word that connotes both familiar and unfamiliar, or homely and homeless, at once), is always already internal to the 'one, unique, punctual present'.

As Derrida puts it towards the end of the 'Tenth Session', in his discussion of presence in 'The Meridian', Celan does not affirm the eternal presence of the sovereign ('the King is dead, long live the King'), but instead 'signals toward an alterity that – within the "I" as punctual living present, as point of the living self-present present, an alterity of the wholly other'. And, moreover, this alterity 'comes along not to include and modalise another living present . . . but here, which is quite different', it involves a 'letting the present *of the other* appear' (*BS1* 270). Against the sovereign time of eternal presence, then, or of each present moment modifying and modalising the others, Derrida posits another majesty of presence – one in which each present moment, each singularity, is also split and conditioned by other present moments or singularities, miraculously without forfeiting its singularity.

Much earlier in this book, I mentioned the possibility of a secret that exceeds sovereignty. I said we would have to circle around, almost indefinitely, before arriving at that possibility. At this point in his text, Derrida comes very close to touching on this issue. Whatever else Celan might mean by 'the secret of an encounter', it is almost certainly something like this secret beyond sovereignty, or beyond the self-contained, self-identical and self-legislating (but also, and paradoxically, self-excluding or self-excepting) entity that our intellectual tradition has dubbed the sovereign. In the next two sections, I will try to explore this in a little more depth by discussing *The Beast and the Sovereign, Volume 2.*

I will start by focusing on what Derrida has to say about the experience of being alone, and his reading of both *Robinson Crusoe* and Heidegger's 1929–30 seminar *The Fundamental Concepts of Metaphysics: World, Finitude, and Solitude*. With respect to the first, and as mentioned above, I will emphasise what Derrida calls 'living death' and his concept of '*survivance*'. With respect to the second, I will pay close attention to what Derrida says about solitude and the act of praying or prayer, and his enigmatic suggestion that all interaction and experience is structured by a kind of prayer. This will lead, finally, to an examination of what Derrida says about death – a secret that, he seems to suggest, exceeds not only the sovereign, but also the distinction between the beast and the sovereign, or everything we typically take to be non-human, on the one hand, and every-thing we typically take to be human, on the other.

Being Alone

What does it mean to be alone? What does it mean to be alone together? We humans are always alone, and always alone together. In the most intimate experiences, in love for example, we are alone and alone together. But even if there were a hundred thousand humans packed into the same building (as at a sporting event, a musical performance, or a massive political rally), they would still not be anywhere near all humans, and thus, in some sense, alone and alone together. Indeed, even if millions of humans were collected together (say, strung out in a line along a series of trenches, facing millions more humans strung out along theirs, as happened in the First World War), they would still be alone and alone together. And why not amplify the claim to the point of complete absurdity? Even if *all* humans were collected together in a single space, even if, after the apocalypse, the last remaining humans found themselves gathered in one spot, they would still be entirely alone, or alone in relation to every other being in the universe. To speak of being at all, in other words, let alone the human being, is to speak of being alone. Only being as such, if we could imagine such a thing, or the totality of all beings, would not be alone. But then we would have to consider, with Plato, that which is greater than or beyond being; and we would be thrown back into the same basic experience – being alone. To be at all is to be alone. Being is being alone. Being is alone. Being alone.

This, I think, is one way of expressing the line of thought with which Derrida begins the very last series of seminars he gave before his death – the seminars that have been published and translated as *The Beast and the Sovereign, Volume 2*. Neither Derrida nor his students at this time knew that he was dying (he was not diagnosed with pancreatic cancer until early 2003, or shortly after the seminars were delivered).[3] And yet, in retrospect, it is hard not to read the text as overdetermined with the encroaching reality of Derrida's own death, or the fact that he about to die. It is as if Derrida was engaged in a performative without knowing it. He speaks about what it might mean to die, just before he is about to do so. Or rather, he speaks about the impossibility of designating the instant of death at just that instant that he, a living man, is poised to die.

Unabashedly, we might say, the philosopher gazes at his navel – at the point (in space, or on his body) that first separated him from the other, or the mother, and at the point (in time, or in his life) at which he is about to be separated again from all others, or from all of the others he has ever known, as well as those he has never known, and from all of the others gathered around him, who do not even know that they are preparing for their loss – their loss of, precisely, him, or the one who is speaking. *The Beast and the Sovereign, Volume 2* is the document of a man watching himself die – watching without watching, we might say, or knowing without knowing. It is the document of what, in it, Derrida repeatedly calls a 'living death', which he also associates with the experience or the nightmare of being buried or eaten alive. Thus, perhaps, reading *The Beast and the Sovereign, Volume 2* is as close as we can get to a representation of the unrepresentable – a representation or account, that is, of the absolute secret, the secret beyond all secrecy, or the secret par excellence.

At the same time, and as always, the particular, discrete or punctual moment is also entirely general. The instant is also an instance. It is a singular universal. For we are all dying. Not only Derrida, and not only in these seminars. That is what it means to be alive. Or, rather, Derrida wonders here whether to be dying – to be mortal – is what we mean by life. And, if so, how do we rigorously distinguish between the two? Can we speak of either life or death as specific phenomena? Should we not, instead, and as mentioned above, speak only of life-death, or the co-implication of the two? What is alive? What is dead? Can we, in any meaningful sense, divide the field of all possible objects across the axis of alive and dead, or even animate and inanimate? And what is the field of all possible objects – present or absent, here or gone? Can we call this 'the world'? But what is the world? What in the world do we mean by the world?

This is, very clearly and explicitly, the enormously expansive range of topics that Derrida has the temerity to open up in *The Beast and the Sovereign, Volume 2* – that is to say, just before he dies. And Derrida does so, or feigns to do so, by applying himself to the close examination of two apparently very different, indeed almost incomparable or incommensurable, texts – namely, Daniel Defoe's canonical novel *Robinson Crusoe*, and Martin Heidegger's 1929–30 seminar *Die Grundbegriffe der Metaphysik: Welt-Endlichkeit-Einsamkeit*, which has been translated as *The Fundamental Concepts of Metaphysics: World, Finitude, Solitude*. In this section, I have no intention of attempting to follow or even begin to explore all of the paths that Derrida tries to set out in *The Beast and the Sovereign, Volume 2*. Instead, as mentioned above, I will focus my attention on two basic elements: first, Derrida's comments, primarily in the 'Fifth Session', on 'living death' and '*survivance*'; and then his consideration of prayer, solitude and, one last time, death, in the 'Eighth Session', the 'Ninth Session' and the 'Tenth Session'.

Throughout *The Beast and the Sovereign, Volume 2*, Derrida repeatedly reminds us of Robinson Crusoe's fear, not of death in general, but of being buried or consumed alive – either by the earth, as in an earthquake, or by an animal, or by another human being, or a cannibal. In the 'Fifth Session', Derrida provocatively asserts that, in fact, Crusoe's worst fear does come true. It does not come true in the narrative, of course, or in the story *Robinson Crusoe* as it is relayed to us by a narrator named Robinson Crusoe. But in another, admittedly quite metaphorical or abstract sense, both the novel and the character are buried alive, or examples of the living dead. For both of them continue to appear in a public forum, or in publication. Both of them can be and are read and reread with enormous frequency. But both are also fundamentally cut off from the animating intention that created them. Both are severed, and severed at their point of origin, as it were, from any determinate origin, or fundamental, singular or discernible meaning. And, for Derrida, the same is true, not only of any book, or any piece of writing, but also for any trace, or any arrangement of anything that might be considered meaningful or legible. 'As is indeed any trace', Derrida writes, 'in the sense that I give this word or concept, a book is living dead, alive and swallowed up alive' (*BS2* 130).

Derrida refers to this phenomenon of the 'living dead' text or trace as '*survivance*'. And, as we have seen him do so often, he attempts to generalise its operation, or to treat it as an, in his words, 'quasi-transcendental' condition for experience in the broadest sense, and perhaps even for existence as such (although we will have to come back to this notion of existence 'as such' below, as it is one that Derrida places into question in his reading of Heidegger). One way to understand what Derrida has in mind here would be to think in terms of the technology of the archive, or the storing and preservation of traces, both official and unofficial (and here we are bushing up against the question of data-politics and the surveillance state again, as we saw at the beginning of the last chapter). Derrida's point is not merely that books or archived traces exist after their author has died. Rather, and in a manner that is closely related to what we saw him say in 'Rams' about the death of the other already haunting my relationship with her from the moment I meet her, Derrida proposes that, in some sense, the archive is already there, from the beginning, as soon as a text is created or a trace inscribed. 'From the first breath, this archive as *survivance* is at work', Derrida maintains. 'But once again, this is the case not only for books, or for writing, or for the archive in the current sense, but for everything from which the tissue of living experience is woven' (*BS2* 132).

Derrida's argumentation here gets quite complex, and even a little obtuse. But one thing this notion of '*survivance*' clearly indicates is the sense in which every text or trace is already, and from the very beginning, given over to the other, or to the one who must seek to read or interpret it without any hope of arriving at its original meaning or intention. Or, to put the same point from another direction, Derrida is proposing that every author (and in this instance he is clearly thinking, not only of Robinson Crusoe or Daniel Defoe, but also of himself) is already at the mercy of the other – completely at their mercy, like a corpse or a jumble of human remains. Thus, for Derrida, the author, or the one whose authority signs and authorises a text, is already and from the beginning not sovereign – not the one who, to recall a familiar locution, decides on the exception, but the one who must accept the decision of the other, and the decision of the other as to what is supposedly inside of them, namely their animating intention or originary meaning or aim. '*Survivance*' then involves, not sovereignty, but what, elsewhere, Derrida sometimes refers to as 'the decision' of 'the other in me' (*AL* 23), or the sense in which my interiority or interior space is first generated or carved out by and through a relation with some other. In other words, there is no inner world, except for the one that is constituted by that which is outer or other.

This brings me, then, to the second point I want to make about *The Beast and the Sovereign, Volume 2,* the point about solitude and prayer, especially as it relates to Heidegger's 1929–30 seminar. The 'Eighth Session' begins with some broad comments on solitude and prayer, which Derrida then, by way of a meticulously close reading, brings to bear on Heidegger's seminar. He begins by pointing out that a prayer is a speech act or a performative in J. L. Austin's sense of the word. It does not refer to anything in the external world, nor does it express a pre-existing inward state or desire. Instead, in its very articulation, the prayer constitutes a world, or a state of affairs. Its referent, if we can call it this, is nothing other than itself. Or, put differently, it does not describe or express a belief, or a desire to be believed. Rather, in and of itself, it is the belief and the desire of which it speaks. Thus a prayer is neither true nor false. It is an appeal to be believed – to have my belief believed by someone else. In this context, Derrida wonders whether it is possible to lie while praying, or to pray dishonestly. The issue here is a little like the *aporia* of self-deception we considered above. Since a prayer constitutes rather than describes a state of affairs, since it has no semantic content external to the act of praying itself, there is no space, as it were, for deception, or no way of concealing a true indication or meaning behind a distorted or confused expression. When we pray, in short, we have nothing to hide.

But Derrida does not stop there. Rather, once again, and as we saw with *survivance* and the living dead a moment ago, not to mention a dozen other places in this book, Derrida seeks to generalise the particular act or experience. That is to say, for Derrida, the specific, singular act of praying becomes a general or universal condition of all language and all interaction. For, as I explained above, in my first chapter, when discussing Derrida's treatment of the oath, even if only by way of a silent implication, we cannot say anything unless we preface it with a 'believe me when I say this', or a 'believe that this is what I believe'. There could be no communication or exchange whatsoever without this appeal to have one's belief believed by the other, or the one to whom I direct my speech. Derrida puts this point in the form of a question: 'can one address oneself to someone or indeed to any living being at all – or even something not living – without some implicit prayer coming to bend, to inflect the discourse', he asks (*BS2* 203).

For Derrida, then, whenever we speak or write or use any sign or inscribe any trace whatsoever, we are also saying something like "'listen to me, please [*je t'en prie*], listen, I pray you, look at me looking at you, please, turn toward me, turn your attention toward what I am saying or doing to you, be present to what is coming from me'" (*BS2* 203). And, Derrida maintains, this implicit prayer or appeal would be at work, not only in benevolent or convivial conversation, but even, and perhaps more so, in acts of cruelty, such as torture or abuse. To make any address whatsoever is also to say 'pray you, hear me now, be here with me now' (203). And, what is more, on Derrida's account, it is also to say something like 'pray you, remember me, or hold on to what I have just said so you might connect it to what I am about to say, and thus comprehend my genuine meaning or intention'. When we interact, when we speak, we are praying for another to remain present with us through time – impossibly, perhaps, to hold together a series of utterly discrete and singular instants, or to make time out of what is properly timeless.

Animal Worlds

Having made these broad points about prayer, and after a fascinating digression on Pascal (on a posthumously published prayer that was found in his coat pocket after he died), Derrida turns his attention towards Heidegger. His basic, and characteristically provocative, assertion is that the lynch pin of the 1929–30 seminar, and perhaps of Heidegger's challenge to what he calls metaphysics in general, can be found in a few passing comments on the topic of prayer. Derrida sets the context of his reading by appealing to a later text (namely the book *Identity and Difference*, which Heidegger published in 1957). There, and as Derrida explains, Heidegger asserts that the god of metaphysics (the god who is a first cause, or the ontic being who creates all other ontic beings) is not a god to whom one would sacrifice or pray. For sacrifice and prayer presuppose a god who is beyond or external to the realm of ontic beings. Indeed, on Heidegger's account (or on Derrida's rendition of Heidegger's account at any rate) the atheist philosopher (that is, Heidegger himself) is in some sense more of a believer than the metaphysical theologian. For the atheist philosopher is able to think the ontological, or Being as such, without reducing it to an ontic being, or some particular and ultimately representable or identifiable thing.

Does this mean that Heidegger's ostensible atheistic philosopher seeks to reinvent or recompose a more authentic religion, or a more authentic experience of god – one that cannot be captured within the framework of metaphysics, and all of its contemporary scientific consequences and expressions? And would Heidegger be suggesting that we might authentically pray to this authentic god? Prudently, Derrida sets that question aside, or places it in the background, and proposes instead to begin with the concept of world, or the central concept of Heidegger's seminar. In particular, Derrida focuses on Heidegger's assertion that 'the stone is without world [*weltlos*], the animal is poor in world [*weltarm*], [whilst] man is world-forming [*weltbildend*]' (*BS2* 134). Derrida primarily addresses Heidegger's claims about the difference between animals and humans. But, as we will see, and as I have already suggested a few times above, his arguments have ramifications for the way we think about 'the stone', or inanimate things, as well.

As Derrida explains, Heidegger follows a long tradition of defining the animal (again, a massively totalising concept, with no clear limits or boundaries) as something that is essentially deprived of a specifically human capacity or power. That is to say, Heidegger defines the animal negatively, off against its ostensible other, or the human. On Heidegger's account, then, of what is the animal deprived? Well, in sum, while the animal can and must experience and understand specific ontic beings (this is food, that is a mate, this is a good place to hide, and so on), it cannot entertain or comprehend the ontological or being as such. That is to say, for Heidegger, the animal has no notion of the totality of beings, and thus no capacity to pose the ontological question: 'why is there something rather than nothing?' The animal has no notion of what Heidegger refers to as the 'as-structure [*als-Structur*]'. Or, as Derrida puts it, here summarising Heidegger: 'Because it cannot conceive being as such', the animal 'lacks the possibility of perceiving as being [*als ein Seiendes*] that to which it is open'. The animal is therefore incapable of what Heidegger calls 'comportment [*Verhalten*]' (*BS2* 218). It can be in the world, we might say, but it cannot comport itself towards the world, or make the world as such, in its totality, one of its objects or things.

As always, Derrida's arguments here get extremely sophisticated, following the letter of Heidegger's texts down into any number of rabbit holes (particularly rabbit holes that have to do with etymology and translation, but others as well). But I think that (while Derrida himself mingles these lines of thought together rather than separating them out analytically as I will here) he essentially has three large claims to make about Heidegger's text. Two of these claims seek to challenge Heidegger's assumptions about the difference between the animal and the human. The other one seeks to expose a hidden, concealed or unconscious logic at work in Heidegger's text – a logic that should, once exposed, properly compel Heidegger and us to reconsider the way we think about all of these issues, and perhaps the way we think about what Heidegger calls 'ontological difference' (the difference between beings and Being), or simply ontology in the most general sense of the term. I will devote the rest of this section to examining the first two points, and, in the next section, turn to the third.

The first of Derrida's two claims about Heidegger's seminar can be stated quite plainly, in terms of questions: First, how can we be so sure that the animal is poor in world, or incapable of an understanding of the ontological as Heidegger defines it? And second, how can we be so sure that the human has a world, or that humans have the power to inhabit and comprehend something like a single world? The third of Derrida's claims about Heidegger's seminar, and indeed about his thought in general, is more complicated, and has significantly more profound implications. But it revolves around Heidegger's use of a single word – namely, the world *Walten*, which is difficult to translate, but which carries connotations of power, domination and violence.

Let us start with the first question: How can we be so sure that the animal is poor in world? For Derrida, this is where Heidegger's brief, or apparently passing and marginal, mention of prayer in his seminar begins to become integral. At a key moment in the seminar, Heidegger examines Aristotle's *Peri Hermeneias* or *On Interpretation*. He wants to show that this text falls within the tradition of metaphysics, and thus fails to ask in a direct manner the question of Being. It fails, in other words, to set out the difference between beings and Being, and thus presents truth in terms of an accurate description of the former, rather than the revelation or unconcealment of the latter. Thus, for Heidegger, Aristotle characterises truth, logic or language in terms of an *apophantikos logos*, or what Heidegger calls an 'enunciative proposition [*Aussagesatz*]' (*BS2* 217). Put as directly as possible, Heidegger maintains that, for Aristotle, the one who speaks must be attempting accurately to represent or reconstitute in propositional form an ontic reality that exists prior to or outside of that representation. And this overlooks or misunderstands the sense in which language not only describes the world around it, or describes beings, but also brings forth, discloses or, we might say, constitutes beings. It overlooks the sense in which language is, not quite the vehicle, but the space or the house of Being.

Here, and as Derrida points out, Heidegger is entering into some very murky territory. For in suggesting that language is not a simple representation of beings, but the house of Being, he is also suggesting that deception or mendacity is as fundamental to language, or simply to what Heidegger refers to as *Dasein*, as propositional truth. In other words, Heidegger is pointing towards what Derrida calls 'the co-originality of truth and untruth for *Dasein*'. As Derrida puts it, on Heidegger's account, 'non-truth does not supervene like an accident, after the fact, on a more originary truth, thus requiring a complimentary or supplementary theory' (*BS2* 241). Rather, and in a very different sense, 'non-truth is as originary as truth. The possibility of error and of lying, of dissimulation in general, is required, originarily required, as possibility, by the possibility of truth or of veracity, and also of unveiling' (241–2). And indeed, on Derrida's reading of Heidegger, this 'co-originality of truth and untruth', or this possibility of an indestructible untruth (one that is not destined to be overcome by the truth, but can potentially exist indefinitely and forever) is crucial to *Dasein's* (or simply the human's) unique capacity to comprehend being as such. Put differently, on Derrida's reading of Heidegger, the interplay of revelation and concealment (in Heidegger's terms, truth as *aletheia*) is what characterises the human's, as opposed to the animal's, experience of the world. It is what makes the human 'world-forming [*weltbildend*]'.

At this point, via a long digression, Derrida reminds us of his consideration of Lacan in the 'Fifth Session' of *The Beast and the Sovereign, Volume 1* – the session I discussed in some detail at the end of my first chapter above. There, as you will recall, Derrida pointed out that, for Lacan, the human is capable of Truth (and thus unlike the animal), because the human is capable of lying – not only concealing some fact from another, be it an enemy or a potential mate, but also taking advantage of the fact that the other knows that I might be lying, or engaging in what Derrida calls 'second degree feint'. In Lacan, as we saw, this means that, while the animal is bound to the imaginary stage, the human can advance or graduate into the symbolic. And, according to Derrida, while their vocabularies are clearly discrete, on this point, Lacan and Heidegger are more or less in agreement. A fundamental component of human speech is the possibility of deception. And this possibility is not added onto the truth, as it were. Rather, it is an ever-present element of truth – one of its basic conditions, and not merely a secondary or ancillary function.

However, Derrida wonders (and this is the key), what about prayer? As we saw above, prayer excludes the possibility of deception. When I pray, I cannot be lying. For the belief expressed in my prayer refers to nothing other than the act of praying itself. There is no other referent or truth that might be concealed and hidden from view. The prayer, in other words, and once again, is a performative and not a constative utterance. And, moreover, according to Derrida, every utterance, indeed every relation, every address, and arguably every experience and perhaps existence as such, presupposes something like a prayer, or a 'pray you believe that this is what I believe' and a 'pray you stay present with me while I unfold my meaning in time'. Prayer is, as Derrida puts it, here using rather poetic language of his own, 'a performative lodged like a pearl in the oyster of the constative' (*BS2* 256). It is already there, as soon as there is any address, and long before there is any effort to represent or describe.

To put the point differently, and in more Heideggerian terms, for Derrida, prayer is not a representation of ontic beings, but a revelation or disclosure of ontological Being. Anything that prays (which is to say, anything that makes any address whatsoever, or anything that comports itself towards another, or that leaves behind what Derrida calls a 'trace') must already have a sense of Being, or some sense of the totality of beings or being as such. And thus, and to return to our question of whether or not we can really say that the animal is 'poor in world [*weltarm*]', inasmuch as the animal does something like address us or anything around it, we must admit that (certainly just as much as the human), the animal dwells in the house of Being.

Having examined the question of whether we can be so certain that the animal is poor in world, or *weltarm*, we can now turn towards the second of Derrida's questions or lines of questioning mentioned above – namely, whether or not we can be so sure that humans are world-forming or *weltbildend*, or merely whether we can be so sure that we humans have something like a world. Here, and quite simply it seems to me, Derrida begins by pointing out that, whatever else it might be, the world (which, for Heidegger, seems to require some conception of the totality of beings or being as such) is not given to our intuition or our sense. Precisely on Heidegger's account, we can have no calculable or empirical experience of it. It is not a being. It is Being. It is not ontic. It is ontological. And therefore we can never be certain that it exists. In fact, it is defined by this impossibility of being pinned down as a kind of ontic certainty.

Another (admittedly a little reductive, but nevertheless instructive) way to understand what Heidegger means by the world would be to think of it in terms of the symbolic space of human interaction – or what, as we have already suggested, and as Derrida suggests as well, Lacan means by the symbolic order. It is the space of interaction or exchange with others that, again in Lacan's terms, gets opened up by the Other. And this supposed world or symbolic order would, as already discussed, entail a kind of 'co-originality of truth and untruth' (*BS2* 241). It would make possible Truth, in Lacan's terms, by being conditioned by the possibility of deception or the lie. But if, in order to communicate in any sense at all, we must in some manner presuppose such a world or symbolic order, then, precisely on its own terms, we can never know for certain whether or not it exists. On Derrida's account, this world might just as well be a happy illusion. There may be no world that unites us and separates us at once, or that holds us together by holding us apart. There is no good reason not to assume that we are all Robinson Crusoes, alone on our islands, and isolated, not only from one another, but also from various elements (or moments) of ourselves.

At this point, and as, throughout this book, I have tried to show he often does, Derrida appeals to our everyday experience. Or rather, he asks us, as it were, to share in his experience of the unsharable, or to agree that it is always impossible to agree. Who, Derrida wonders, can avoid or deny 'the feeling that the worlds in which we live are different', or that they are 'absolutely unsharable'? And who is not suspicious of 'the vague comforting feeling of understanding each other' or engaging 'in consensual communicative action'? (*BS2* 267). The hypothesis of a world, let alone one we share, or one in which we can assume that others carry with them and presuppose some (at least unconscious) understanding of the totality of beings, or being as such, and that they communicate with us on the basis of this understanding, may very well be a ruse or a fantasy. Indeed it may very well be the case, and (as Derrida, who presented these seminars just as the Second Gulf War was breaking out, notes as well) a great deal of evidence suggests that it is the case, that there is no single human world governed by the possibility of consensus and exchange, but instead an infinite number of worlds, or an infinite number of solitudes, eternally at war, and engaging with one another, not through discourse, sympathy and concord, but through violence, antagonism and strife.

Dominance and Death

This brings me, finally, to the last point I want to make about *The Beast and the Sovereign, Volume 2*, and the last point I will make in this chapter. Throughout the final three sessions of his last seminar, and interspersed among the other themes he takes up, Derrida strings together an extended reflection on Heidegger's use of basically one word – the German word *Walten*, which could be translated as dominate or prevail, and which has connotations of sovereignty or reign, as well as simply power and mastery. By way of a meticulously close analysis of Heidegger's text, Derrida proposes that, from Heidegger's perspective, something like *Walten* generates or is at the source of the ontico-ontological difference, or what first separates beings from Being. The set of moves that Derrida makes here is exceptionally intricate, and operates on a level that is deeply internal to another very difficult thinker – namely Heidegger. I can make no claim to understanding everything that is at stake. But I think if we can capture the overall pattern of the argument, it will help us illuminate the theme of this book (or the secret) and of this chapter (or time and death). It will also give us a glimpse of that enigmatic notion we have mentioned a handful of times already – the notion of a secret that exceeds sovereignty, and that cannot be contained within a sovereign order or design.

The basic claim that Derrida makes in this regard, or at least his point of departure, is lexical. Derrida notes that, while we can find it here and there in the earlier work, it is only in the 1929–30 seminar that Heidegger begins to develop a vocabulary of *Walten*, or to use it and its cognates with any degree of consistency or regularity. Even more precisely, Derrida claims that this word begins to appear around the same time that Heidegger discusses the phenomenon of prayer. We will recall that, for Derrida, Heidegger slightly misunderstands or underestimates the significance of prayer. For while he appears to recognise that it is what, since Austin, we have called a performative rather than a constative (it refers only to its own act of enunciation, and not to any ontic thing in the world), Heidegger does not appear to see, or to want to see, that this means prayer has some affinity with the ontological, and with a conception of truth, not as adequation, but as revelation and disclosure of Being. At any rate, Derrida's hypothesis here is that the appearance of a vocabulary of *Walten* around the same time Heidegger discusses prayer is not accidental, but suggests a deep affinity between his conception of religion and his treatment of this theme.

This puts the matter a little crudely, no doubt, but I think that Derrida's underlying concern here is whether or not, for Heidegger, *Walten* might constitute something like a non-metaphysical, non-onto-theological or properly ontological rather than merely ontic god. As we saw earlier, for Heidegger, all theology, even perhaps of the negative sort, has effectively tried to conceive of god in ontic terms, or avoid the ontological question of Being and reduce god to one being among many. A non-metaphysical, non-onto-theological or properly onto-logical approach to god would have to escape or elude many if not all of the themes and tropes that theologians have employed to discuss god. In particular, it would have to escape or elude the dominant understanding of god's sovereignty, and along with it the entire discourse of political theology.

Walten, then, is the power that first separates beings from Being. But where would such a power come from, and how would we even begin to conceive of it? We could not speak of it in historical or scientific terms. We could not speak of its originary status, or of its coming before all the beings we experience. Nor, obviously, could we seek to provide an ontic representation of it, or grasp it according to the rules of orderly description. For, inasmuch as it generates the distinction between beings and Being, it is already a condition for both the notion of origin and that of representation. Somewhat mysteriously, it 'comes before' the logic or the way of thinking (that is, the metaphysics and the onto-theology) that would give priority to that which comes before, or that looks for truth by tracing back a chain of causes and effects to some original *causa sui* or first cause.

As Derrida puts it, for it to escape or elude metaphysics and onto-theology, this *Walten* of which Heidegger speaks would have to be 'foreign to the attributes or power and of sovereignty, of height and of causal and fundamental principality' (*BS2* 215). If we had to understand 'this God more divine than the God of onto-theology' in terms of 'sovereignty', it would have to be 'another sovereignty', one that remains 'foreign to ontic power, and therefore foreign to political theology and to creationism, and to fundamentalism, in all senses of the term, in particular in the sense that refers to a founding God' (215). In other words, and as Derrida explains a little earlier in the text, this *Walten* god would have somehow to remain 'foreign or heterogeneous, excessive even, with respect to this ontic and therefore theological and theological-political sovereignty'. It would have to constitute what Derrida calls 'an ontological super-sovereignty, at the source of the ontological difference' (208). The god called *Walten*, then, would have to be a sovereignty beyond all sovereignty – a height higher than the highest, more powerful than the most powerful, greater than the greatest, indeed higher and more powerful and greater than the entire logic of the high, the powerful or the great, beyond any measure that might seek to measure the immeasurable, an infinity larger and of more magnitude than the infinite.

This is the point in Derrida's reading of Heidegger where what he has to say exceeds my capacity to comprehend and relay in clear or lucid terms. It is the point where, as Derrida puts it, 'Heidegger's writing can sometimes look like an unjustified and annoying game'; but it is also 'the moment when the most subtle differences are also the most decisive' (*BS2* 252). Here I am simply going to admit my lack of capacity, and submit to the complexity of what is being discussed. But I can say that, essentially, Derrida associates Heidegger's vocabulary of *Walten* with his use of the term *Austrag*, a term that is equally difficult to translate, but that, as Derrida suggests, entails a kind of ruling that brings a dispute to an end (perhaps, then, something like a decision). At any rate, the consequence of this extremely difficult and elaborate reading is that, for Derrida's image of Heidegger, *Walten* becomes 'the event, the origin, the power, the force, the source, the movement, the process, the meaning, etc. – whatever you like – of the ontological difference, or the becoming-ontological-difference of the ontological difference, of the supervening of Being and the arrival of beings' (256).

At this moment, and not incidentally, Derrida too becomes a little confused, or at least affects a posture of confusion. 'But what does "excess of sovereignty" mean', he writes, referring to all of the hyperbole that we associated with *Walten* at the end of the paragraph preceding the last, 'if sovereignty, in essence and by vocation, by its structure, signals and signifies itself primarily as excess itself, as normal abuse, surplus and transcendence beyond or compared with any determinable measure?' (*BS2* 279).

After suggesting that, for Heidegger, it has something to do with the question of nothingness (something that the positive scientist cannot begin to comprehend, but the poet and the philosopher can), Derrida turns to Heidegger's consideration of the opening words of Sophocles' *Antigone*, which seem to speak about something essentially human, and which, Derrida says, 'are usually translated thus: "Manifold is the uncanny, yet nothing / uncannier than man bestirs itself, rising up beyond him"' (285). The word translated as 'uncanny' here (or, in the German, *unheimlich*) is the Greek *deinon*, which might also be translated as 'wonder'. The human, then, is uncanny – not only in the world, but also to itself. The essence of the human is to be a wonder, we might say, but also to wonder, or to wonder about itself.

This line of thinking is quite clearly connected to what Heidegger says in *Being and Time* about questioning, and his conception of *Dasein* as the being for whom Being is a question. But more importantly, in the context of Derrida's reading of Heidegger in *The Beast and the Sovereign, Volume 2*, this notion of the human being as a wonder that also wonders is one more expression of Heidegger's, as it were, deep seeded humanism, or continued effort, despite so much of what his own thought would appear to indicate, to draw a sharp line between the human and the animal. Or rather, at this point, it becomes clear that Heidegger's use of a vocabulary of *Walten* could be read in two different and opposed ways. On the one hand, we could see it as yet another justification of human exceptionalism. On this reading, which Derrida summarises but does not submit to, 'the violence that grips man is indeed that of the *as such* of beings that *Dasein* is and that he must take upon himself, it is *Walten*, as such' (*BS2* 288). Alternatively, however, and without abandoning any element of Heidegger's own logic, we could read the same vocabulary of *Walten* as describing a force, power, or violence that tears open the distinction between beings and Being, and that therefore is prior to every being, including the human being. In other words, on the second reading (which is the one Derrida appears to be pursuing), *Walten* is not something that humans grip; rather, it is something that grips them.

We have covered quite a bit of ground in a very short space. As I mentioned above, my discussion of Derrida's final reading of Heidegger on the concept of *Walten* is limited, not only by the space constraints I have, but also by my own ignorance. I think, however, that I have provided some sense of the overall trajectory of Derrida's claims. And yet, and importantly, this is not where Derrida leaves the issue. At the very end of the 'Tenth Session' – again, the last session of his last seminar – Derrida himself begins to wonder whether there might be another force opposing or exceeding or somehow escaping this 'super-sovereignty', as he puts it, of *Walten*. Or rather, he begins to wonder whether Heidegger offers us the possibility of thinking another force. Here Derrida quotes Heidegger: "'*Nur an* einem [underlined] *scheitert alle Gewalt-tätigkeit unmittelbar* (There is only *one* thing against which all violence-doing, violent action, violent activity, immediately shatters"', Derrida (or rather Heidegger) writes. Then Derrida comments: 'Notice that, as much as the failure and limit of violence, of the outbidding of *Walten*, of *Gewalt*, what seems to count here is immediate in this limit that imposes failure on *Gewalt* and *Walten* (*unmittelbar* is the last word).' Then Derrida's seminar manuscript has a note to himself, or a kind of stage direction for the reading: '(Repeat German and French)'. And, finally, at the very end, quoting Heidegger one last time: "'*Das ist der Tod* [it is death]"' (*BS2* 290).

This is all presented, of course, as a reading, and even a simple quotation, of Heidegger. But it is a quotation that Derrida at least appears to be affirming. Thus, if we had to put the matter in plain terms, we might say that, for Derrida, the only thing that exceeds not only sovereignty in the political theological sense, but also the 'super-sovereignty' that Heidegger dubs *Walten*, is death. That would be, then, the secret that eludes or exceeds sovereignty, and in fact eludes every effort we might make to comprehend, think, know, understand, or even just experience it. It is too easy, I believe, to miss the profundity of this thought by assuming that we understand it, or that, having read Heidegger, or even just Plato's *Phaedo*, we have already allowed ourselves to think the unthinkable, and are thus done, at home, or at peace with it. Not only death, but the mere thought of death – these are not things that one can be done with. Death – and not only our own death, but death, if we can put it this way, as such – is the omnipresent secret organising everything we do, every time we do it. And whether we know it or not, we think it all of the time, or rather at each and every instant, each time for the first time, in horror and in wonder.

I have just two points left me make here. The first one goes to the question of Derrida's relationship with religion and theology, and the supposed 'religious turn' in his later work. The second concerns Derrida's enigmatic and hyperbolic notion, discussed a few times in this chapter, that each single death constitutes the end of the only and entire world ('*toute fin est la fin de tout*', as I put it, aping and playing on Derrida's '*tout autre est tout autre*'). In the first case, I am simply affirming, as I did in my Introduction above, Martin Hägglund's notion that Derrida was a 'radical atheist'. For here, in the final sessions of *The Beast and the Sovereign, Volume 2*, we can see that, while Derrida explores the possibility that *Walten* is something like a god ('Can one pray to *Walten*?', Derrida queries at one point [*BS2* 215]), or a god beyond every onto-theological and metaphysical determination, he nevertheless gives the last word to finitude and death. If *Walten* is god, death is greater than god, and therefore, by every definition of what god means with which I am familiar, god is not god – there is no god.

But we are still left with this question: how could we imagine that each and every death of a unique living creature (in principle, at least, from mitochondria to monkeys to human beings) constitutes, not merely the end of a world, or the world that belonged to them, and that they formed by way of their life, but the end of the only and the entire world? As I suggested earlier, I am not sure I can understand such a claim, either rationally or affectively. But if one could understand it – if one could even begin to think or feel it – then this would certainly suggest that death, whatever else it might be, is greater than the greatest sovereignty, and even greater than the super-sovereignty that Derrida finds Heidegger referring to, from about the time of the 1929–30 seminars onwards, as *Walten*. If death is more than that which makes possible a world (or a notion of the totality of beings or being as such), if death is more than the ontological question of Being (or why is there something rather than nothing?), if it is even more than the nothing or nothingness with which it is often associated, then yes, each and every one of its manifestations would be the end of the only and entire world, or all of the only and entire worlds that we (whoever we are), when doing that thing we call living (whatever that is), inhabit, constitute and compose.

Notes

1　See Derrida, *The Work of Mourning*; Balfour (ed.), Late Derrida, a Special Issue of *The South Atlantic Quarterly*; Mitchell and Davidson, *The Late Derrida*.

2　For a subtle discussion of *Melancholia*, which reads it through the lens of Winnicottian psychoanalysis, see Honig, 'Out Like a Lion: *Melancholia* with Euripides and Winnicott'.

3　See Peeters, *Derrida: A Biography*, 521–2.

Conclusion: Secretions

Mirror Back

The image is Francesca Woodman's, a New York artist who worked in the 1970s and early 1980s, until she killed herself at the age of twenty-two. It is a photographic self-portrait. She is a woman holding a mirror up to her face – a fairly common trope in our artistic tradition, and one with which Woodman often engaged and manipulated throughout her tragically brief career. But the reflective side of the mirror is not directed at her, as we often see in such pictures. Rather, it is directed at us, or whoever happens to be looking at the image. In the mirror, we should see our face, or us looking back at ourselves, narcissistically, no doubt, or confidently self-aware. But we do not see ourselves. Rather, we see her back and the back of her head. In other words, and paradoxically, she faces us with her back turned towards us. She looks out at us looking at her refusing to look at us. Or is that the best and most felicitous interpretation? I am not sure. For, obviously, with the back of the mirror pressed up against her nose, she cannot see us either. We look at her not looking at us, facing forward, with her back to us. Or, perhaps, we somehow occupy her position, turning her back on herself, even as she, or we, are still able to watch her do so. We watch her watch us not watch herself – or ourselves. From her perspective, we look on as she refuses to look. We look as she refuses to look at herself produce this image that we can but cannot see, or that makes us see that we can but cannot see, precisely, her.

I am ripping Woodman's self-portrait out of its context. I am not considering it in relation to either her other works, or the many other works to which it appears to refer, and alongside of which we might seek to make sense of it. Nevertheless, and acknowledging the violence inherent in my gesture, this singular photograph – this instant that is also an instance – does seem to capture much of what I have been trying to articulate in this book. We all look at one another with our backs turned towards one another. And we all see in the mirror, not (or not only) our own face, but also (the back of) another. Every other is every bit other – looking at us by looking away, or engaging with us only in so far as they disengage as well. We are held together by what holds us apart, or by what forever comes in between us, namely a mirror in which we should properly hope to see ourselves. We are nothing but this game of infinite self-reflection (or rather other-reflection), right up until that instant when we die (whatever that might mean, and none of us will ever know). We are all Francesca Woodman on death's door, trying somehow to show (by not showing or refusing to show) someone else who we are (and will never be). Perhaps that is what it means to be alive, and thus already dead, or 'living dead'. But, of course, and again, no one will ever know. For death also holds a mirror up to its face, showing only its back, or the back of another – the one who has already died, tragically, too young, before she had time to say what she could not possibly have known.

In this conclusion, I would like to open up the terrain of my investigations so far, and to begin to compare Derrida's treatment of the secret with that of others – to suggest ways in which various understandings of the secret reflect and fail to reflect one another. I am calling my conclusion 'Secretions' in part because I want to suggest that, while I have focused quite intensely on his thought, what I say cannot be reduced to a commentary on Derrida, or on his body of work, but seeps out of that body as well, and relates it, from the inside, to things that are not contained therein. The more specific reference, however, is to Gilles Deleuze's and Félix Guattari's *A Thousand Plateaus*, in which we can find a brief but important discussion of the secret, in a section called 'Memories of the Secret'. At the crux of this section is the strange notion of 'the secret as secretion'.[1] That is, for Deleuze and Guattari, the secret, like the body, is never fully closed off or self-contained, but always and only exists in relation to its outside, or to its own betrayal or exposition.

In the rest of this section, then, I will discuss Deleuze and Guattari's treatment of the secret, and show how it both fits and does not fit with Derrida's. I maintain, in essence, that Derrida would agree with their definition or conception of the secret; but he would also point out that it is far from exhaustive, and that it ignores or leaves unexplored far more than it illuminates or brings to light. Derrida's primary point of disagreement, however, would probably be over the way Deleuze and Guattari link their discussion of the secret to their larger critique of psychoanalysis, and especially the way they characterise the un-conscious as something that must be created or composed rather than discovered or revealed. Something like this is true, no doubt; but the particular way that Deleuze and Guattari express this claim opens the space for a kind of sovereign subjectivism, voluntarism or even humanism – as though the unconscious were not the register of the signifier, or what Derrida calls the trace, but something that an individual or an assemblage might wilfully and intentionally generate and control.

'Memories of the Secret' appears in the middle of the tenth chapter of *A Thousand Plateaus*, or '1730: Becoming-Intense, Becoming-Animal, Becoming-Imperceptible'. As suggested, it forms part of Deleuze's and Guattari's critique of psychoanalysis, and of the psychoanalytic conception of the unconscious and the Oedipus complex. Its primary thrust is to consider the subject of the secret without submitting to a 'binary machine',[2] or the simple opposition between revelation and concealment. The secret is not merely something hidden that, with proper techniques, might be revealed (which is how Deleuze and Guattari characterise the Freudian unconscious and the Freudian analysis). It is not about the imperceptible as opposed to the perceptible, but instead a becoming-imperceptible. Thus, for Deleuze and Guattari, it is not only the case that the perception or detection of the secret is always part of the structure or operation of the secret (the secret exists, in part, by already being exposed, as in 'the first rule of fight club is never to talk about fight club', or what, above, we called the *Fight Club* problem); it is also the case that this perception or detection will itself be secretive. 'What counts is that the perception of the secret must necessarily be secret itself', Deleuze and Guattari maintain: 'the spy, the voyeur, the blackmailer, the author of anonymous letters are no less secretive than what they are in a position to disclose, regardless of their ulterior motives'.[3]

If it is the case that the secret is already exposed, and that its exposure is itself invariably secretive, it is also the case that the secret circulates and roams even while remaining a secret. As Deleuze and Guattari put it, 'the secret has a way of spreading that is in turn shrouded in secrecy. The secret as secretion. The secret must sneak, insert, or introduce itself into the arena of public forums.'[4] Crucially, then, from Deleuze and Guattari's perspective, the secret is not private in any sense of the word. Indeed, its operation is fundamentally public or, as Deleuze and Guattari also say at this moment in their text, social. 'The secret was invented by society', they write; 'it is a sociological notion. Every secret is a collective assemblage.' Indeed, for Deleuze and Guattari, the secret can never be anything 'static' like a private property. Rather, and now referring to some of their own technical concepts or vocabulary, 'only becomings are secrets'. Which also means that 'the secret has its origins in the war machine; it is the war machine and its becomings-woman, becomings-child, becomings-animal that bring the secret'.[5] That is to say, the secret can only be nomadic. It can never be contained by a fixed and located form. Rather, and in a manner that closely resembles Simmel's work (and in a footnote here, they do refer to Simmel on the secret),[6] Deleuze and Guattari suggest that the content of the secret itself becomes the form, or that the secret involves a collapse of any simple opposition of content and form in a process of interminable becomings (what Manuel De Landa might call a 'flat ontology' of deception).[7]

The rest of Deleuze and Guattari's discussion of the secret is organised around two basic topics: paranoia, on the one hand, and sexual difference, or rather becoming-woman, on the other. In essence, Deleuze and Guattari propose that, once we reject the notion of a secret as something hidden that might be revealed (or the 'binary machine', as we saw above), and try to think of it instead in terms of becomings, we also shift, in more psychoanalytic terms, from 'hysterical childhood content' to 'virile paranoid form'.[8] That is to say, analysis can no longer be about exposing a childhood trauma (that is itself related to and structured by the Oedipus complex). It now must reckon with the eternal semiosis, or the unending signifying chain, of the paranoid mind – a mind that, as soon as one claims to have exposed a hidden truth that is the cause for its symptomatic belief in a fantastic conspiracy, absorbs that supposed truth back into the conspiracy. As Deleuze and Guattari put it, the paranoid mind might be seen to operate in one of two ways. 'On the one hand', they write, 'paranoids denounce the international plot of those who steal their secret . . . or they declare that they have the gift of perceiving the secrets of others'. Here the model of the secret as concealment and revelation retains some force. 'On the other hand', however, 'paranoics act by means of, or else suffer from, rays they emit or receive . . . Influence by rays, and doubling by flight or echo, are what now give the secret its infinite form, in which perceptions as well as actions pass into imperceptibility.'[9]

On Deleuze and Guattari's account, this shift from the 'hysterical childhood content' to the 'virile paranoid form' has profound consequences for analysis. For what it amounts to is the affirmation of analysis without endpoint or goal. 'Interminable analysis', as Deleuze and Guattari write. And, in turn, this means that 'the Unconscious' gets 'assigned the increasingly difficult task of itself being the infinite form of secrecy, instead of a simple box containing secrets'.[10] With the shift from the hysteric to the paranoid, we leave behind the model where there is some traumatic truth hidden behind the neurotic symptom, and adopt instead one where the revelation of secrets is bottomless and infinite. And what this means in practice, Deleuze and Guattari appear to be saying, or in the clinical practice of psychoanalysis, is an elevation of the unconscious to a pure form of secrecy, and thus a hyperbolic emphasis, not on the experiences of the analysand, but on the formal categories of psychoanalysis itself, and especially the Oedipus complex. But the analysand comes to recognise this secret rather quickly. She gets savvy, we might say. And her engagement with psychoanalytic categories gets absorbed into her symptoms, rendering the whole process ineffectual and obsolete. 'The news travels fast that the secret of men is nothing', Deleuze and Guattari go on to explain, 'in truth nothing at all. Oedipus, the phallus, castration, "the splinter in the flesh" – that was the secret? It is enough to make women, children, lunatics, and molecules laugh.'[11]

This is where Deleuze and Guattari begin to discuss becoming-woman. One way of understanding the move from the hysteric to the psychotic, or hidden childhood trauma to infinite semiosis or becoming, would be to view it as the end of the secret as such, or of the category of the secret. For, as it turns out, in psychoanalysis, there is nothing to hide, and nothing has ever been hidden. For Deleuze and Guattari, however, this would be a mistake. Despite the shift from hidden content to infinite semiosis, Deleuze and Guattari claim, 'the secret does not as a result disappear'. However, 'it does take on' what they call 'a more feminine status' (and here, parenthetically at least, we must point out that Deleuze and Guattari are talking about analytic categories and not fixed gender identities, and that, for them, there is no sexual identity as such, only sexual becomings). So Deleuze and Guattari wonder at how, unlike men, it is possible for a woman to 'be secretive while at the same time hiding nothing'. This is possible because of what Deleuze and Guattari call 'celerity' or speed as opposed to 'gravity'. 'Men adopt a grave attitude', Deleuze and Guattari propose, 'knights of the secret'. They put on display the burden they must carry because of the secret they must keep, betraying their secret in the process. Thus, and as Deleuze and Guattari put it, 'they end up telling everything – and it turns out to be nothing'. Women, however, are entirely different. They 'tell everything, sometimes in appalling technical detail, but one knows no more at the end than at the beginning'.[12]

As I mentioned above, much of what Deleuze and Guattari say about the secret resonates with Derrida's work on the subject. In particular, the notion that the secret is already shared, that it is a secretion, and that it is not a private but a social phenomenon, sits very well alongside everything I have been trying to explore in this book, and perhaps especially alongside Derrida's notion, as expressed in 'How to Avoid Speaking', for example, that 'there is no secret', or no secret 'as such' (given that part of the structure of the secret is its already having been shared or exposed). At the same time, and as I noted a moment ago, I am sure that Derrida would suggest that this brief section in *A Thousand Plateaus* on the secret is far from exhaustive, and that what it overlooks or avoids is as interesting as what it addresses. For example, there is here no discussion of the lie (and thus the problem of intention or intentionality), or of the relationship between the lie and perjury (and thus the law), or of the oath, or of the relationship between the history of the secret and that of the sacred, or religion in general, and so forth. Derrida would also likely propose a subtler approach at many points, perhaps especially with respect to the question of sexual difference, which Deleuze and Guattari discuss in a fairly cavalier manner, as if their own positions (or becomings, if you prefer) had no bearing on what they were saying (or doing, in the performative mode).

But I think the more pressing issue for Derrida would be the treatment here of psychoanalysis, and especially the psycho-analytic concept of the unconscious. First of all, and as I think we could even get a contemporary Deleuzo-Guattarian to agree, the characterisation of Freudian analysis at this point is little more than a straw-person. Freud most certainly did not create or propagate a conception of the unconscious as simply a hidden content that, once exposed, would alleviate the painful symptom. Quite the contrary, Freud was fully aware of the fact that the analytic session itself in part constitutes the unconscious thought, and that the complex process of transference between the analyst and the analysand cannot be divorced from the history or experience or dreams (or whatever) being explored. Moreover, and more importantly, at crucial moments in their discussion of the secret and becoming-imperceptible (and doubtless elsewhere as well), Deleuze and Guattari appear to trade the Freudian unconscious (with what they take to be its hidden desires that must be revealed, all of which are organised around the Oedipal drama) for an unconscious that can be actively constructed or created – as if by a subject, or an agent, or perhaps an assemblage that comes to make up such a thing.

A good example of this tendency can be found just before Deleuze and Guattari consider the secret in 'Memories of the Secret'. Thus, while discussing becoming-imperceptible, they once again challenge what they take to be Freud's basic distinction between the unconscious and the conscious, or 'the perception-consciousness system'. This 'dualism machine' is designed, they seem to suggest, to separate the experience of affect in the present from the unconscious desires or traumas being revealed by the analyst. 'Everything is different on the plane of consistency or immanence', Deleuze and Guattari write, 'which is necessarily perceived in its own right in the course of its construction.' That is to say, the unconscious is not merely discovered in analysis; it is actively created there. Here 'experimentation replaces interpretation' and 'the unconscious no longer designates the hidden principle of the transcendent plane of organisation, but the process of the immanent plane of consistency as it appears on itself in the course of its construction'. And then, finally, to hammer the point home: 'For the unconscious must be constructed, not discovered.'[13]

I think in terms of psychoanalytic or even just psychological practice, there is a great deal to be said for this line of thought. One could imagine very different kinds of sessions based on them – one where the analyst-father was dismantled, in favour of collective assemblages and experiments. At the same time, and as I think Derrida would point out as well, Deleuze and Guattari are presenting a rather truncated or simplified version of the unconscious. It never was, for Freud or any other serious thinker, simply the hidden truth of the symptom. But it is tricky, or a seat of trickery. It conceals, distorts, confuses, transfers, obstructs, and a thousand other things. And it would be able to do this, even when one thought one was constructing rather than interpreting or exposing it. To put the point differently, what Deleuze and Guattari say might hold if we think exclusively in terms of the signifier. But it does not if we adopt Derrida's language, and think in terms of the trace. As Derrida says, and as we discussed much earlier in this book, when considering one of his engagements with Lacan, it is the nature of the trace, not to be effaced or exposed by something else, or some outside agent, but to efface itself. It is, as it were, always already concealed, and that concealment or effacement is a condition of its ever being revealed.

In my discussion of Deleuze and Guattari I have, I hope, established the agenda of this conclusion – namely, to let my work on Derrida's secret secrete a little, or spill out into discussions of other thinkers who have taken up the issue, and to relate some of what they say to Derrida's work. In the next section, I want to continue with this project by discussing and comparing the work of Carl Schmitt, Hannah Arendt and Georges Bataille. I will use these three thinkers to set up a kind of interpretation machine for the secret, or a secret-machine, if you will. The stakes here will be particularly political, as all three consider the secret in relation to the problem of the sovereign, and the relationship between sovereignty and dissimulation. What they all miss, however, is what I attempted to examine here and there throughout the four chapters of this book, and especially towards the very end – namely, the possibility of a secrecy that exceeds the order of the sovereign. In the next and final section of this Conclusion, I will turn my attention briefly towards Giorgio Agamben. Here I will take issue with Derrida's own rather dismissive comments on Agamben in *The Beast and the Sovereign, Volume 1*, and try to suggest instead some more robust connections and differences between their work, especially with respect to the concept of the oath. But first, Schmitt, Arendt and Bataille.

Secret Machine

In 1938 (a significant date, no doubt), Carl Schmitt published a short book called *The Leviathan and the State Theory of Thomas Hobbes: Meaning and Failure of a Political Symbol*. Prior to this text, Schmitt rarely missed an opportunity to praise Hobbes, or at least his own particular interpretation of Hobbes, which was organised around the dictum '*auctoritas, non veritas facit legem*' – authority and not truth makes law. But here, the emphasis is on the failure mentioned in the subtitle. Essentially, Schmitt argues that Hobbes's leviathan state failed in so far as it lost the personal sovereign, or the specifically political figure at its core, and thus degenerated into a state apparatus that could be occupied and operated by any number of non-political interests. So long as the Hobbesian sovereign remained specifically political, and not the representation of non-political interests, it was a 'mortal god who brings peace and security' and 'an irresistible instrument of quietude' with 'all objective and subjective rights on its side'. But in the absence of that political authority, the leviathan state became a 'technically neutral instrument' that could fall into the hands of 'the most varied political constellations', or parties that might 'carry out their actions under the guise of something other than politics – namely religion, culture, economy and private matters – and still derive the advantages of state'.[14] Thus the state might be run by the self-proclaimed representatives of the working class or by a cabal of religious zealots or by a collection of free-market economists; for Schmitt, it all amounts to the same thing, namely an erasure of what is specifically political, and thus a reduction of politics to struggles over essentially non-political concerns.

Setting aside for a moment the question of which non-political interests or concerns erroneously wielding the political power of the state Schmitt might have had in mind in 1938, we must consider just how, on his account, Hobbes's personal sovereign lost or forfeited its position. In this respect, Schmitt is quite explicit. Hobbes's error, and the reason for the failure of his leviathan, was his willingness to allow for a distinction between public power and private right, especially with respect to religion. In short, Hobbes questioned religious freedom only when it resulted in turmoil in the public realm. Otherwise, one's inward beliefs could be left relatively untouched by the leviathan. This, for Schmitt, was Hobbes's singular mistake. For its consequence was the composition of an inner world, or a distinction between the inner and the outer, that threatened the leviathan's authority, and thus amplified the distinction between personal (or group) interest and pubic order. 'When political power wants to be only public', Schmitt writes, 'when state and confession drive inner belief into a private domain, the soul of a people betakes itself on the "secret road" that leads inward.' And, on Schmitt's account, this process invariably results in the 'emergence of a distinction between inner and outer that becomes for the mortal god a sickness unto death'.[15]

We can, without betraying the spirit of Schmitt's argument, articulate this set of claims in a slightly different way. For Schmitt, the Hobbesian leviathan failed because it failed to establish what, earlier, I referred as a monopoly, not just on violence, but on secrecy as well. Of course the leviathan, as part of its absolute public authority, has the right, and quite frequently the responsibility, to keep secrets, both from external enemies and from internal subjects. 'To every great politics', Schmitt writes in his earlier but here relevant book on *Roman Catholicism and Political Form*, 'belongs the "*arcanum*"'.[16] Indeed, without such secrecy, there is, for Schmitt, no way for political order to transcend or remain detached from the eternal competition of non-political interests that it must both protect and restrain. But, as the text on Hobbes indicates, there can be no reciprocal right to secrecy among those whom the sovereign governs. Indeed, the possibility for secrecy among the governed, or the 'distinction between the inner and the outer' that allows for such a thing, constitutes a 'sickness unto death' for sovereign power.[17] Only the sovereign right to secrecy ensures that its political power transcends non-political interests. And the private right to the same secrecy can only result in a breeding ground for those interests, or a breeding ground for the assumption that there might be a politics that, rather than monopolising all right, articulates directly one particular right, or one particular set of essentially non-political positions or claims.

This Schmittian conception of the sovereign as a monopoly on secrecy might be fruitfully counterpoised to arguments articulated by Hannah Arendt in her posthumously published lectures on 'Some Questions of Moral Responsibility' (lectures that were originally delivered at the New School for Social Research in 1965, in the wake of the controversy sparked by Arendt's *Eichmann in Jerusalem: A Report on the Banality of Evil*). The gesture in these lectures is, in a sense, to provide a depiction, not of the banality of evil, but of the exceptional nature of good. Against a long tradition that suggests we understand morality in terms of our relationships with others, Arendt insists that, in fact, it concerns first and foremost our relationship with ourselves. Morality, Arendt argues, is organised around the Socratic proposition that 'it is better to be at odds with the whole world than, being one, to be at odds with myself'.[18] The moral person, that is to say, is not the one who treats others in a certain manner, either according to the standards of an absolute duty or according to conventional mores; rather, the moral person is one who refuses to live in contradiction with herself. To recall the phrase from ancient philosophy that I mentioned in the Introduction (and that, as is well known, fascinated Michel Foucault in his later work as well), morality is first and foremost a question of 'care for self'.[19]

For the same reason, Arendt insists on a rather rigid distinction between politics and morality or politics and ethics. For Arendt, politics is concerned with action, or with the capacity to create something new through engagement with others. In so far as it involves relating to oneself, or care for self, morality, on the other hand, 'has nothing whatsoever to do with action'. Indeed, Arendt suggests that, 'politically speaking', morality 'is irresponsible'. And this is so because, unlike politics, 'its standard is the self and not the world'.[20] At the same time, Arendt continues, there is one sense in which morality has political consequence, or one manner in which it relates to the political. Specifically, on Arendt's account, 'morality is politically relevant only in times of crisis', or when, as happened during the Nazi regime, political action gets displaced by criminal violence. The 'self' of morality 'is politically a kind of emergency measure', Arendt maintains. It is 'important only in exceptional circumstances'. It applies in what Arendt calls 'borderline situations'.[21] While the immoral person, such as Eichmann, adapts thoughtlessly to the criminal situation, the moral self, unable to live in contradiction with herself, does not, thus constituting a bulwark, however small, against the spread of evil.

Now, while she does not make the connection explicit, it is, I would suggest, hardly accidental that when Arendt describes the significance of the moral self in times of political crisis (or what, elsewhere, she calls 'dark times') she adopts the language of the sovereign exception. Thus the self is, in her words, an 'emergency measure' that applies in 'exceptional circumstances'. Indeed, in speaking about 'borderline situations', Arendt even appears to be indirectly referencing Schmitt, whose work she knew quite well, and who, in his *Political Theology*, speaks of the sovereign exception as a 'borderline concept [*Grenzbegriff*]' in that it applies to the 'outermost sphere' of political existence.[22] The implication is partly ironic, as elsewhere Arendt makes it very clear that she rejects that concept of sovereignty, and even believes that it should be expelled from political discourse. Thus, in her essay 'What is Freedom?', for example, Arendt associates sovereignty with the commanding will of the internally unified subject (whether individual or collective), which she opposes to the plurality of positions and debates that properly constitute the political sphere, and political freedom in particular. 'If men wish to be free', Arendt writes in that essay, 'it is precisely sovereignty they must renounce.'[23] Nevertheless, it seems clear that, for Arendt, the moral self, or the inner world that will not live in contradiction with itself, operates as a kind of sovereign exception – not a figure of exceptional violence, but one, as it were, of exceptional passivity.

We have, then, two different understandings of the political significance of inner life, and thus one possibility of the secret. Or, more accurately, we have two different evaluations of the same understanding. For Schmitt, private secrecy represents a threat to sovereign authority, which should properly enforce a monopoly on secrecy. For Arendt, on the other hand, it *is* the sovereign authority, or the only sense in which anything like a sovereign exception should play any role in political life whatsoever. That is to say, while for Schmitt the sovereign must exclude private secrecy, for Arendt, private secrecy operates as the last line of defence against an authority that endeavours to be total. And if Schmitt thinks that secrecy is ultimately a breeding ground for non-political interests, or for efforts on the part of non-political interests to appropriate the apparatus of the state, Arendt thinks of it as the space of morality, or the possibility of a form of life that exceeds both the agonism and glory of the public sphere, on the one side, and the instrumental functionality of the private one, on the other. On the one hand secrecy and inner life are the first steps in the direction of crass self-interest;

on the other, they are the first steps in the direction of morality, ethics and care for self.

Of course, this opposition between Schmitt and Arendt by no means exhausts the possibilities of secrecy, and the manner in which it configures the relationship between inner life and politics. Indeed, if only for heuristic purposes, it is helpful at this moment to add a third voice to this hypothetical conversation, namely that of Georges Bataille. Inasmuch as he also addresses the problem of sovereignty, and has a predilection for exceptional states, Bataille is often, and I think incorrectly, represented as a kind of left-wing version of Schmitt – 'left fascism', as Richard Wolin succinctly puts it in the title of his essay on the topic.[24] But it is precisely with respect to the question of the secret that we can draw a definitive line between Schmitt and Bataille, and between the former's concern with the exception and the latter's fascination with transgression. If, for Schmitt, the secret is necessarily a state secret, and thus kept in the interests of some state-determined end (specifically, or at least typically, security), for Bataille, the secret should properly serve no external ends, but instead be preserved as a kind of end in itself, or rather a pure means without end. For those not familiar with Bataille's work, this probably sounds a little odd, so I will now explain.

As Wolin and others are correct to note, Bataille like Schmitt was fascinated with the question of sovereignty. But Bataille explicitly sets out to distinguish that concept from other political issues, or from any other determinate political institution of a programme. 'Sovereignty', Bataille maintains, 'has little to do with the sovereignty of states, as international law defines it.'[25] While, in the past, some cultures or societies might have latched onto this 'aspect', and organised power structures around it, what actually defines sovereignty, Bataille maintains, or what distinguishes the servile from the sovereign, is not a particular social relation, political position or legal status, but an experience of time. While it is always servile 'to employ the present time for the sake of the *future*', Bataille says, it is always sovereign to 'enjoy the present time without having anything else in view than the present time'. Or, to put the same point in different terms, 'life beyond *utility* is the domain of sovereignty'.[26]

Bataille's examples of such 'life beyond utility' are notorious, and probably the sort of thing most frequently associated with his name – excess, waste, expenditure, eroticism, sacrifice, intoxication, violence, and ultimately and perhaps most importantly, death. But, as Bataille never ceased to point out, because these experiences or phenomena are 'beyond utility', they are also, in a sense, beyond discourse and language. They thus constitute a kind of secret – something unknowable, because it cannot be reduced to the vehicle of knowledge. As Bataille puts it, 'knowledge is never given to us except by an *unfolding in time*'. It requires 'a *discourse*, which is necessarily deployed in duration'. Consequently, 'to know is always to strive, to work'. It is always 'a servile operation, indefinitely resumed, indefinitely repeated'.[27] For this reason, knowledge is 'never sovereign', for 'to be *sovereign* it would have to occur in a moment'. The only way to approximate sovereignty in knowledge, or approximate some representation of it, would be via something Bataille calls 'unknowing', or by 'cancelling . . . every operation of knowledge within ourselves'.[28]

Bataille's secret is, then, in some sense absolute. Enigmatically, impossibly, it is somehow kept even from those who keep it. It attempts to designate everything that exceeds, not only this or that discourse, but discourse and exchange in general. Efforts might be made to arrive at (or at least get closer to) it through the cultivation of secrecy in the conventional sense – that is, two or more parties entering into a pact, or agreeing to conceal something from someone else. Indeed, Bataille himself is known to have participated in any number of such secret societies, most notably the *Acéphale* group, who are sometimes rumoured to have planned (but never executed) the sacrifice of one of their members (and Bataille himself was probably the one to have put his neck on the line). But these sorts of games cannot capture or contain the absolute secrecy that Bataille intends. If Schmitt's secret is shared by those in power, and Arendt's is shared, in a sense, only with oneself, Bataille's secret almost cannot be shared, but is instead a singularity that eludes the very notion of the share. It is thus an experience of the pure event, one that might be personal or collective, but one that also cannot enter into language, or be characterised as a means to any further end. It is an end in itself, or a means without end. It is both. And it is neither.

A Hidden Pact

Despite all of their many differences, then, and despite the very different ways that they conceive of secrecy in particular, Schmitt, Arendt and Bataille all appear to associate it with sovereignty, and with the enigmatic or extraordinary figure of the sovereign. Secrecy is thus a feature of the sovereign exception, whether we understand that in terms of the personal leviathan at the head of the state, or the moral individual who excludes themselves from a criminal political order, or the voluptuously transgressive deviant who acts with no concern for the future, and thus eludes any logic of discourse or explanation. As we have seen throughout this book, Derrida certainly understands secrecy in all of these ways as well. But he also posits something like a secrecy that exceeds the sovereign. And, while we have to be very careful of jumping to conclusions, or believing that we have comprehended this point simply because we have been informed of it, Derrida associates this secrecy beyond sovereignty with death – a death, however, that cannot be represented simply in terms of the end of life, or that cannot simply be located at the end of something called life, but that instead is an omnipresent aspect of life, informing all of its elements, and each of its instances. Derrida's conception of the secret is, therefore, simply more profound and extensive than the ones we find in Deleuze and Guattari, Schmitt, Arendt and Bataille. And this is so, not because of any superior capacity on Derrida's part, but merely because he opens the question of the secret up in a more extensive manner, and links it to significantly more alternative questions, problems and themes.

That said, there is one theorist who, in my estimation, at least keeps pace with Derrida on a number of these themes. I am thinking, as I suggested above, about Agamben. In the opening section of the third chapter of this book, I made a brief reference to Agamben's *The Kingdom and the Glory*, and to his concept of the 'bi-polar machine' of sovereignty and governance, which I related to so-called neo-liberalism, and to what I dubbed the deregulating regulation of politics and law today. I also pointed out that an entire, and entirely different, book could be written on Agamben's thought and the question of the secret. I proposed that such a book might begin by considering, not only what Agamben has to say about the secret (or what he sometimes calls 'the enigma'),[29] but also by tracing the way his rhetoric, his writing and his thought put the secret to work. As anyone who has read even a few pages of Agamben will know, he has a predilection for hermeticism and the arcane. His texts typically operate by feigning to reveal a heretofore unknown or unnoticed moment buried deeply in our intellectual tradition, and showing how attention to this moment suddenly casts the present in an entirely new light, forcing us to rethink the most basic assumptions we make about ourselves and our world.

This is a rhetorical ploy that, in the 'Third Session' and the 'Eleventh Session' of *The Beast and the Sovereign, Volume 1*, Derrida attacks, and attacks in a manner that, in my estimation, is rather dismissive, reactive, and even a little unjust. Focusing on Agamben's *Homo Sacer: Sovereign Power and Bare Life*, Derrida basically maintains that Agamben's style is itself an assertion of sovereign power – indeed, according to Derrida, the most classical, and perhaps the crassest, mode of that power. I will not explore the entirety of this episode here, but in essence, Derrida provides a quick synopsis of *Homo Sacer*, and goes on to critique Agamben's penchant for pretending to uncover a secret history underneath the dominant history of western metaphysics or philosophy as 'his most irrepressible gesture', or the primary characteristic of his argumentation. 'I point this out with a smile', Derrida tells his students, 'only to recall that this is the very definition, vocation, or essential claim of sovereignty' (*BS1* 92). That is to say, for Derrida, the essential claim of sovereignty is the claim to possess arcane but nevertheless determinate and essential knowledge.

This, I think, is not Derrida at his best. In fact, it may even be him at his worst. And it does suggest one thing we must be cautious of when reading the seminars. In my Introduction above, I speculated that, in a sense, the seminars are probably seminal to the later Derrida, and that they probably contain what, from the perspective of the publications alone, can look like an otherwise missing project or body of work. I will not back down from this speculation. But I will note that, when reading Derrida's seminars, we must always be aware of the genre and the context at hand. These are unpolished and unfinished pieces, written for spoken presentation, and thus more than a little spontaneous. And, while he was obviously very profound, Derrida was also a person and an academic like any other, and thus prone to all of the jealousies and antagonisms that characterise academic life. If his students were discussing Agamben, and he wanted them to remain focused on what he is saying, Derrida was obviously capable of trying to brush Agamben aside in a few words, or dismissing rather than genuinely dealing with his work. And, it seems to me, something like that is going on at this point in his text. So if we are going to take the seminars seriously, we will need to be on guard, as it were, for these kinds of moments, and to try to sift through the apparently petty stuff in search of the more important arguments and debates.

Now, to be clear, one could certainly take what Derrida says in the 'Third Session' and the 'Eleventh Session' of *The Beast and the Sovereign, Volume 1*, and use those comments as the basis of a robust contrast between Derrida and Agamben. In my opinion, my former colleague Amy Swiffen has done a commendable job of this in her paper 'Derrida Contra Agamben: Sovereignty, Biopower, History'. Here, however, I want to propose a slightly different approach. Leaving aside Derrida's explicit comments on Agamben, I want to compare their respective treatments of just one topic related to the secret – a topic that I explored in some detail in the opening chapter of this book, namely the oath. The work I am doing here in the last section of my Conclusion is decidedly preparatory, and by no means systematic or exhaustive. I will simply want to try to show that, in his work on the oath (which we find in a short book, and one element of the larger, multi-volume *Homo Sacer* project, called *The Sacrament of Language: An Archeology of the Oath*), Agamben appears to be departing from Derrida in both senses of the word – that is, both relying on and escaping from Derrida's influence. And even if this is not bibliographically true (even if Agamben in fact is not thinking about Derrida at all in this text), we can certainly read and try to make sense of it in that fashion.

I have here, then, two tasks. First, I will briefly reiterate Derrida's theory of the oath, which I set out in detail in the first chapter. Then, I will provide an analysis of Agamben's *Sacrament of Language*, and of the alternative approach to the oath that Agamben sets out there. As we will see, while I think that Agamben's approach to the oath contrasts quite explicitly (and perhaps even intentionally) with Derrida's, I also think that Agamben's conclusions concerning the oath have real affinities with what Derrida says about testimony and the kind of subjective truth (or more accurately, singular truth, or a truth beyond objectively verifiable truth and falsehood) that, on Derrida's account, testimony entails.

For Derrida, as you will recall, the oath is something like a prior condition of any interaction or relation. It is grounded in this insight that 'every other is every bit other'. Put simply, because we cannot see inside one another's heads, every time we say anything at all, or even just exchange a glance, we are compelled to ask the other to believe that what we are saying is what we genuinely believe. And, conversely, when we are the addressee, or the subject of an address, we are compelled to believe that the other is saying what they believe as well. Even someone who wants to deceive the other, or to betray their trust, relies on this exchange of belief, or what I called this act of faith. The oath, then, is already there, in advance of anything anyone says at any time to anyone at all. It structures and even makes possible all of our relations with one another, from the moment those relations begin.

In many ways, Agamben's *The Sacrament of Language* appears to be designed to take aim at precisely this conception of the oath. Unlike Derrida, whose concept of the oath is very abstract, and refers to a kind of *a priori* condition of interaction and exchange, Agamben approaches it more anthropologically, in terms of the history and the operation of the specific and concrete act of swearing to god. The argument in *The Sacrament of Language* takes shape in opposition to what Agamben characterises as a long scholarly tradition (central to anthropology, linguistics and philology, as well as legal and religious history) that treats the oath as a remedy for the fact that language is ambiguous, and that humans have the capacity to lie. For Agamben, this long and consistent tradition locates the origin of the oath in a 'magico-religious' stage in human history, or a time when humans genuinely feared divine retribution. It thus relies on what he calls the 'scientific mythologeme' of 'the primordiality of the sacred',[30] or the myth that human history proceeds from a primitive belief in the reality of the sacred realm to an increasingly rational juridical and scientific codification of that belief.

According to Agamben, however, this theory is a mistake. On his account, religion, law and science have always comingled in human history. Or, at any rate, we cannot understand human history in terms of progressive stages, where we move from the first, through the second, to the last. Thus it is of no use to try to conceive of the oath as a remnant of a primitive age, or to assume that the gods that it invokes originally functioned as omniscient witnesses who would punish anyone who deigned to speak falsely, or say something that they themselves did not genuinely believe. To swear to god is not to fear god's power or reprisal. Rather, Agamben proposes, it is to invoke, and even to partake of, the, as it were, godlike power of language itself, or the power that language has to name the world. The oath, in other words, is not what Agamben calls a 'sacrament of power'; it is what he calls 'a sacrament of language'.[31]

The simplest way of explaining what Agamben means here is to say that, for him, the oath is a speech act, or a performative rather than a constative statement. In other words, irrespective of the truth or falsehood of what I say while under oath, the oath itself, or the act of swearing, refers to nothing other than itself, or that very act. Thus, Agamben claims, it 'cannot be contested or verified in any way'. Rather, it 'coincides with the call and is accomplished and extinguished together with it'.[32] Or, to put the same point in slightly different terms, in the oath as in the speech act, the expression and its referent are consubstantial. There is an immediate connection between the world of language on the one hand and that of actions or things on the other. Thus, and once again in opposition to the traditional understanding, the oath is not designed to compensate for a gap between words and things, or an abyss that separates signifier and signified. Rather, as a pure performance, or pure performative, it allows these two registers to come into being simultaneously. And in this sense the oath 'concerns not the verification of a fact or an event but the very signifying power of language'. It testifies, not to a particular state or affairs, but to what Agamben calls 'the positive force of language', or 'that which unites words and things'.[33]

Agamben elaborates on this point by way of an important digression on the problem of naming god, which is typically characterised in terms of representing the unrepresentable, but which Agamben associates with the speech act as well. Referring to the nineteenth-century philologist Hermann Usener's 1896 monograph *Götternamen* or 'the name of god', Agamben maintains that 'all the names of the gods are initially names of actions or brief events'. Or, as he says a little later: 'the god who presides over the singular activity and the singular situation is nothing other than the very name of the activity and the situation'.[34] Originally, then, to name a god is to name an activity or event, such that the god, its name (or its being named) and the activity or event itself are effectively one, and cannot be separated out. The shift in human society from polytheism to monotheism serves to abstract or formalise this naming process. That is to say, with the emergence of monotheism, 'the potentially infinite dissemination of singular, divine events of naming gives way to the divinization of the logos as such' or 'to the name of God as archi-event of language that takes place in names'.[35] What we mean by god, in other words, is not the unrepresentable, or that which cannot be named. Rather, god is the act of naming – the event of language that, again, miraculously unites words and things. In effect, god is invoked in the oath because god is the oath, or the kind of speech that the oath entails.

It would appear, then, that Agamben's conception of the oath differs from Derrida's. We might even conjecture that *The Sacrament of Language* contains a kind of esoteric critique of Derrida. For one thing, the proposition that the oath entails the power of language to unify, or simultaneously bring into being, words and things, or signifiers and signifieds, clearly challenges the structuralist conception of semiotics, where the meaning of a sign is given, not by reference to the world, but by its difference from other signs – a notion that, because of his engagement with it in his early work, many assume Derrida adopts as well. But more importantly, and like the anthropologists Agamben challenges, Derrida does seem to suggest that the oath has something to do with the ambiguity of language, and the fact that we can have no certain or direct perception of what another person genuinely thinks or believes; whereas, for Agamben, the oath involves something else entirely – namely the unambiguous power of language to constitute a world.

Whether it is intentional and esoteric or unintentional but still instructive (and here it is worth noting in passing that we will never know, a point that goes in Derrida's favour), the opposition between Agamben and Derrida becomes even sharper when Agamben begins to consider what he calls the 'peculiar virtue' of human as opposed to animal language. For Agamben, this 'peculiar virtue' is not found 'in the tool itself', or in human language's instrumental capacity to communicate with others or represent the world. Rather, it is to be found 'in the place it leaves the speaker' or 'the ethical relation that is established between the speaker and his language'. As Agamben puts it, 'the human being is that living being that, in order to speak, must say "I", must take the word, assume it and make it his own'.[36] The peculiar virtue of human language, then, is the sense in which it implicates the speaker herself in the truth of what she says, or the sense in which, every time we speak, and even when we speak falsely, we are investing our subjectivity, indeed our very being, in the truth of what we say. It concerns, in other words, a particular relationship between the subject and truth – one in which the subject does not merely represent the world, but discloses it, or calls it forth into being, or rather is the event of being.

While I am certain such a project would be fruitful, this is not the place to begin an engagement with Agamben's treatment of the animal, and the way that it differs from Derrida's.[37] Rather, I want to consider what Derrida might say about the conception of the 'I', or the relationship between subjectivity and truth, that Agamben gestures towards in this passage. I think he would agree that, whenever a subject speaks, and even when they speak falsely, they invest themselves in their statement. As we have seen numerous times, for Derrida, to speak or engage with another at all is always already to have sworn an oath, or promised to say what you believe and believe what the other says. But, and as we have also seen numerous times, it is also always and already to have broken that oath, and to have broken it in the very act of taking or swearing it. Indeed, for Derrida, I can be accountable for what I say, and I can give an account of myself (to another or to myself) only because what I say might not be what I believe, or on the condition that my speech might be false. To be sure, the oath is like a speech act – curiously, perhaps, an often silent or unspoken speech act that binds me to the other precisely in so far as it separates me from her as well. But it is also constitutively unfulfilled, or split at the point of origin. And this is not something that happens to it by accident, or something that haunts it as a future possibility or potential. It is part of what it means to take the oath, and thus to speak, to engage, or to interact in any manner whatsoever.

For Derrida, then, and to repeat what I have said many times in the course of this book, we always share precisely that which divides us. We are always held together in so far as we are held apart – not only from others, but from ourselves as well. I can only be 'I' in so far as I am held apart from myself – an enigma or a secret to myself. Or, as Derrida puts it in *Monolingualism of the Other*, every identity consists of a '*disorder of identity* [trouble d'identité]' (*MO* 14). And this disorder – this secret, I want to say – is precisely what opens the space for both identification and relation, both the self and the other. And this is true, arguably, not only for humans, and not only for language, but for everything that leaves a trace, every time a trace is left. Moreover, it does not stop happening once a sentence is complete or an engagement fulfilled. It starts happening before the sentence begins, and, in equal measure, it starts after it is complete. It survives into an indefinite future yet to come. And this principle holds, not only for sentences, but for any relation – be it seducing a Queen, testifying in front of the Senate Intelligence Committee, addressing one's students in an academic seminar, responding to an animal, encountering a poem, or, indeed, writing a book.

Notes

1 Deleuze and Guattari, *A Thousand Plateaus*, 317.
2 Deleuze and Guattari, *A Thousand Plateaus*, 316.
3 Deleuze and Guattari, *A Thousand Plateaus*, 316.
4 Deleuze and Guattari, *A Thousand Plateaus*, 317.
5 Deleuze and Guattari, *A Thousand Plateaus*, 317.
6 Deleuze and Guattari, *A Thousand Plateaus*, 681.
7 See De Landa, *Intensive Science and Virtual Philosophy*.
8 Deleuze and Guattari, *A Thousand Plateaus*, 318.
9 Deleuze and Guattari, *A Thousand Plateaus*, 318.
10 Deleuze and Guattari, *A Thousand Plateaus*, 318.
11 Deleuze and Guattari, *A Thousand Plateaus*, 319.
12 Deleuze and Guattari, *A Thousand Plateaus*, 319.
13 Deleuze and Guattari, *A Thousand Plateaus*, 313.
14 Schmitt, *The Leviathan and the State Theory of Thomas Hobbes*, 74.
15 Schmitt, *Leviathan*, 61.
16 Schmitt, *Roman Catholicism and Political Form*, 34.
17 Schmitt, *Leviathan*, 74.
18 Arendt, 'Some Questions of Moral Responsibility', in *Responsibility and Judgment*, 100.

19 See Foucault's *The Hermeneutics of the Subject: Lectures at the Collége de France, 1981–1982*.

20 Arendt, 'Some Questions', 79.

21 Arendt. 'Some Questions', 106.

22 Schmitt, *Political Theology*, 5.

23 Arendt, 'What is Freedom?', in *Between Past and Future*, 165.

24 See Wolin, *The Seduction of Unreason: The Intellectual Romance with Fascism from Nietzsche to Postmodernism*, 153, and Jay, 'The Limits of Limit-Experience: Bataille and Foucault'. For a critique of this approach to Bataille, see Barbour, 'The Sovereign Without Domain: Georges Bataille and the Ethics of Nothing'.

25 Bataille, *The Accursed Share: An Essay on General Economy, Volume 1, Consumption*, 197.

26 Bataille, *The Accursed Share*, 198.

27 Bataille, *The Accursed Share*, 201.

28 Bataille, *The Accursed Share*, 200.

29 See Agamben, *Stanzas: Word and Phantasm in Western Culture*, 138.

30 Agamben, *The Sacrament of Language: An Archaeology of the Oath*.

31 Agamben, *The Sacrament*, 71.

32 Agamben, *The Sacrament*, 33.

33 Agamben, *The Sacrament*, 34.

34 Agamben, *The Sacrament*, 46.

35 Agamben, *The Sacrament*, 49.

36 Agamben, *The Sacrament*, 71.

37 See Agamben, *The Open: Man and Animal*.

Bibliography

Works by Jacques Derrida

Acts of Religion, ed. G. Anidjar (New York: Routledge, 2002).

Adieu to Emmanuel Levinas, trans. P.-A. Brault and M. Naas (Stanford: Stanford University Press, 1999).

The Animal That Therefore I Am, trans. D. Wills (New York: Fordham University Press, 2008).

Aporias, trans. T. Dutoit (Stanford: Stanford University Press, 1996).

Archive Fever, trans. E. Prenowitz (Chicago: University of Chicago Press, 1996).

The Beast and the Sovereign, Volume 1, trans. G. Bennington (Chicago: University of Chicago Press, 2009).

The Beast and the Sovereign, Volume 2, trans. G. Bennington (Chicago: University of Chicago Press, 2010).

'Circumfession', in G. Bennington and J. Derrida, *Jacques Derrida* (Chicago: University of Chicago Press, 1993).

'*Demeure*: Fiction and Testimony', trans. E. Rottenberg, in M. Blanchot and J. Derrida, *The Instant of My Death / Demeure: Fiction and Testimony* (Stanford: Stanford University Press, 2000).

Dissemination, trans. B. Johnson (Chicago: University of Chicago Press, 1981).

The Gift of Death and *Literature in Secret*, trans. D. Wills (Chicago: University of Chicago Press, 2008).

Glas, trans. J. P. Leavey and R. Rand (Lincoln: University of Nebraska Press, 1986).

'How to Avoid Speaking: Denials', trans. K. Frieden and E. Rottenberg, in J. Derrida, *Psyche 2: Inventions of the Other*, ed. P. Kamuf and E. Rottenberg (Stanford: Stanford University Press, 2008).

Margins of Philosophy, trans. A. Bass (Chicago: University of Chicago Press, 1982).

'Marx & Sons', trans. G. M. Goshgarian, in M. Sprinker (ed.), *Ghostly Demarcations: A Symposium on Jacques Derrida's* Specters of Marx (London: Verso, 1999).

Memoirs of the Blind: The Self-Portrait and Other Ruins, trans. P.-A. Brault and M. Naas (Chicago: University of Chicago Press, 1993).

Monolingualism of the Other; or, The Prosthesis of Origin, trans. P. Mensah (Stanford: Stanford University Press, 1998).

Of Grammatology, trans. G. C. Spivak (Baltimore: Johns Hopkins University Press, 1976).

Of Hospitality, trans. R. Bowlby (Stanford: Stanford University Press, 2000).

Of Spirit: Heidegger and the Question, trans. G. Bennington (Chicago: University of Chicago Press, 1991).

On the Name, ed. T. Dutoit (Stanford: Stanford University Press, 1993).

Parages, trans. T. Conley, J. Hulbert, J. P. Leavey and A. Ronell (Stanford: Stanford University Press, 2010).

'Passions: "An Oblique Offering"', trans. D. Wood, in D. Wood (ed.), *Jacques Derrida: A Critical Reader* (London: Wiley-Blackwell, 1991).

Politics of Friendship, trans. G. Collins (New York: Verso, 1997).

Positions, trans. A. Bass (Chicago: University of Chicago Press, 1981).

Psyche 1: Inventions of the Other, trans. P. Kamuf and E. Rottenberg (Stanford: Stanford University Press, 2007).

Psyche 2: Inventions of the Other, ed. P. Kamuf and E. Rottenberg (Stanford: Stanford University Press, 2008).

Rogues: Two Essays on Reason, trans. P.-A. Brault and M. Naas (Stanford: Stanford University Press, 2005).

Specters of Marx: The State of the Debt, the Work of Mourning, and the New International, trans. P. Kamuf (New York: Routledge, 1994).

Speech and Phenomena: And Other Essays on Husserl's Theory of Signs, trans. D. B. Allison (Evanston: Northwestern University Press, 1973).

Sovereignties in Question: The Poetics of Paul Celan, ed. T. Dutoit and O. Pasanen (New York: Fordham University Press, 2005).

A Taste for the Secret, with Maurizio Ferraris, trans. G. Donis (Cambridge: Polity Press, 2001).

The Truth in Painting, trans. G. Bennington and I. McLeod (Chicago: University of Chicago Press, 1987).

Without Alibi, ed. P. Kamuf (Stanford: Stanford University Press, 2002).

The Work of Mourning, ed. P.-A. Brault and M. Naas (Chicago: University of Chicago Press, 2001).

Other Works Cited

Agamben, Giorgio, *Homo Sacer: Sovereign Power and Bare Life*, trans. D. Heller-Roazen (Stanford: Stanford University Press, 1997).

Agamben, Giorgio, *The Kingdom and the Glory: For a Genealogy of Economy and Government*, trans. L. Chiesa (Stanford: Stanford University Press, 2011).

Agamben, Giorgio, *The Open: Man and Animal*, trans. K. Attell (Stanford: Stanford University Press, 2003).

Agamben, Giorgio, *The Sacrament of Language: An Archaeology of the Oath*, trans. A. Kotsko (Stanford: Stanford University Press, 2011).

Agamben, Giorgio, *Stanzas: Word and Phantasm in Western Culture*, trans. R. T. Martinez (Minnesota: University of Minnesota Press, 1993).

Agamben, Giorgio, *State of Exception*, trans. K. Attell (Chicago: University of Chicago Press, 2005).

Almond, Ian, 'Derrida and the Secret of the Non-Secret: On Respiritualizing the Profane', *Literature and Theology*, 17:4 (2013): 457–71.

Arendt, Hannah, *Eichmann in Jerusalem: A Report on the Banality of Evil* (New York: Penguin, 2006).

Arendt, Hannah, *On Revolution* (New York: Penguin, 1977).

Arendt, Hannah, 'Some Questions of Moral Responsibility', in *Responsibility and Judgment*, ed. J. Kohn (New York: Schocken Books, 2003).

Arendt, Hannah, 'Truth and Politics', in *Between Past and Future* (New York: Penguin, 1977).

Arendt, Hannah, 'What is Freedom?', in *Between Past and Future* (New York: Penguin, 1977).

Augustine, Saint, 'On Lying', in *Nicene and Post-Nicene Fathers, Volume 3*, ed. P. Schaff (New York: Cosimo, 1957).

Austin, J. L., *How to Do Things with Words* (Oxford: Oxford University Press, 1962).

Avaramides, Anita, *Other Minds* (Abingdon: Routledge, 2001).

Bajorek, Jennifer, *Counterfeit Capital: Poetic Labour and Revolutionary Irony* (Stanford: Stanford University Press, 2009).

Balfour, Ian (ed.), Late Derrida, a Special Issue of *The South Atlantic Quarterly*, 106:2 (2007): 205–420.

Barbour, Charles, 'The Acts of Faith: On Witnessing in Derrida and Arendt, *Philosophy and Social Criticism*, 37:6 (2011): 629–45.

Barbour, Charles, 'The Hazard of Truth: Perjury and Oath in Derrida's Later Work', *Law, Culture and the Humanities*, forthcoming (online first).

Barbour, Charles, 'The Maker of Lies: Simmel, Mendacity and the Economy of Faith', *Theory, Culture and Society*, 29:7–8 (2012): 218–36.

Barbour, Charles, 'The Sovereign Without Domain: Georges Bataille and the Ethics of Nothing', in C. Monagle and D. Vardoulakis (eds), *The Politics of Nothing* (New York: Routledge, 2011).

Bataille, Georges, *The Accursed Share: An Essay on General Economy, Volume 1, Consumption*, trans. R. Hurley (New York: Zone Books, 1991).

Bennington, Geoffrey, 'Derrida and Politics', in T. Cohen (ed.), *Jacques Derrida and the Humanities: A Critical Reader* (Cambridge: Cambridge University Press, 2001).

Bennington, Geoffrey and Jacques Derrida, *Jacques Derrida*, trans. G. Bennington (Chicago: University of Chicago, 1993).

Bernet, Rudolf, 'The Secret According to Heidegger and "The Purloined Letter" by Poe', *Continental Philosophy Review*, 47:3 (2014): 353–7.

Birchall, Clare, 'Aesthetics of the Secret', *New Formations*, 83 (2014): 25–46.

Bounegru, Liliana, 'GetHub as Transparency Device in Data Journalism, Open Date and Data Activism', http://lilianabounegru.org/category/data-visualization.

Caputo, John D., *The Prayers and Tears of Jacques Derrida: Religion Without Religion* (Bloomington: Indiana University Press, 1997).

Caputo, John D., *The Weakness of God: A Theology of the Event* (Bloomington: Indiana University Press, 2006).

Celan, Paul, *The Meridian: Final Version – Drafts – Materials*, trans. P. Joris (Stanford: Stanford University Press, 2011).

Chalmers, David J., *The Conscious Mind: In Search of a Fundamental Theory* (Oxford: Oxford University Press, 1996).

Chalmers, David J., 'Facing Up to the Problem of Consciousness', *Journal of Consciousness Studies*, 2:3 (1995): 200–19.

Coleridge, Samuel Taylor, *Coleridge's Criticism of Shakespeare* (Detroit: Wayne State University Press, 1989).

Coward, Howard and Toby Foshay (eds), *Derrida and Negative Theology* (Albany: State University of New York Press, 1992).

Curtius, Ernst Robert, *European Literature and the Latin Middle Ages*, trans. W. R. Trask (Princeton: Princeton University Press, 2013).

Davidson, Donald, 'Who is Fooled?', in *Self-Deception and Paradoxes of Rationality*, ed. J. P. Dupuy (Stanford: CSLI Publications, 1998).

De Landa, Manuel, *Intensive Science and Virtual Philosophy* (London: Bloomsbury, 2002).

De Ville, Jacques, 'Derrida's *Purveyor of Truth* and Constitutional Reading', *International Journal for the Semiotics of Law*, 21 (2008): 117–33.

De Ville, Jacques, *Jacques Derrida: Law as Absolute Hospitality* (Abingdon: Routledge, 2011).

de Vries, Hent, *Religion and Violence: Philosophical Perspectives from Kant to Derrida* (Baltimore: Johns Hopkins University Press, 2002).

Dean, Jodi, *Publicity's Secret: How Technoculture Capitalizes on Democracy* (Ithaca: Cornell University Press, 2002).

Deleuze, Gilles, 'Postscript on the Societies of Control', October, 59 (1993): 3–7.

Deleuze, Gilles and Félix Guattari, *A Thousand Plateaus*, trans. Brian Massumi (Minnesota: University of Minnesota Press, 1987).

Durkheim, Emile, *Elementary Forms of Religious Life*, trans. J. W. Swain (Mineola: Dover, 2008).

Fritsch, Matthias, 'Derrida's Democracy to Come', *Constellations: An International Journal of Critical and Democratic Theory*, 9:4 (2002): 574–97

Fingarette, Herbert, *Self-Deception* (Berkeley: University of California Press, 1969).

Foss, Jeffrey, 'Rethinking Self-Deception', *American Philosophical Quarterly*, 17 (1980).

Foucault, Michel, *The Hermeneutics of the Subject: Lectures at the Collége de France, 1981–1982*, trans. G. Burchell (New York: Picador, 2005).

Gadamer, Hans-Georg, *Truth and Method*, trans. J. Weinsheimer and D. G. Marshall (London: Bloomsbury, 2013).

Gasché, Rodolphe, *The Tain of the Mirror: Derrida and the Philosophy of Reflection* (Cambridge: Harvard University Press, 1986).

Gilbert, Jeremy, 'Public Secrets: "Being-With" in the Era of Perpetual Disclosure', *Cultural Studies*, 21:1 (2007): 22–41.

Gratton, Peter, 'Post-Deconstructive Realism: It's About Time', *Speculations: A Journal of Speculative Realism*, IV (2013): 84–90.

Gratton, Peter, *Speculative Realism: Problems and Prospects* (London: Bloomsbury, 2014).

Guerlac, Suzanne and Pheng Cheah (eds), *Derrida and the Time of the Political* (Durham, NC: Duke University Press, 2009).

Hägglund, Martin, *Radical Atheism: Derrida on the Time of Life* (Stanford: Stanford University Press, 2008).

Hart, Kevin, *The Trespass of the Sign: Deconstruction, Theology and Philosophy* (New York: Fordham University Press, 2000).

Hazlitt, William, *Characters of Shakespeare's Plays* (London: John Templeman, 1838).

Heidegger, Martin, *Being and Time*, trans. J. Stambaugh (Albany: State University of New York Press, 1962).

Heidegger, Martin, 'The Question Concerning Technology', in *Basic Writings*, ed. D. F. Krell (New York: Harper Collins, 1993).

Herodotus, *The Histories*, trans. T. Holland (New York: Penguin, 1994).

Honig, Bonnie, 'Out Like a Lion: Melancholia with Euripides and Winnicott', *Theory & Event*, 18:2 (2015).

Jay, Martin, 'The Limits of Limit-Experience: Bataille and Foucault', *Constellations*, 2:2 (1995): 155–74.

Jay, Martin, 'Pseudology: Derrida and Arendt on Lying in Politics', in P. Cheah and S. Guerlac (eds), *Derrida and the Time of the Political* (Durham, NC: Duke University Press, 2009).

Kamuf, Peggy, 'Preface: Toward the Event', in J. Derrida, *Without Alibi*, trans. P. Kamuf (Stanford: Stanford University Press, 2002).

Kant, Immanuel, *Critique of the Power of Judgment*, trans. P. Guyer and E. Matthews (Cambridge: Cambridge University Press, 2000).

Kant, Immanuel, *The Metaphysics of Morals*, trans. M. Gregor (Cambridge: Cambridge University Press, 1996).

Kantorowicz, Ernst H., *The King's Two Bodies: A Study in Medieval Political Theology* (Princeton: Princeton University Press, 1957).

Kearney, Richard, *The God Who May Be: A Hermeneutics of Religion* (Bloomington: Indiana University Press, 2011).

La Caze, Marguerite, 'It's Easier to Lie If You Believe It Yourself: Derrida, Arendt, and the Modern Lie', *Law, Culture and the Humanities*, forthcoming (online first).

Lacan, Jacques, 'Seminar of "The Purloined Letter"', trans. J. Mehlman, *Yale French Studies*, 53 (1975): 31–113.

Lacan, Jacques, 'The Subversion of the Subject and the Dialectic of Desire in the Freudian Unconscious', in *Écrits: The First Complete English Edition*, trans. B. Fink (New York: Norton, 2006).

Lambert, Gregg, *Return Statements: The Return of Religion in Contemporary Philosophy* (Edinburgh: Edinburgh University Press, 2016).

Lawlor, Leonard, *Derrida and Husserl: The Basic Problem of Phenomenology* (Bloomington: Indiana University Press, 2002).

Lefort, Claude, *Democracy and Political Theory*, trans. D. Macey (Oxford: Polity Press, 1988).

Lefort, Claude, *The Political Forms of Modern Society: Bureaucracy, Democracy, Totalitarianism*, ed. J. B. Thompson (Cambridge, MA: MIT Press, 1986).

Leitch, Vincent B., 'Late Derrida: The Politics of Sovereignty', *Critical Inquiry*, 33 (2007): 229–47.

Levinas, Emmanuel, 'Essence and Disinterestedness', in *Basic Philosophical Writings*, ed. A. T. Peperzak, S. Critchley and R. Bernasconi (Bloomington: Indiana University Press, 1996).

Levinas, Emmanuel, *God, Death, and Time*, trans. B. Bergo (Stanford: Stanford University Press, 2000).

Levinas, Emmanuel, *Otherwise than Being, Or Beyond Essence*, trans. A. Lingis (Dordrecht: Martinus Nijhoff, 1998).

Levinas, Emmanuel, *Totality and Infinity: An Essay on Exteriority*, trans. A. Lingis (Dordrecht: Martinus Nijhoff, 1969).

Levinas, Emmanuel, 'Truth of Disclosure and Truth of Testimony', in *Basic Philosophical Writings*, ed. A. T. Peperzak, S. Critchley and R. Bernasconi (Bloomington: Indiana University Press, 1996).

Lüdelmann, Susanne, *Politics of Deconstruction: A New Introduction to Jacques Derrida* (Stanford: Stanford University Press, 2014).

Meillassoux, Quentin, *After Finitude: An Essay on the Necessity of Contingency*, trans. R. Brassier (London: Bloomsbury, 2008).

Meillassoux, Quentin, 'Iteration, Reiteration, Repetition: A Speculative Analysis of the Sign Devoid of Meaning', in A. Avanessian and S. Malik (eds), *Genealogies of Speculation: Materialism and Subjectivity Since Structuralism* (London: Bloomsbury, 2016).

Mele, Alfred R., 'Real Self-Deception', *Behavioural and Brain Sciences*, 20 (1997).

Mele, Alfred R., 'Recent Work in Self-Deception', *American Philosophical Quarterly*, 24 (1987).

Michelfelder, Diane P. and Richard E. Palmer (eds), *Dialogue and Deconstruction: The Gadamer-Derrida Encounter* (Albany: State University of New York Press, 1989).

Mitchell, W. J. T. and Arnold I. Davidson, *The Late Derrida* (Chicago: University of Chicago Press, 2007).

Moyn, Samuel, *Christian Human Rights* (Philadelphia: University of Pennsylvania Press, 2015).

Moyn, Samuel, *The Last Utopia: Human Rights in History* (Cambridge: Harvard University Press, 2010).

Naas, Michael, *Miracle and Machine: Jacques Derrida and the Two Sources of Religion, Science, and the Media* (New York: Fordham University Press, 2011).

Naas, Michael, *Taking on the Tradition: Jacques Derrida and the Legacies of Deconstruction* (Stanford: Stanford University Press, 2013).

Nancy, Jean-Luc, *Being Singular Plural*, trans. R. Richardson and A. O'Byrne (Stanford: Stanford University Press, 2000).

Nedelmann, Brigitta, 'The Continuing Relevance of Georg Simmel: Staking Out Anew the Field of Sociology', in G. Ritzer and B. Smart (eds), *Handbook of Social Theory* (London: Routledge, 2001).

Negri, Antonio, *The Politics of Subversion: A Manifesto for the Twenty-First Century*, trans. J. Newell (Cambridge: Polity Press, 2005).

Panagia, Davide, 'On Datapolitik', http://www.academia.edu6875336/On_Datapolitik.

Peeters, Benoit, *Derrida: A Biography* (Cambridge: Polity Press, 2013).

Peterson, Christopher, 'The *Gravity* of *Melancholia*: A Critique of Speculative Realism', *Theory & Event*, 18:2 (2015).

Plato, *The Republic*, trans. T. Griffith (Cambridge: Cambridge University Press, 2000).

Poe, Edgar Allan, 'The Purloined Letter', in *Poe's Tales of Mystery and Terror* (New York: Prestige Books, 1967).

Ryle, Gilbert, 'Thinking and Self-Teaching', *Journal of Philosophy of Education*, 5:2 (1971): 216–88.

Sallis, John (ed.), *Deconstruction and Philosophy* (Chicago: University of Chicago Press, 1987).

Sartre, Jean-Paul, *Being and Nothingness: A Phenomenological Essay on Ontology*, trans. H. E. Barnes (New York: Washington Square Press, 1992).

Schmitt, Carl, *The Concept of the Political*, trans. J. H. Lomax (Chicago: University of Chicago Press, 1996).

Schmitt, Carl, *The Leviathan and the State Theory of Thomas Hobbes: Meaning and Failure of a Political Symbol*, trans. G. Schwab and E. Hilfstein (Chicago: University of Chicago Press, 2008).

Schmitt, Carl, *Political Theology: Four Chapters of the Concept of Sovereignty*, trans. G. Schwab (Chicago: University of Chicago Press, 2005).

Schmitt, Carl, *Roman Catholicism and Political Form*, trans. G. L. Ulmen (Westport: Greenwood Press, 1996).

Searle, John, 'Reiterating the Differences: A Reply to Derrida', *Glyph* 1 (1977): 198–208.

Shakespeare, William, *Othello* (New York: Penguin, 2005).

Shaviro, Steven, *Discognition* (New York: Repeater, 2015).

Shell, Marc, *The Economy of Literature* (Baltimore: Johns Hopkins University Press, 1983).

Sherwood, Yvonne and Kevin Hart (eds), *Derrida and Religion: Other Testaments* (New York: Routledge, 2005).

Simmel, Georg, 'A Contribution to the Sociology of Religion', in *Essays on Religion*, ed. H. J. Helle (New Haven: Yale University Press, 1997).

Simmel, Georg, 'How is Society Possible?', in *Georg Simmel on Individuality and Social Forms*, ed. D. N. Levine (Chicago: University of Chicago Press, 1971).

Simmel, Georg, 'The Maker of Lies', trans. T. Kemple, *Theory, Culture and Society*, 29:7–8 (2012): 273–5.

Simmel, Georg, *The Philosophy of Money*, ed. D. Frisby (London: Routledge, 2004).

Simmel, Georg, 'Religion', in *Essays on Religion*, ed. H. J. Helle (New Haven: Yale University Press, 1997).

Simmel, Georg, 'Sociological Aesthetics', in *The Conflict of Modern Culture and Other Essays*, trans. P. Etzcorn (New York: Teachers College Press, 1968).

Simmel, Georg, *Sociology: Inquiries into the Construction of Social Forms*, 2 Volumes, trans. A. J. Blasi, A. K. Jacobs and M. Kanjirathinkal (Leiden: Brill, 2009).

Simmel, Georg, *The Sociology of Georg Simmel*, trans. K. H. Wolff (New York: The Free Press, 1950).

Simmel, Georg, 'Sociology of the Meal', in D. Frisby and M. Featherstone (eds), *Simmel on Culture: Selected Writings* (London: Sage, 1997).

Simmel, Georg, 'The Sociology of Secrecy and Secret Societies', *The American Journal of Sociology*, 11:4 (1906): 441–98.

Simmel, Georg, 'Zur Psychologie un Soziologie der Lüge', in *Gesamtausgabe in 24 Bänden: Band 5*, ed. H. J. Duhme and D. Frisby (Frankfurt: Suhrkamp, 1992).

Simons, William, 'The Third: Levinas's Theoretical Move from An-Archical Ethics to the Realm of Justice and Politics', *Philosophy and Social Criticism*, 25:6 (1999): 83–104.

Sprinker, Michael (ed.), *Ghostly Demarcations: A Symposium on Jacques Derrida's Spectres of Marx* (London: Verso, 2007).

Staten, Henry, *Wittgenstein and Derrida* (Lincoln: University of Nebraska Press, 1984).

Stauffer, Jill, *Ethical Loneliness: The Injustice of Not Being Heard* (New York: Columbia University Press, 2015).

Swiffen, Amy, 'Derrida Contra Agamben', *Societies*, 2:4 (2012): 345–56.

Talbot, W. J. T., 'Intentional Self-Deception in a Single Coherent Self', *Philosophy and Phenomenological Research*, 55 (1995).

Taylor, Mark C., *Erring: A Postmodern A/theology* (Chicago: University of Chicago Press, 1987).

Taylor, Mark C., *Nots* (Chicago: University of Chicago Press, 1993).

Vardoulakis, Dimitris, *The Doppelgänger: Literature's Philosophy* (New York: Fordham University Press, 2010).

Weber, Max, *The Protestant Ethic and the Spirit of Capitalism*, trans. T. Parsons (New York: Dover, 2003).

Whyte, Jessica, 'The Fortunes of Natural Man: Robinson Crusoe, Political Economy, and the Universal Declaration of Human Rights', *Humanity*, 5:3 (2014): 301–21.

Wills, David, *Matchbook: Essays in Deconstruction* (Stanford: Stanford University Press, 2005).

Wills, David, *Prosthesis* (Stanford: Stanford University Press, 1995).

Wisdom, John, *Other Minds* (Berkeley: University of California Press, 1968).

Wolin, Richard, *The Seduction of Unreason: The Intellectual Romance with Fascism from Nietzsche to Postmodernism* (Princeton: Princeton University Press, 2006).

Wood, David (ed.), *Derrida: A Critical Reader* (London: Blackwell, 1992).

Wood, David and Robert Bernasconi (eds), *Derrida and Différance* (Evanston: Northwestern University Press, 1988).

Index

melancholy, 192, 196, 197, 202, 204, 205, 207
messianic, 48
miracle, 52, 128–9
Moyn, Samuel, 115–16, 134

Naas, Michael, 35, 47
Negative Theology, 80, 112, 158, 177–9
neo-liberalism, 151, 153, 156, 268
Nietzsche, Friedrich, 207–11

oath, 25–6, 32, 38–9, 47–9, 51, 53–5, 59, 61–3, 67, 82, 86, 90, 122, 143, 145, 179–81, 207, 231, 256, 259, 270–6
other minds, 29, 149, 190

Panagia, Davide, 98, 157
paranoia, 170, 253
perjury, 9, 11, 13, 38, 53–5, 59, 61–9, 121, 143, 265
phenomenology, 19, 79, 126, 185
Plato, 1–8, 126, 172, 174, 226, 246
Poe, Edward Allan, 28, 99–109, 110, 117
prayer, 198, 204, 225, 228, 230–3, 235, 237–8, 241–2
privacy, 11, 14, 27, 95–7, 116, 176
promise, 23, 26, 48–52, 54–5, 60, 68, 119, 143, 179–80, 183, 276

psychoanalysis, 88, 106, 178, 251–6

Rancière, Jacques, 97
reflective judgement, 120
rights, 96–7, 115–16, 132, 134–8, 141
Russell's Paradox, 107
Ryle, Gilbert, 4, 107, 179

sacred, 47, 52–4, 256, 272
Sartre, Jean-Paul, 159, 163–4
Schmitt, Carl, 259–62
Searle, John, 22, 36
secret, 69–71, 75–81, 110–13, 139–45, 175–83, 249–77
self-deception, 150, 158–67, 170, 173–4
Senate Intelligence Committee, 8–9, 15
sexual difference, 213, 215, 253, 256
Shakespeare, William, 39–45, 48
Simmel, Georg, 8, 26, 35, 39, 69–82, 93, 102, 113, 158, 171–4, 210, 253
singular universal, 28–9, 33, 41, 68, 99, 107, 110, 117, 119, 120, 123–4, 128, 133, 142, 148, 186, 196, 203, 205, 212, 216, 227
Snowden, Edward, 9–10, 14, 27, 96–7, 154–5
social bond, 25, 26–7, 38, 51, 81, 90, 142, 176, 179, 183, 202, 207

EU Authorised Representative:

Easy Access System Europe Mustamäe tee 50, 10621 Tallinn, Estonia

gpsr.requests@easproject.com

Printed and bound by CPI Group (UK) Ltd, Croydon, CR0 4YY

27/06/2026

02149880-0001